Gettysburg as the
Generals Remembered It

Gettysburg as the Generals Remembered It

Postwar Perspectives of Ten Commanders

Edited by
ROBERT P. BROADWATER

McFarland & Company, Inc., Publishers
Jefferson, North Carolina, and London

LIBRARY OF CONGRESS CATALOGUING-IN-PUBLICATION DATA

Gettysburg as the generals remembered it : postwar perspectives
of ten commanders / edited by Robert P. Broadwater.
    p.   cm.
Includes bibliographical references and index.

ISBN 978-0-7864-4995-8
softcover : 50# alkaline paper ∞

1. Gettysburg, Battle of, Gettysburg, Pa., 1863– —Personal
narratives. 2. Generals—United States—Biography.
3. Generals—Confederate States of America—Biography.
I. Broadwater, Robert P., 1958–
E475.53.G3937   2010
973.7'349—dc22   2010017736

British Library cataloguing data are available

Cover image ©2010 Shutterstock

Manufactured in the United States of America

McFarland & Company, Inc., Publishers
 Box 611, Jefferson, North Carolina 28640
 www.mcfarlandpub.com

Table of Contents

Introduction

In 1891, the *North American Review* published, in serial form, articles on the battle of Gettysburg penned by several of the leading Union generals involved in that conflict. The Comte de Paris, a noted military historian, and, for a time, a volunteer officer in the Union army, was making a trip to America to visit the battlefield. In October of 1890, General Daniel Butterfield assembled a group of the surviving Union generals to accompany the Count. In this assemblage were all of the living corps commanders of the Army of the Potomac, save Pleasonton and Gibbon. The group met on that field, the first time that they had all been there together since the battle had taken place, and conducted a tour for the Count. As the party examined each of the sites made famous by the fighting during the epic battle, each commander described the events that had taken place on his portion of the line. A visit by so many famous military personalities was cause for celebration for the town of Gettysburg, and the dignitaries were given a welcome befitting their status. Each of the leading participants in the battle in attendance recorded his impressions not only of the visit, but of their service there twenty-seven years before. These personal recollections will provide the reader, it is hoped, with the kind of insight that can only be derived from a first-hand account of the Battle of Gettysburg.

There can also be seen the seeds of controversy that have survived to our time concerning the actions of certain officers. In particular, the article of John Gibbon refutes several of the statements made by brother officers, and casts aspersions on their intentions in making them. Gibbon was not in attendance during the October visit to the battlefield, and wrote in response to reading the articles submitted by those who were there.

This material has been brought together to enable students of the battle of Gettysburg to "experience" the greatest gathering of Union commanders to occur on the battlefield in the years that followed the historic event. One can almost hear the rattle of musketry and the roar of cannon in their descriptions of the action, and one can feel the nostalgia in the descriptions of deep-seated memories. They returned to the site of their greatest fame, no longer the young men who had commanded an army of soldiers, but rather, men in their declining years. Many of their comrades had already passed from this life, and those that remained were interested in telling their stories before joining them.

Doctor Carol Reardon, a respected expert in military history, has long defined the difference between history and memory, as it pertains to memoirs and first-person histories of the war. Many of the regimental and general histories that have been handed down to us were written a few decades after the war. Time dulls one's memory, and events become distorted in the retelling. There was also the fact that, following the war, many personal reputations were at stake. Many ranking officers were attempting to defend their actions during the war from attacks by historians and brother officers.

In the following pages the reader will first get to read the remembrances of the surviving Union corps commanders who attended the guided tour that General Butterfield put together for the Comte de Paris. Each general's words will be followed by an historical examination that will try to uncover how accurate, or inaccurate, the general's statements were. The historic events that unfolded on that field will be compared to the articles written by the generals. Other memoirs and statements about the battle from these same men will also be examined, to explore any discrepancies in a general's different accounts of the same event. In the end, it is hoped that the reader will gain a clearer understanding of what actually happened, how the generals remembered it, and why some of them may have chosen to remember events as they believed or wanted them to be, and not as the historical record proved them to be.

In the case of the Southern generals who fought on the fields of Gettysburg, no gathering like the one that took place for the Comte de Paris occurred in the years following the war. This did not prevent these officers from reliving those epic events in the media, however. Just as with the Union officers, a controversial public debate was initiated that continues to this day. In fact, the Southern war of words that resulted predated the articles in the *North American Review* by more than a decade. The remembrances that appeared in the Southern Historical Society Papers in 1878–79 initiated the same sort of controversy as the Northern generals' articles. General Dan Sickles served as the catalyst for the Union leaders, and General James P. Longstreet assumed the same role for the Southern leaders. Longstreet's attempts to explain his actions at Gettysburg elicited responses from Generals Fitzhugh Lee and Jubal Early, sparking a debate that has yet to end. Regrettably, most of the primary Confederate leaders at Gettysburg were no longer alive by the time this public debate began. Robert E. Lee had died in 1872. Longstreet was the only surviving corps commander of the Army of Northern Virginia, Richard Ewell having died in 1872, and Ambrose P. Hill being killed in the final days of the war. J.E.B. Stuart, the Southern cavalry commander, had lost his life at the battle of Yellow Tavern. When General Longstreet agreed to write a detailed account of the Gettysburg Campaign for the Philadelphia *Times,* in 1877, his remembrance of the events that transpired on that field were called to question by generals who had not served under his command, or even on the portion of the battlefield occupied by his corps. Longstreet's version of the chain of events at Gettysburg laid a large portion of the blame for the defeat on the shoulders of Robert E. Lee. Lee's supporters quickly rallied to his defense, and alleged that it was Longstreet, not Lee, who was responsible for the failure of the Pennsylvania Campaign. We will examine the charges and countercharges of these generals and attempt to separate fact from fiction, reality from partisanship.

As we stand on the threshold of the 150th anniversary of the battle of Gettysburg, may the insight gained through the words of the Union and Confederate commanders who fought on that field provide us a fuller understanding of the greatest battle ever to take place on the North American continent.

The Comte de Paris, USA

Louis-Philippe Albert d'Orléans, Comte de Paris (the Count of Paris), was born on August 24, 1838. He was the grandson of Louis Philippe I, king of France, and became heir to the throne when his father, Prince Ferdinand Philippe, was killed in an accident in 1842. In 1848, his grandfather abdicated the throne, introducing the advent of the French Second Republic. A historian and journalist, the Comte de Paris volunteered, along with his younger brother, the Duc de Chartres, to serve in the Union army. He was commissioned to the rank of captain, and was assigned to the staff of Major General George B. McClellan. The Comte de Paris served in the army for approximately one year, and he distinguished himself during the Peninsula Campaign. Upon his return to Europe, he began writing a history of the Civil War, which became a standard reference work on the subject.

The fall of Napoleon III in 1873 led to the establishment of a National Assembly favorable to the reinstatement of the monarchy, placing the Comte de Paris in line to become king of France. He withdrew his claim to the throne in favor of the Comte de Chambord, who was childless, but the Comte de Paris' claim to the throne was never legitimized by the Comte de Chambord. Upon the Comte de Chambord's death in 1883 the Comte de Paris was recognized as Phillip VII of France by most monarchists but the succession was disputed by the Bourbon kings of Spain. The Comte de Paris lived in England, as had his grandfather following his abdication of the throne. He died there on September 8, 1894.

A Remarkable engraving, called "The Midnight Review," is very popular in France and may be known in America. It represents innumerable lines of phantom warriors mustering through the moonlit clouds to march past before the ghost of Napoleon, under whose leadership each of them had met a soldier's death.

This weird scene had made a deep impression on my mind when I was a child, and its remembrance suddenly flashed upon me when I entered, some weeks ago, the Great National Cemetery of Gettysburg, over whose peaceful graves presides the bronze statue of the gallant Reynolds. My imagination first retraced to me the real midnight scene which the then small cemetery of Gettysburg witnessed on the historical night of July 1, 1863, when the illustrious General Meade, hastening to grasp with a firm hand the command of the army so recently entrusted to him, set his foot upon that key-position where his weary soldiers, sleeping among the citizen's tombs, seemed, under the pure rays of the moon, as so many statues recording the memory of the departed.

How many among those young and healthy men slept that night for the last time and now rest forever in the long rows of white stones, drawn like regiments on the parade-ground, with their officers in front, which extend all over the hallowed ground, and whose martial order cannot fail to strike every visitor's mind!

It required, indeed, a small amount of imagination to conceive another midnight scene, where, under the call of some mysterious power, in the stillness and dubious light of that hour, the form of every dead soldier would grow out of the small marble slabs to form a powerful array on the ground where they had generously given up their life to save their country in the most critical moment of its history.

However, this is perhaps too pagan a thought for a Christian cemetery, where the memory of the dead is honored by words of peace and hope, and not of vengeance and retaliation. As General Howard so eloquently said on that same evening at the meeting of the citizens of Gettysburg, the watchword must be "Charity for all." It is only a feverish brain which could in its dream call the spirits of the Confederate soldiers out of their scattered tombs to lead them in the darkness of the midnight hour to the assault of those heights which were soaked with their blood a quarter century ago. And taking this view, I must confess that I regretted to see our late enemies' remains excluded from the ground dedicated by a reunited people to the memory of the victims of the war, where every one bows before the emblem of our common redeemer. I felt this regret more keenly when, some days later, I saw in Quebec the common monument erected by the British nation to the memory of the two valiant soldiers, Wolfe and Montcalm—a great example of impartiality before the equality in deaths and glory!

But why evoke the dead while in broad daylight I could behold a more extraordinary sight in an historical point of view that the midnight review? To the call of General Butterfield, chief of staff of the Army of the Potomac in that decisive battle, had answered nearly all the surviving chiefs who were the principal actors in this great drama. Instead of the ghostly legions marching in an unearthly silence, I had around me all the living leaders whose names will always be associated with the history of the battle of Gettysburg. It was, indeed, a high compliment which they paid to a true friend of their country, who, after having served with them in the same army, had undertaken to write an impartial account of the great struggle. This compliment I once more gratefully acknowledge.

The citizens of Gettysburg were right to appreciate the remarkable character of the visit which took place on the 15th of October, for I believe that there is not one of the innumerable battlefields of old Europe which has been revisited by such a number of the leaders of the victorious army, assembled on the same day to go together on the historical ground and combine their remembrances of a quarter of a century past, to enrich, if I can say so, their common fund of information.

I understand that each of them has promised to give his personal impressions of that visit. Nothing could be more interesting for the student of history and the military critic. In company with such high authorities I cannot presume to add to their statements anything which would be of interest for the one or the other. Moreover, if the impressions of a European officer may be of some value to the readers of this, I shall yield the pen to my friend and companion, Colonel de Parseval, who has already recorded these impressions in a French military paper, where they have been duly appreciated.

However, this I can say: that, having minutely described the field of battle, and mastered, I believe, all the operations which were conducted upon it, without having seen the ground, I was very anxious to know whether the personal inspection of this ground would correspond or not with the ideas I had formed by the study of the maps. That my expectation was fully realized speaks volumes in favor of the accuracy of those maps. I confess that only by a very natural process of the mind I had imagined that every inequality of the ground, except perhaps the bold profiles of the Round Tops and Culp's Hill, was more marked than I found it to be in reality.

It was only when we were crammed on the platform of the belfry of the theological seminary that I clearly understood the strength and importance of the ridge to which this building gives its name. From there also it was easy to recognize the natural weakness of the position in which the Eleventh Corps had to support the brunt of Ewell's attacks. That the whole line occupied on the afternoon of the 1st of July by the two Federal corps d' armes was bound to crumble to pieces as soon as it should be strongly assailed from the north and northeast was so evident that any discussion upon the connection between these two corps seemed to be quite out of order: a happy result, for the narrow platform was no place to debate upon such a burning question.

In the afternoon our drive took us first to Culp's Hill, the rugged ground of which must be seen to understand the nature of the bloody fight which took place on its eastern slope. But to realize fully its importance for the defense of the Federal lines, it is necessary at the same time to look a moment westward so as to see how near it lies to the part of those lines which occupied Cemetery Ridge and extended further south. It is impossible then not to be struck by what must be called Lee's capitol error in the disposition of his forces on the second and third days of the battle. It is no disparagement of the great Confederate chieftain's abilities to point out the error, for which some causes may be found, for as the general result of the battle was the defeat of his army, the cause of this defeat must be found somewhere, and I do not hesitate to ascribe it principally to the extension of his left opposite Culp's Hill.

While in an hour or two at the utmost reinforcements could be taken from there to Cemetery Ridge and Round Top, and vice versa, it would have required a whole day's march for a column leaving the shores of Rock Creek, at the foot of Culp's Hill, to reach the positions from which Pickett's division moved to its celebrated charge. This excessive development of Lee's front, which gave his adversary the advantage of the interior lines in a degree rarely seen on any field of battle, deprived him not only of the power of concentration, but also of the means of securing combined action. For even his messengers were greatly delayed in carrying his orders, and when he directed his lieutenants, in order to act in concert, to take the cannonade on one wing as a signal for an attack of the other, this plan lamentably failed. If we ask why he threw in that way his left around Culp's Hill, and why he did not correct this when discovered, as he no doubt did very soon, that it was a mistake, the answer should be, I think; First, that on the evening of the 1st he did certainly not expect to meet next morning on Cemetery Hill the unconquerable resistance which alone prevented his two wings from being strongly connected together. Neither the condition of the Federal troops that evening when they lost Gettysburg nor the aspect of Cemetery Hill as seen from the seminary could justify such an expectation. Second, that it was the very greatness of the defeat of his position which prevented him from correcting it. If he had drawn in his left to reinforce his centre, this would have, no doubt, enabled Longstreet, in turn, to extend to the right and to strike south of Round Top a blow which would probably have caused the retreat of the Federal army. But to accomplish that transfer a full day would have been consumed, during which Ewell's forces would have been practically annulled and the whole of the Federal right left free to join either the centre or the left in a general attack against Hill or Longstreet. This risk General Lee could not afford to run, and so he was more and more fatally entangled by the consequences of the first move of Ewell down the valley of Rock Creek.

Having retraced our steps, we turned first south-southwest and then due east at the crossroads, in an angle of which lies the celebrated peach orchard. This was the ground soaked by the blood of the gallant soldiers of the Third Corps. After these streams of blood, streams of ink flowed in the controversy upon the merits or defects of the position taken on this ground by our brave friend General Sickles. In this controversy we were not disposed to enter again, and I was more anxious to have the glorious cripple show us the exact spot where he parted with his shattered leg than to sit in judgment upon officers, dead or living, who had all acted with unsurpassed bravery and devotion, and been inspired only by their desire to serve faithfully their common cause. The only observation which a careful study of the general aspect of the ground will suggest here is that this aspect is, if I can say so, of a very deceitful nature. I mean that, at a certain distance, one can easily be mistaken upon the real value of a position which appears to have a certain command over the neighborhood, and which, on closer inspection, turns out to be very weak. This applies to all the ground crossed by the Emmetsburg road, but not, of course, to the bold profile of Little Round Top, on whose rocky summit our next steps brought us.

On the importance of this place, consecrated by the death of Weed, Vincent, and so many of their brave followers, there is no room for discussion. The bronze statue of Warren, standing like a living man on a protruding boulder, reminds a visitor of the happy initiative which secured to the Federals the possession of Little Round Top. I must confess that I was deeply moved at the sight of this monument raised to the memory of this gallant officer, whose heart was broken forever by the unjust prosecution of which he was a victim.

There is no striking natural feature to distinguish the place where Pickett's undaunted soldiers met in the most desperate hand-to-hand conflict (Webb's) Philadelphia brigade, and were hurled back by the fighting crowd which gathered before them at the call of Hancock. The place is perhaps the more impressive on account of its plainness. A crumbling stone-wall, a foot high, dividing two fields, one of which gently slopes towards the southwest, a few stunted trees behind, marks the high-tide line upon which broke the last, the most powerful wave of the Confederate invasion. A few yards beyond, the place is pointed out, and should always be in memory of a gallant soldier, where, like the block of stone hurled by this wave before its final receding, General Armistead fell dying in the thickest of his enemies. I have not space enough to dwell upon our very interesting excursion to the east, where General David McM. Gregg explained to us in such a clear and forcible way the details of the cavalry fight, which, although it took place some miles from the positions of the contending hosts, had a great influence upon the issue of the battle. For Stuart, who had been carried too far away by unforeseen circumstances, and whose absence had been such a source of weakness to the Confederate army, might have retrieved his error by falling upon the Federal line of communication, if he had not been stopped in this dangerous movement by the prompt and decisive action of Gregg's cavalry. The latter general was kind enough to remind me that I have been the first to give full value to the service he rendered to that army in that fight, which had been rather overlooked by other writers on the same subject.

I shall conclude this sketch of our day's work by the visit to the small wooden country house, which stands unaltered since 1863, where Meade had his headquarters near which Butterfield received a glorious wound, and which derives its historical importance from the council of war in which it was decided to fight out the greatest battle of the war in the positions in which a mere accident had placed the two contending hosts. There is an old proverb which says that councils of war never fight. The stern resolution to which this council came makes a most remarkable exception to the general rule of military history, to the credit of those who endorsed it. But there is another rule which must never be forgotten; it is that whatever may be the opinion of a council of war, it is nothing but an opinion, and that the whole responsibility of any decision rests entirely and only upon the commander-in-chief. With the responsibility goes naturally the credit when success rewards the course which he has pursued. Therefore I think it must be most emphatically asserted that, whatever may have been General Meade's utterances in the council of war, he must reap the whole benefit of the decision he indorsed and carried into effect. And he will be praised by future generations for having inspired himself from the short sentence uttered by our valiant Marshal McMahon when he entered, sword in hand, the ruin of Fort Malakoff: "J'y suis, j'y reste"—"Here I am and shall remain."

From the little room where the chief of staff and four out of seven generals who commanded the army corps on the 2nd of July, the three others being dead, have met again after more than twenty-seven years, our last step will be to the spacious chapel where, on the evening of the 15th of October, the inhabitants of Gettysburg, both ladies and gentlemen, met to give a cordial greeting to our party. Young and old, mothers and children, belonging to every profession, came to see, sitting together on the same platform, most of the generals whose names were familiar to all of them. To some, belonging to our generation, not only their names, but their faces were familiar, and it was not without emotion that this sight carried them back to the days of their youth, when the tremendous storm of war suddenly broke upon their peaceful town. But to most of them the sight was a perfectly historical event, like the battle of Marathon, and most of our auditors must at first have doubted whether the gentlemen quietly sitting before them, who, notwithstanding for some of the loss of a limb, for others the color of the hair, seemed full of life and activity, were really some of the chief actors in the great events to which their town owes its celebrity. I hope a full account of the proceedings of that evening will be published. I conclude by expressing my gratitude to General Butterfield for having organized with such perfect success our visit to Gettysburg, and to all our companions for having so cheerfully answered his call.

The Comte de Paris

At the time of his visit to Gettysburg, the Comte de Paris was a king without a kingdom, living in a foreign land. Indeed, his fame owed more to his talents as a military historian and writer than to his position as a world leader, for while he had a legitimate claim to the throne, he was not the recognized leader of France. The Comte de Paris was in his declining years when he visited Gettysburg, and would die four years later. His time spent in the Union army was one of the high points of his life, and his study and journal-

istic endeavors concerning that war had been a lifelong passion. He had already written his history of the battle before he traveled to Gettysburg, and the trip was not a fact-finding mission, or an attempt to gather information for his research. It was, instead, an opportunity to walk the fields he had already written about, to see with his own eyes the places where the dramatic events had taken place, and to experience the grandeur of that hallowed battlefield shrine. It was also an opportunity to renew old acquaintances with several of the friends of his youth, with whom he had served in the Union army, a chance to relive the glory days. His accounts of the battle are those of an historian, and not a participant, and as such are different from the other accounts contained herein. The Comte de Paris obtained his information through correspondence, over the years, with the leading officers in the battle, and he compiled his history based largely upon this first-person research. In the following remembrances we will read the words of the generals who commanded upon that field, men who had forged history, and not merely written about it. With the Comte de Paris, they will serve as our personal guides to the battle of Gettysburg.

General Oliver Howard, USA

General Howard speaks little of the actual battle. Instead, he concentrates on the many visible changes in the physical appearance of his old comrades. Howard's words are more nostalgic than historic, and he seemed to delight in being reunited with these friends and peers of younger days.

Oliver Otis Howard was born on November 8, 1830, in Leeds, Maine. He graduated from West Point in 1856, fourth in a class that included a long list of officers who would achieve distinction in the Civil War. Much of Howard's pre-war service was spent at West Point, where he was an assistant professor of mathematics. Howard began the war as colonel of the 3rd Maine. He commanded a brigade at 1st Manassas, and received a general's star following that battle. He continued to command a brigade, during the Peninsula Campaign, where he lost his right arm at the battle of Seven Pines. After the war, he would receive the Congressional Medal of Honor for his part in the battle. In less than three months, Howard was back on active duty, and assumed command of 2nd Division of the II Corps, which he led at Antietam and at Fredericksburg. In November of 1862, he had been promoted to the rank of major general, and in March of 1863 was assigned to the command of the XI Corps. It was Howard's corps that was totally flanked and surprised by Stonewall Jackson's attack at Chancellorsville. Howard had neglected to obey a direct order from General Hooker to protect his exposed flank, and must be held responsible for the Union defeat on that field. In spite of this negligence, Howard continued to lead the XI Corps, and led this corps at Gettysburg, where he found himself in command of all Union forces on the field on July 1, following the death of General John Reynolds, and prior to the arrival on the field of General Hancock, assuming that command by virtue of his seniority over General Doubleday. During that period, he displayed a lack of decisive action in handling the troops, which could have ended in disaster. He was, nonetheless, voted the thanks of Congress for his action at Gettysburg.[1]

Perhaps no occasion was more consonant with the wishes of the Comte de Paris and all others concerned than the Washington dinner, given by our army commander, General Schofield. It was at the Metropolitan Club rooms. There was perhaps in the feast itself nothing to distinguish it from other such joyous gatherings. There were no speeches to record; yet many happy ones were made, but none publicly; each to his neighbor condensed a word of experience into the concrete. The Hon. Secretary to my right told me a half-dozen tales, which have never yet gotten into print, that came from the lips of Abraham Lincoln. Without permission I could not repeat them for publication, but two hearers near the Secretary laughed till they cried, as they were made to feel that Mr. Lincoln so often gained the mastery by his richest gift of humorous and pointed story-telling. It was a satisfaction to the Comte to meet the many distinguished comrades gathered around the board, such as Rosecrans, Augur, Wright, Butterfield, Casey, of the army, Admiral Franklin, of the navy, Secretaries Noble and Rusk, of the President's Cabinet, and others. Each alternative plate was for the Comte and for each of his six visiting companions. There were, near the close of the banquet, little groups of twos and threes; and in each group a hearty and happy interchange of thoughts and recollections had place. There was a lingering, after rising from the table, to multiply the words of sympathy and friendship.

I was obliged to return to New York when the party went out to southern fields, and did not rejoin it till the 15th of October, at Gettysburg. On the 14th, going north from Fort McHenry, Lieutenant Treat and I had two stops, one at York and the other at Hanover. York was full of reminiscence. Here we met soldier and citizen. How proud the gray-headed veteran to bring forward the roster of his company as it was when discharged at the close of the war. How his eyes sparkled as he told us how he happened to be at home at that period on Confederate Early's arrival; and how he followed up Early's great division, numerous in "effectives," as it marched off to Gettysburg, where it arrived and impinged upon General Howard's right flank the first day of July, 1863. This restaurant-keeper (for he is now so employed) was before us again, a vigorous Yankee soldier, and we fared well, be assured, at his table. There was the elderly citizen who barbered us, across the way from the engine-house and tower, where we took in the hills and fields that the Confederates had held for a day or two by their numerous infantry and thundering artillery. He talked glibly of the past events. He was fifteen then. "Our governors paid some $28,000 or $30,000 in cash, and gave their notes for the balance of one hundred thousand; not long since some citizens met Mr. Early in Washington, and he, Early, showed the old notes and laughed." "Are these not good still?" he inquired. Never did the barber trim one better while he talked of the past. It was a startling time, that visit of '63, and it made a deep and lasting impression.

We had plenty of time at Hanover to find Kilpatrick's cavalry position before the battle there of June 30. We found the square where the Northern and Southern horsemen first came into collision. They have changed that "square" old fence lot into "a round," and the market-house has been demolished. A fleshy veteran lumber merchant, with white head and bending shoulders, pointed to the hills held by J.E.B. Stuart, the Confederate cavalry leader, and to the other heights opposite, where the brave Custer came in. As we worked our way to the edge of the town, we exercised but little imagination to revive the scene. How surprised must friend Stuart have been when, in his long column, Pleasonton's men, under Kilpatrick and Custer, came smashing into his flank, and the wicked shells screeched their way across his lines! No wonder he fended the Yankees off, and went on via "Hanover Junction" to the coveted cover of Robert E. Lee's infantry.

At last, after enforced halts, we arrived at Gettysburg and found our party. Six had been corps commanders; and one had led a great cavalry division. Generals Gobin and Orland Smith were now prominent railroad managers. Three cars, a president's coach, then a Pullman, and then General Orland Smith's own moving palace! Another feast was already spread in them from front car to rear. General Smith gave royal welcome and hospitality that night. At sunrise I took a preliminary trip to the Cemetery Heights. Captain Morhain, of the Comte's party, shook his head as I asked him to walk. "Oh no; must I not walk all day?" And as I moved off I heard the words, "But, General, you do not walk—you run!" It took quick work to go from the railroad to the cemetery and return.

But weren't we disappointed! The evergreens with their lovely broad tops and dark shadows covered all the First Corps' front, and hid the grounds of conflict down by that wall. At the old or citizen's gate—"Where is that good woman, Mrs. Thorn, who gave us a cup of coffee, the sweetest one ever drunk, the night of the first of July after the battle?" "Oh, sir, she is not here. She has moved over there a few miles—over towards Baltimore." The north side of the Baltimore Pike is called the "North Cemetery," and has a tall iron fence around it; in front of the one near the town, where the "Louisiana Tigers" came up the evening of the second of July,

'63, for their fierce fight, is a reservoir which itself already looks old; but it was not there twenty-seven years ago. A high tower now stands on the prominent height behind the place of Steinwher's division. Later in the day as many of our party as could crowd the top took from that point satisfactory views of the great monumental field of Gettysburg.

Going back to breakfast, a Pennsylvania German, who still lisps his English, though seventy years of age, encountered the writer.

"May I ask, sir, if you might be one of the strangers?"

"Oh, yes, I came last night."

"But, no"—the brightening hope dying down. "You might not be a —?"

As he hesitated, the writer added: "Frenchman? No, no, I am only an old soldier—an American."

He gave cordial and polite thanks for the name; but he wanted, rather, to see the Comte and the other strangers from France.

We enjoyed our second breakfast that morning. Think of it, comrades, what we saw in the genial sunshiny presence of our guests.

We saw the gray locks thrown back from a high forehead; twenty-seven years ago, they had another and a darker hue.

We saw bright eyes beaming with gentleness; they were as full, but more fiery, then.

We saw a weighty man with but one foot; he was then, July 1, of slight build, quickstep, and had two feet.

We saw deep wrinkles, dimming sight, and a feeble step; this one was then a strong young man with a solid tread.

We saw a tall, soldierly figure, erect still, but with such pleasant ways and growing peace of look! He was sturdy once, almost fierce in his battle-charge.

Years have crowned that sensitive man of middle life and not lessened his manhood. He had then a fair completion and flaxen head.

And here the very happy face, that is round and fresh as the morning, but with an aged beard! He then could work all day and all night, and make a hundred thousand others do the same. There sat among them the Comte de Paris—whom the soldiers pleasantly dubbed "Captain Paris." He is as tall as in '62, but time has left his mark upon him. There are lines of care and thought; there is a higher forehead and fuller form. Years agone we remember the youth, bright and strong, whose twenty-two summers gave evidence of a hearty young life full of hope, full of enthusiasm, very like that of the favorite son by his side, the Duke d' Orleans.

Others will name the profitable work of that 15th of October, 1890, but could we have a better pictorial view of history than the Gettysburg breakfast-table on the railroad train?

Later, after the Gettysburg trip, we were publicly accused, I saw, of changing our views, as compared with the older expressions of opinion, and of affirming what we formally denied. Perhaps so. At any rate, several old feuds and misunderstandings, both here at New York and at Gettysburg, essentially gave way. The great healer and good hearts usually work goodly changes. There may have been errors; there is no shame in their confession and correction. There may have been a too heated rivalry and consequent injustice. Being brought together by the Comte's cheery and friendly visit, in his conciliating presence, the rivalry may now be over; the injustice seen and acknowledged. Why not?

Oliver Otis Howard
Major-General U.S. Army

Though Howard's conduct at Gettysburg is open to criticism, it appears that his Congressional recognition is well deserved. On July 1, his corps, consisting of 9,019 men and 26 cannon, was at Emmetsburg, some ten miles from Gettysburg. He started his men on the march at about 8:00 A.M., and by 10:30 was within sight of the town when he received word from Reynolds that the battle had been joined. Howard led his men through Gettysburg, to the scene of the morning's fight. At 11:30, he was informed of Reynold's death, and assumed command of the troops on the field. As such, he became the fourth Federal commander on the field that day. John Buford had commanded until Reynolds reached the field, and upon his death, Abner Doubleday assumed command until Howard was on the field, assuming the top spot because of seniority.[2] Howard declined to ride forward to inspect Reynold's lines, or to meet with the generals of the I Corps. Instead, he retired to Cemetery Hill, where he established his headquarters and formed his reserve, consisting of von Steinwher's division. Hancock described the position as "the highest point north of the Baltimore Pike," and stated that it "commanded every eminence within easy range. The slopes toward the west and south were gradual, and could be completely swept by artillery. To the north, the ridge was broken by a ravine running transversely." By 1:00 P.M., General Shurz's division marched through Gettysburg, and Howard directed it to a position north of the town. Barlow's

division followed Shurz's, and Howard accompanied it into its place in the line. It was during this time that he first sent dispatches to Generals Slocum and Sickles, informing them of the situation in Gettysburg, but he did not request reinforcements, or urge either general to make haste in coming to the town. A second set of couriers was sent about a half hour later. This time, Howard was asking for help, and ordering Slocum and Sickles to march for Gettysburg with all dispatch. At about 2:00 P.M., he sent a message to General Meade informing him of the situation and of his orders to bring the other two corps forward. Only after all of this activity did he finally get around to making a personal inspection of Doubleday's position outside of town. General Buford's warning about the approach of A.P. Hill's corps, on the Heildersburg and York roads, caused him to place two of his divisions at a right angle to Doubleday's to guard against this new threat, coming from the north. "About this time (2:5 P.M.) the enemy showed himself in force in front of the Eleventh Corps. His batteries could be distinctly seen on a prominent slope between the Mummasburg and the Harrisburg Roads. From this point he opened fire upon the Eleventh Corps, and also more or less enfilading Robinson's division, of the First Corps. The batteries attached to the First and Third Divisions, Eleventh Corps, immediately replied, and with evident effect." With the battle joined in his front, Howard sent word to Slocum that he was engaged, and repeated his request for support. Slocum's Corps, was, at this time, "reported to be at Two Taverns, distant between 4 and 5 miles from Gettysburg." Sickles' corps was near Emmetsburg, where Howard's corps had started from in the morning.

"At 3:20 P.M. the enemy renewed his attack upon the First corps, hotly pressing the First and Second Divisions. Earnest requests were made upon me for Reinforcements, and General Shurz, who was engaged with a force of the enemy much larger than his own, asked for a brigade to be placed en echelon on his right. I had then only two small brigades in reserve, and had already located three regiments from these in the edge of town and to the north." After 3:45, the Confederates turned Doubleday's left, and Howard's right. At 4:00 P.M., Howard sent word to Doubleday that if he could not hold against the Rebel onslaught he should fall back to Cemetery Ridge to reform. Slocum was, at this time, only about a mile outside of town. He had already ordered one of his divisions to proceed to the right of the Union line, and upon receiving word from Howard directed a second division to the left. Slocum refused to come forward himself, declining to assume the command of the Union forces that was rightfully his. At 4:10, Howard's corps was forced from its position north of town, and made a running fight in withdrawing to the site selected

at Cemetery Ridge. By 4:30, Howard's men were forming on the ridge, supported by artillery already placed there. It was at approximately this time that General Hancock arrived on the field, with orders from Meade to assume overall command of the army until Meade could arrive.[3] Although Howard had selected the position for the Union troops to rally upon, Hancock at once took over responsibility for the placement of men and guns on the hill, and in a very short time, the Union divisions were reformed and ready to face another attack.[4] The Confederates, seeing the strength of the position, "made no further attempts to renew the engagement that evening." At approximately 7:00 P.M., General Meade arrived on the field, joined by General Slocum.[5] This last statement is somewhat confusing. Slocum had been on the field for about an hour before the arrival of Meade, and had, by virtue of seniority, assumed command of the Union forces gathered there. When he joined Meade, it was to turn over command to the army commander.

Though the Eleventh Corps assisted, by detachments, in the fighting that took place over the next two days, its primary role in the battle was now ended. Overall, Howard's performance on the field had been very beneficial to the Union cause. True, he had failed to fully assume command of the situation, or to make any decisions regarding the First Corps for almost three hours following the death of Reynolds, and he had not grasped the gravity of the events unfolding necessary to urge Slocum's and Sickle's corps forward to the point of crisis for that same period of time. However, his Eleventh Corps, along with the First Corps, had held out against a largely superior force from 10:00 A.M. until 7:00 P.M., giving Meade the chance to consolidate his army to face the Southern threat. He was also responsible for selecting the position on Cemetery Ridge for the remnants of those two corps to reform their line upon, ensuring that the Union army would hold the strongest position available on the field when the contest resumed the following day. It was for these two reasons that Congress voted him its thanks for his contributions in the battle.

Following Gettysburg, Howard's corps was transferred to the Western Theater, where it took part in the battle of Chickamauga in September of 1863. Howard and his corps would never again rejoin the Army of the Potomac. Instead, it fought under General William T. Sherman in all of the battles of the west until the end of the war. Howard would rise to command of the Army of the Tennessee in the North Carolina Campaign. After the war, he served as the first director of the Freedman's Bureau, was instrumental in establishing Howard College, was superintendent of West Point, and commanded the Division of the East until his retirement in 1894. General Howard died at his home in Burlington, Vermont, on October 26, 1909.[6]

General Henry W. Slocum, USA

General Henry Warner Slocum was born on September 2, 1827, at Delphi, New York. He graduated from West Point in 1852, and saw service against the Seminoles, in Florida, and garrison duty at Charleston, South Carolina, before resigning his commission in 1856 to begin a career in law. Slocum maintained a connection with the military, however, becoming a colonel of artillery in the New York State Militia. At the outbreak of the Civil War, he was commissioned colonel of the 27th New York Infantry. He led his regiment as the battle of 1st Manassas, where he was wounded in the thigh. When Slocum returned to active duty, he was given command of a brigade in William B. Franklin's division, and when Franklin was elevated to command of the VI Corps, Slocum assumed command of Franklin's old division, which he led during the Peninsula Campaign and at Antietam. Following the Antietam Campaign, he was assigned to command of the XII Corps. His corps did not participate in the battle of Fredericksburg, but was heavily engaged at Chancellorsville. The XII Corps was severely bloodied in this battle, losing 2,755 men in the fighting. After this battle, Slocum became one of the leading critics of General Hooker, advocating his replacement as army commander.[1]

I recently heard a warm discussion between two gentlemen of an event connected with one of the battles of our Civil War.

Mr. A. said: "My authority is an article recently published in one of our magazines."

Mr. B. replied: "My authority is the statement of an officer who was present and took part in the battle."

A. yielded the point, considering that B.'s authority was better than his own.

As to the value of the authorities quoted I think both gentlemen were in error. It by no means follows that the opinion of one who took part in a battle is superior to that of the historian who was not present.

Many of the reporters who came to Gettysburg the day after the battle knew more of the true history of the great struggle than did the great mass of the officers and soldiers who were engaged in it. Not an officer or soldier on Culp's Hill or in the cavalry under General Gregg saw anything of Pickett's charge, or knew anything of the result, except as they learned from others.

The position of a line officer is with his own men, and he rarely sees or knows, during a battle, anything of it outside of his immediate locality.

Nearly all our great battles were fought on fields where one portion of the line was hidden from another. The commanding officer of the right of the line at Gettysburg saw nothing of the operations on the left. His duty was with his own command, which was entirely hidden from the left. When he left Gettysburg, after the close of the battle, he had seen nothing of the first day's operations; had not been on Little Round Top; nor had he seen the Devil's Den; had not visited the field of Gregg's magnificent cavalry fight. On his return to the field after the close of the war, all these scenes were visited, and a far clearer knowledge of the events of the great contest was obtained.

The recent visit in company with the Comte de Paris was the most profitable of all the visits he has ever made at Gettysburg, not excepting the one made in company with General Longstreet and other Confederate officers. The count visited the field to enable him to verify his history of the battle. He is an exceedingly painstaking and conscientious historian. He was accompanied by a representative of each corps of the Union army. Not a point on the field escaped his observation.

His questions were numerous and of a character proving that he already had a thorough knowledge of the field and of the movements and positions of the troops on both sides. The replies of Generals Howard and Doubleday to his questions on the field of that first day of the battle gave me a clear idea of what had occurred, and convinced me that our troops had fought a hard battle and had been handled with skill. I was also convinced that it was a fortunate thing for our army that we were compelled to leave that field. As an officer who was with us expressed it, "On the first day we were pounded into a splendid position."

The position assumed on the morning of the 2nd of July, and held by us to the close of the battle, was far stronger than that on the first day.

Our visit to Little Round Top served to increase my admiration of General Warren, and my sense of the great debt due him for his services on the field. His military knowledge enabled him to discover in Little Round top the key of the field, and soldierly instinct prompted him, without waiting orders, to seize it. Any delay on his part would have been fatal. His field artillery could not be drawn up by horses; so the men were ordered to dismount and drag the pieces to the summit by hand.

Our visit to the extreme right of our line caused me to appreciate more clearly than ever before the value of the services of the command under General Gregg, one of the most modest and unassuming, but one of the bravest and most skillful, of our great cavalry leaders. A large force of cavalry under Stuart, while attempting to turn our right and reach the Baltimore Pike in our rear, where were parked all our reserve artillery and our trains, was met by the command of General Gregg, defeated and driven back.

We called at the house which has always been an object of interest to all who visit the field. Near the line occupied by the brigade under command of General J.B. Carr, of Troy, N.Y., stands a little one-story house, which at the time of the battle was occupied by a Mrs. Rogers and her daughter. On the morning of July 2 General Carr stopped at the house and found the daughter, a girl about eighteen years of age, alone, busily engaged in baking bread. He informed her that a great battle was inevitable, and advised her to seek a place of safety at once. She said she had a batch of bread baking in the oven, and she would remain until it was baked and then leave. When her bread was baked, it was given to our soldiers, and was devoured so eagerly that she concluded to remain and bake another batch. And so she continued to the end of the battle, baking and giving her bread to all who came. The great artillery duel which shook the earth for miles around did not drive her from her oven. Pickett's men who charged past her house found her quietly baking bread and distributing it to the hungry. When the battle was over, her house was found to be riddled with shot and shell, and seventeen dead bodies were taken from the house and cellar; the bodies of wounded men who had crawled to the little dwelling for shelter.

Twenty years after the close of the war General Carr's men and others held a grand reunion at Gettysburg; and learning that Josephine Rogers was still living, but had married and taken up her residence in Ohio, they sent for her, paid her passage from her home to Gettysburg and back, and had her go to her old home and tell them the story which they all knew so well. They decorated her with a score of army badges, and sent her back a happy woman. Why should not the poet immortalize Josephine Rogers as he did Barbara Fritchie?

We visited another house which was an object of great interest to me. It was the little one-story hovel in which General Meade held his celebrated council of war on the night of July 2. I have passed the house a score of times since the battle, but did not recognize it till I entered the room in which Meade and his corps commanders met. Then the scene came back to me, and I could point to the place occupied by each officer then present. The room was unchanged, except that at the time of the council a little rickety bed stood in one corner and a cheap pine table in the centre of the room.

I remember each corps commander was first asked as to his losses during the day and the number of fighting men he could put into battle the next morning. These questions answered, then came the commanding general's all-important query: "What shall be the order of the day for to-morrow?"

There is a remarkable similarity between Waterloo and Gettysburg in the numbers engaged and the losses suffered. In Major Fox's valuable book of reference for the military student, "Regimental Losses during the War," I find the following statistics:

At Waterloo the Allies had 72,000 men and 186 guns.

At Gettysburg the Union army had 82,000 men and 300 guns.

At Waterloo the French had 80,000 men and 252 guns.

At Gettysburg the Confederates had 70,000 men and 250 guns.

The total loss of the Allies was 23,185 men.

The loss of the Union army was 23,003 men.

The total loss of the French was 26,300 men.

The total loss of the Confederates was 27,535 men.

Who can estimate the effects of these two great battles? Who can tell the consequences that might have followed the defeat of Wellington at Waterloo or the defeat of Meade at Gettysburg?

H.W. Slocum

General Slocum's account, like that of Howard, is very reminiscent, but it does give more information specific to the battle than the latter's. His open-

*ing statements concerning the relative merits of the historian versus the first
hand authority are both accurate and revealing. Slocum was conceding that
even though he was present on that great field, and had taken a leading role
in the events that transpired there, others may have known more about what
actually took place, on the whole, than he did. His comments that this visit
to the field was the most important one made, "not excepting" the one that
had been made with General Longstreet and other Confederate officers, is also
revealing. In many cases, troops on a battlefield will share more in common
with the enemy they faced across the field than with other members of their
own army, because they were engaged in the same actions. Union troops fighting on Culp's Hill shared memories with the Confederates they were fighting
against, and not with fellow Northerners who were engaged in fighting on Little Round Top. For this reason, there was always a sort of brotherhood that
existed between former enemies when they attended reunions of the great battles. The old vets could be seen visiting one another's camps, seeking out members of the units they had fought against on those fields, to discuss the events
that had become a common bond between them.*

*In retelling the story of Josephine Rogers, the brave young girl who con-
tinued to bake bread for the army despite the constant danger of a battle being
fought all around her house, Slocum gives readers evidence of yet another civil-
ian hero of Gettysburg to be remembered, along with John Burns and Jennie
Wade.*

*At Gettysburg, Slocum's XII Corps contained 9,534 men and 20 can-
non. His conduct on that field, on the first day of the conflict, is open to examination. Upon receiving the plea from General Howard to bring his corps
forward to reinforce the beleaguered Union forces at Gettysburg, Slocum stalled
and hesitated, unwilling to assume the responsibility of command that would
have been his by virtue of his rank. Indeed, he spent the entire afternoon of
July 1 trying to maneuver himself out of accepting this tough assignment. His
delay was not caused by cowardice, or by any feelings that his command abilities were inadequate to the situation, but rather because he felt that fighting
a battle at Gettysburg was contrary to the wishes of General Meade and to his
Pipe Creek strategy. Slocum did not want to be responsible for altering the
plans of the commanding general, and thus reacted with contemplation and
caution, earning him the nickname in the army as "Slow Come." He was not
possessed of the aggressive nature of a Reynolds, Hancock, or Sickles, and did
not feel compelled to march to the sound of the guns without assurance from
his commander that his course of action was approved. While he pondered,
however, the fate of the Union army hung in the balance at Gettysburg, and*

had it not been for the tenacious fight waged by the members of the I and XI Corps, the fortunes of the battle, and the war, may have gone in favor of the Confederates.

In his official report, Slocum states that his corps was at Two Taverns on the morning of July 1, when he received word from Howard that the I and XI Corps were engaged, "when the march was at once resumed."[2] *This statement is obviously untrue, as the historical record shows. Howard had marched his corps twice the distance Slocum had to cover, and had done so in two and one half hours. It took Slocum six hours to reach Gettysburg from a distance of four to five miles. Had he responded in the same fashion as had General Reynolds, he could have been on the field himself, in advance of his men, in less than an hour. Slocum's statement that he put his troops on the march as soon as he received word from Howard was obviously an attempt to cover what he himself, in retrospect, felt to be an unnecessary delay.*

Once Slocum did arrive on the field, at approximately 6:00 P.M., he strengthened the Union defenses by ordering General John Geary's division to take up position on Little Round Top and directing General Alpheus Williams' division to Wolf's Hill, on the right of the line. These moves both extended and strengthened the Federal position, and, in the case of the latter, were influential in causing General Richard Ewell to decline carrying out Lee's discretionary orders to occupy the heights on Culp's Hill on the evening of July 1.

July 2 found the XII Corps holding the right of the Union line, from Culp's Hill to Spangler Spring, with General George Sykes' V Corps to their right, forming the flank of that portion of the line. Slocum was given overall command of the right wing, consisting of the XII and V Corps, to make a proposed attack on the Confederates. Slocum opposed the attack, and was successful in convincing Meade that the wooded and rocky terrain of Culp's Hill territory was too rugged from which to launch an offensive. With no further action contemplated for this part of the line, Meade directed the V Corps to be shifted to the Union left, leaving the XII Corps as the right flank of the army. With no attack to be made, there was no longer a reason to have a wing commander, but Slocum continued to assume the title, appointing Alpheus Williams to command the XII Corps, while he himself continued to exercise a role that no longer mattered. The XII Corps was called to battle in the afternoon, following Longstreet's attack on the Union left at the Round Tops, Devil's Den, the Peach Orchard, and the Wheat Field. Sickles' III Corps was being roughly handled, and the reinforcements Meade was funneling into the fray were being torn up by the Confederate onslaught. Meade ordered Slocum to leave one brigade to guard Culp's Hill and march the remainder of his corps in support of the left and center. Units from the I, V, and VI Corps were also ordered into the breach to try to stem the gray tide. General Williams led the XII Corps column in the direction where he heard the most firing, He had no definitive instructions, and no guide. General Slocum continued to supervise the "right wing" even though no such military structure yet existed. Williams' men arrived on the field in time to slam into General William Barskdale's Confederate brigade, which had just fought its way through the Peach Orchard. Barksdale's men were exhausted and almost fought out when the vanguard of the XII Corps arrived in its front, and the pressure from this fresh column forced the Rebel attack to crumble. Slocum, in his statement, refers to the fighting on the left on July 2, but he does not allude to the contributions of the XII Corps in that conflict, presumably because he was not present with his men when it took place.[3] He does, however, praise General Warren for realizing the importance of Little Round Top, and for seizing it, without orders, thus saving this all-important defensive point for the Union army. The fact is that Warren was ordered to Little Round Top by General Meade, who upon discovering the unauthorized move of Sickles' III Corps feared for the safety of his line. Warren is to receive full credit for the defense of Little Round Top that took place following his arrival at that spot, but he cannot be credited with going to that place on his own initiative, as Slocum states.

Slocum alludes to the council of war, held by Meade on the evening of July 2, to canvass the opinions of his generals as to whether the army should stay and fight on July 3, or whether it should be withdrawn. Slocum's answer was short and curt: *"Stay and fight it out."* He was equally stoic when he was later informed that General Edward Johnson's "Stonewall Division" had captured the breastworks vacated by his corps when it was sent to reinforce the Federal left. *"We'll drive them out at daylight,"* was his only response. *"Orders were at once issued for an attack at daybreak, for the purpose of regaining that portion of the line which had been lost. The artillery of the Twelfth Corps, consisting of Battery F, Fourth U.S. Artillery; Battery K, Fifth U.S. Artillery; Battery M, First New York, and Knap's Pennsylvania battery, was placed in position during the night by Lieutenant-Colonel Best, and opened the battle at 4 A.M. on the following morning, and during the entire engagement all these batteries rendered most valuable aid to our cause."*[4]

Johnson's Confederates had been reinforced during the night, and it took Slocum's men all morning to drive them back and recover their breastworks, but drive them back they did. The action on Slocum's front was ending just as the drama was shifting to the center, preparatory to Pickett's Charge. Slocum's role at Gettysburg, as well as that of the XII Corps, was ended.

Following the battle, Slocum and the XII Corps were unintentionally slighted in the official report of General Meade, who minimized their contribution to the outcome. For Slocum, this was a fortunate turn of events. Had his own performance received a thorough examination, he would most probably have been called to answer for his unwarranted delay in answering Howard's calls for help, and if the I and XI Corps had failed to hold on July 1, Slocum would definitely have had to shoulder a majority of the blame for the Union loss. As it was, Gettysburg neither enhanced nor diminished Slocum's reputation in the army. As with Howard, he was not to be associated with the Army of the Potomac for much longer. His XII Corps was sent south to reinforce General Rosecrans' army, just as was Howard's XI Corps, in time to take part in the Chickamauga Campaign. Joseph Hooker was in command of the two corps, and because of a personal difference between Hooker and Slocum the latter was assigned to duty at Vicksburg. Following Hooker's resignation, Slocum once again assumed control of his corps, and led it in the Atlanta Campaign and the March to the Sea. During the Carolinas Campaign, Slocum commanded the left wing of Sherman's army, while Howard commanded the right. Slocum would end the war in command of this wing, designated the Army of Georgia.

Following the end of the war, Slocum practiced law, served three terms in Congress, and was appointed as a member of the Board of Gettysburg Monument Commissioners. In this capacity, he visited the field of Gettysburg on many occasions. Henry Warner Slocum died at Brooklyn, New York, on April 14, 1894.[5]

General Abner Doubleday, USA

Abner Doubleday was born at Ballston Spa, New York, on June 26, 1819. Doubleday graduated from West Point in 1842 in a class that included such Confederate notables as Gustavus Woodson Smith, A.P. Stewart, D.H. Hill, Lafayette McLaws, Earl Van Dorn, and James Longstreet. Following graduation he was assigned to the artillery, and served with this branch in the Mexican-American War. The outbreak of hostilities in 1861 found him serving as an officer at Fort Sumter, in Charleston Harbor, where he was credited with aiming the first gun to reply to the Confederate bombardment. Doubleday saw service in the Shenandoah before being commissioned a brigadier general and assigned to command a brigade in Irvin McDowell's corps during the Second Manassas Campaign. At Antietam he was promoted to command of the First Division in the I Corps, and he continued in that position at Fredericksburg. His division was not engaged at Chancellorsville, being held in reserve. Gettysburg would prove to be his greatest contribution in the war, and would be his only opportunity to exercise independent or corps command.[1]

Not having been at Gettysburg for several years, I had formed the idea that it was covered with monumental abortions, and was agreeably surprised to see so many beautiful and attractive memorial structures. All over the wide fields marble soldiers are represented as kneeling, loading, and firing, and the effect is very striking and picturesque. The Count of Paris said that there is no battlefield in Europe so magnificently adorned. Gettysburg is now the Waterloo of our country, and deserves a visit from every tourist; not only on account of its historical associations, but as one of the art-centers of America.

Upon reaching the ground, I found everything as familiar to me as it was twenty-seven years ago, when the First Corps came upon the scene to relieve Buford, who was holding on with his cavalry to those perilous ridges and looking anxiously to the south for help. Reynolds had been placed in command of the First, Third, and Eleventh Corps, and was eager to meet the enemy. He was not one of your retiring generals, nor was he in favor of making an everlasting war of positions. He saw the hordes of the enemy ravaging his native State, and, proud of the men he commanded, determined to fight the invaders d' outrance as soon as he could get at them. The Confederate forces at this time were impoverishing a large part of Pennsylvania by their merciless requisitions. It might almost be said of them as of the old Danes when they landed on the coast of England:

> With hands of steel and tongues of flame
> They ranged the country through;
> And where the Norseman sickle came
> No crop but hunger grew.

There seems hardly room in the short space allotted me to dwell upon many of the episodes of the battle, but perhaps a brief statement of the opening scenes of the contest on the first day may not be inappropriate.

Two roads lead into Gettysburg from the west, and come together on the edge of the town. These are cut by ridges which run north and south, and by a small stream beyond the second ridge, called Wiloughby's Run. Our cavalry, through some misapprehension, reported that the enemy were advancing on both roads, and this rendered General Reynolds and myself unnecessarily apprehensive as regards our communication with the south. Buford's cavalry since early morning had been holding on desperately to the ridge nearest the water, contending with two large divisions of Hill's corps; while the First Corps was five miles away to the south on Marsh Creek. As it was all quiet there and the stress of battle lay with Buford, Reynolds hastened forward with the nearest troops at hand—two small brigades of Wadsworth's division—and directed me to bring the remainder of the corps as soon as possible. Having withdrawn the pickets and put the other two divisions en route, I galloped ahead and reached the field just as the contest began between Cutler's brigade on the right against Davis's Confederate brigade. Meredith's brigade was still on its way a quarter of a mile to the rear. In the mean time I had sent an aid to ask for orders, and received this message from General Reynolds in reply: "Tell Doubleday I will hold on to this road, and he must hold on to that one."

This was the last order he ever issued. Archer's Confederate brigade, however, which formed the right of the attacking column, did not advance by the lower road, but attempted to take possession of a piece of woods between the two roads. Reynolds imprudently rode in there, almost unattended, to reconnoiter. As he turned his head to the rear to see how near we were, one of the enemy's sharpshooters must have seen him, and put a bullet through his neck, killing him instantly. As Meredith's men came on, I made a short address to them, telling them that this was the decisive battle of the war and that the result would decide whether the Confederate President or Abraham Lincoln was to rule the country. I urged them to take the wood and hold it at all hazards. Full of the memory of their past achievements, they replied: "If we can't hold it, where will you find the men who can?" They went forward enthusiastically, entered the grove, and not only overpowered Archer's brigade, but captured him and the greater portion of his men. While this was going on, I had gone almost down to the stream on the left to see if any enemies were approaching along the more southern road. As there were none in sight, I returned, and the prisoners were brought up to me. I said, somewhat inconsiderably, to General Archer, who had been an old comrade of mine in Mexico: "I am glad to see you Archer!" To which he angrily replied: "I am not a damned bit glad to see you, sir!"

I now found that, while we had been fortunate on the left, we had met with a check on the right, where Davis's Confederate brigade had flanked that of Cutler and had obliged it to fall back a short distance. I soon remedied this, however, by sending a force under Colonel Dawes, of the Sixth Wisconsin, reinforced by another under Colonel Fowler, of the Fourteenth Brooklyn, to attack Davis in flank. The Confederates rushed into a cut in the railroad for shelter. There they were enfiladed and partially surrounded, and after a desperate hand-to-hand struggle most of them surrendered. This cleared my front temporarily of enemies and left me a period of repose.

If Hill had only known what a meagre force we had, he might have swept us away by a resolute advance, for he could easily have turned both flanks; but the absence of the cavalry had cut off all sources of information from him. Two of his brigades had been roughly handled, and he imagined that the whole Army of the Potomac confronted him. He therefore waited until he could be reinforced by the arrival of Ewell's corps before making any further attempts.

This delay enabled the remainder of the First Corps to reach the field. The Eleventh Corps arrived soon after, and made immediate dispositions to cover the right flank of the First against the advance of Ewell, who had now appeared in sight. They did not succeed, however, in preventing Ewell from taking possession of a prominent elevation, upon which he established his batteries which enfiladed my line, rendering a new formation necessary.

A combined attack was now made by Hill's and Ewell's forces against the Union line, but, as regards the First Corps, it was handsomely repulsed, and almost an entire brigade—that of Iverson—was captured by General John C. Robinson's division on the right. The concentration of Lee's army, however, was going on rapidly. The whole country was filled with troops who were advancing from the north and northwest. My line had now become very weak and thin. I had lost fully one-half of my force, and when the enemy brought on their strong reserves, further resistance became impossible. We accordingly fell back in a leisurely way, aided by Buford's cavalry on the left, turning every hundred yards to face the enemy again, until we reached Cemetery Hill, which was held by Steinwher's division of the Eleventh Corps. As we passed through the streets, the women came out, pale and frightened, to offer us coffee and refreshments and to implore us not to desert them.

Toward the close of the contest Hancock rode up and told me that he had been sent to assume command of the field. He was our good genius, for he at once brought order out of confusion and made such admirable dispositions that he secured the ridge and held it. As he was junior in rank to General Howard, he had no right, technically speaking, to supercede the latter. Meade had assigned him to that duty, it is true, but under the law only the President himself could place a junior officer over a senior. Howard did not recognize him as his superior, and I think Hancock, as he rode over to me, was in some doubt as to whether I, as commander of the First Corps, would acknowledge him as Howard's superior. Had I refused to do so, the battle of Gettysburg, in all probability, would have had a different termination. As Hancock ranked me, however, the question did not concern me personally, and I saw plainly enough that, if I refused to acknowledge his delegated authority, both the First and Eleventh Corps would be surrounded and captured. I had no desire to see the men of my command sent to adorn the prisons of the Confederacy, and I therefore did not insist on any technicality which would be certain to produce that result.

There were several reasons why the enemy did not advance at once and crush us.

First—Both Ewell's and Hill's corps had suffered heavy losses during the day, as General Lee testifies in his official report; in consequence of which they did not feel in a very adventurous mood.

Second—Kilpatrick had started north to meet Stuart's cavalry, which was coming from Carlisle. Ewell saw this movement and, fearing that it foreboded an attack against his rear, weakened his main line by detaching a considerable force to meet it.

Third—The dispositions made by Hancock were calculated to deceive the enemy and make them think that we had been largely reinforced; and,

Fourth—A party sent by Ewell to ascertain how far our line extended south of Culp's Hill encountered the Seventh Indiana Regiment of Wadsworth's command, who had been directed to reconnoiter in that direction. The Seventh heard the enemy approaching, lay in wait for them, captured some who were in advance, and drove the others off. The latter returned and reported that they found Union troops in position far south of Culp's Hill. This implied, of course, that our line had been strengthened.

The final result was that the Confederate leaders thought it would be prudent to defer further action until daylight came and enabled them to see how much ground we occupied.

So ended the first day of the battle of Gettysburg. I have not attempted to give a detailed account of the operations of the Eleventh Corps, as I suppose General Howard will do so in the article he intends to write for this series.

Abner Doubleday

Doubleday does less nostalgic retrospection and more actual historic narrative than either of the two preceding generals. His surprise to find that the field had not been desecrated by gaudy, tasteless statues, but was instead filled with artistic tributes, shows a reverence for the ground where he and so many of his comrades fought a desperate struggle that immortalized friend and foe alike, and became a national symbol of the sacrifice both armies made on the road to a reunited nation. The hills, woods, and fields were hallowed ground, and a shrine to those who had fallen. One can readily see, from his statements, that Doubleday was pleased with the way the monuments added to the sanctity of the ground.

At Gettysburg, the I Corps contained 11,997 men and 28 cannon. As such, it was the largest of the Federal corps on the field for the first day's fight. When Doubleday was thrust into corps command, following the death of General

Reynolds, he inherited a corps that was not yet positioned for battle. Reynolds had arrived on the field a little after 10:00 A.M., in advance of his men. By the time of his death, at about 11:00 A.M., only Cutler's Brigade and Hall's Battery had been brought on line. Reynolds was in the process of leading the Iron Brigade onto the field when he was struck down by a sniper's bullet. In his official report, Doubleday reports the time of Reynolds' death to be a little earlier. He wrote that he "learned, with deep sorrow, that our brave and lamented commander, Major-General Reynolds, had just been shot, and was no more. This melancholy event occurred in the beginning of the attack referred to, about 10:15 A.M." To Doubleday, therefore, fell the task not only of fighting the battle, but of establishing the line upon which it would be waged. It was Doubleday who formed the battle line, and he was responsible for shifting those forces to meet the flowing tide of the battle. An overwhelming number of Confederates threatened to swallow up Doubleday's forces. Wadsworth's brigade had been ordered, by its commander, to withdraw to Seminary Ridge, Hall's battery had lost one of its cannon and was in danger of being overrun, and the 147th New York was cut off, with the Confederates firmly blocking its line of retreat. Against this backdrop, Doubleday ordered the 6th Wisconsin, of the Iron Brigade, to change front and charge into the flank of the Confederates. The 95th New York and the 14th Brooklyn were added to the charge. General James Archer's brigade was turned back, with Archer himself being taken prisoner, the first Confederate general to be captured since Lee had assumed command of the army. The Union counterattack swept forward to engage two regiments of Davis's brigade that had taken refuge in a railroad cut, and were blocking off the retreat of the 147th New York. A bayonet charge was made upon the Confederate position, with the result being the surrender of the two Southern regiments that occupied it, "the release of the One hundred and forty-seventh New York Volunteers, which had been cut off, and the recapture of one of Hall's pieces." Doubleday states, "I immediately directed the original line of battle to be resumed, which was done. All this was accomplished in less than half an hour, and before General Howard had arrived on the field or assumed command."[2]

Even after the arrival of Howard on the field, Doubleday continued to manage the battle on the left wing of the Union army, and to meet the Confederate threats with skill and dogged determination. It was his opinion that "there never was an occasion in which the result could have been more momentous upon our national destiny. Final success in this war can only be attained by desperate fighting, and the infliction of heavy loss upon the enemy; nor could I have retreated without the full knowledge and approbation of Gen-

eral Howard, who was my superior officer, and who had now arrived on the field." Doubleday's corps certainly did its share of desperate fighting that day. The I Corps sustained losses of over 6,000 men at Gettysburg, or over 60 percent of its strength, with most of them being lost during this period. They were hammered by the corps of A.P. Hill, and Richard Ewell, and were seriously outnumbered, but held on for a period of about four hours, before being forced to retire to Cemetery Ridge. Their actions had bought General Meade, and the rest of the Union army, precious time with which it could concentrate at Gettysburg to meet Lee's army, and they had been able to hold on to the Cemetery Ridge, the strongest position on the field. In so doing, they had not only staved off defeat, but had ensured the final victory for the North. They had withstood the attack of more than 16,000 Confederate veterans, and had crippled seven of the ten Southern brigades thrown against them, inflicting casualties of from 35 to 50 percent.[3]

Following General Meade's arrival on the field, General Doubleday suffered possibly the most serious slight of any general to fight in the battle. Thus far, he had managed his part of the engagement with skill and daring, and, upon examination, had performed in a manner more credible than had Howard or Sickles. However, he was not a favorite with General Meade, who had him replaced with General John Newton, as commander of the I Corps. Doubleday had been nicknamed "Forty-eight Hours" in the army, and Meade doubted his initiative and celerity, despite the positive evidence to the contrary his performance on the field had just shown. The appointment of Newton caused hard feelings not only with Doubleday, but also with the veterans of his corps, who felt that their commander had done an admirable job in managing the battle and resented being placed under the command of an officer who was not even from their corps. For Doubleday, his service was over. He spent the remainder of the war serving in Washington. Following the end of the war, he was made a colonel and assigned to the command of the 35th Infantry, a post he held until his retirement in 1873. Doubleday would die at his home in Mendham, New Jersey, on January 26, 1893. Though modern historians have endeavored to do justice to his contributions on the field of Gettysburg, he remains today as the most underappreciated general to have fought in that engagement. The tenacious stand of the I Corps, under his immediate supervision, and despite the staggering losses it sustained, prevented the routing of two Union corps, and gave Meade the opportunity to win the most dramatic battle ever to be fought upon American soil.[4]

Following the war, he would become embroiled in controversy concerning statements he made alleging that General Meade contemplated a retreat from Gettysburg on July 2. He was roundly criticized for these remarks, and repeatedly attacked in the press. William Swinton, who wrote "History of the Army of the Potomac," avowed that there was not "a Scintilla of evidence" to support Doubleday's assertion, causing the latter to present that evidence. Doubleday was quick to respond: "Mr. Swinton takes the ground that it was an attack on Gen. Meade's reputation to assert that he ever thought of falling back. I am aware that it may seem ungracious to speak thus of Gen. Meade's intentions. As he did remain and fight it out, he is entitled to the credit of doing so. I, therefore, would not have mentioned the subject at all if it had not been for a circumstance that has escaped Mr. Swinton's notice. The desire to retreat was supplemented by acts which form part of the history of the battle. He sent for Gen. Pleasonton on the 2nd of July, his Chief of Cavalry, and directed him, late in the afternoon, to collect what cavalry and artillery he could, proceed with it to the rear, and take up a position to cover the retreat of the army. As a faithful historian, if I refer to Gen. Pleasonton's movements at all, I must state the origin of it. Mr. Swinton forgets that the Congressional Committee on the Conduct of the War reported that there was evidence that Gen. Meade desired to retreat." Indeed, the historic record supports Doubleday's contention, but George G. Meade had already died by the time that it became so controversial, and Meade's supporters, fearing that the reputation of the dead hero would suffer, continued to blast Doubleday for even suggesting that Meade ever contemplated retiring from the field. As his commander, Meade had taken his corps away from him, and now the memory of Meade was challenging his very reporting of the events he had lived through.[5]

Doubleday's name would become more familiar to most Americans than the majority of the generals who had fought at Gettysburg, but it would not be a result of his service during the war. Instead, he would achieve everlasting fame for being credited, incorrectly, with inventing the game of baseball.

General Daniel Sickles, USA

Daniel Sickles was born in New York City on October 20, 1819. After attending New York University, where he studied law, he went into politics, becoming a key figure in the Tammany Hall machine, serving in the capacity of legal counsel. Sickles left Tammany Hall to become secretary of legation, in London. He spent the years immediately prior to the Civil War serving in elected office, as a New York State Senator and a representative in the United States Congress. In 1859, Sickles murdered his wife's lover, the son of Francis Scott Key, within sight of the White House. In the trial that followed, Sickles was acquitted of the murder charge, in the first use of an insanity plea in United States judicial history. The lawyer who represented Sickles in the case was none other than Edwin Stanton, the man who would later become Abraham Lincoln's Secretary of War.

Because of his political ties, and the fact that he was a War Democrat, the Lincoln administration readily accepted Sickles' services in the military, granting him the rank of brigadier general in September of 1861. Sickles commanded the famed Excelsior Brigade until November of 1862, when he was promoted to the rank of major general. In this capacity, he commanded a division at Fredericksburg, and was elevated to command of the III Corps at Chancellorsville. At Chancellorsville, Sickles' command reported the flank movement of Stonewall Jackson, and Sickles pushed forward two-thirds of his corps to pursue the Confederates, leaving Howard's XI Corps completely isolated on the right flank and open to the crushing attack that Jackson later made. Sickles act in leaving his assigned position in the line was a major factor in the disaster that followed, which led to the crushing defeat of Hooker's army. Sickles had often been guilty of quarrelling with his superiors, and following Chancellorsville, he entered into a nasty feud with Joseph Hooker, who felt Sickles' actions to be a large reason for the disgrace his army had suffered on that field. At Gettysburg, Sickles would continue to display a tendency to overstep his authority, and to circumvent the wishes of his superiors when he once more moved his corps from the place that had been assigned to it in the battle line.[1]

It was indeed an event of rare interest to meet on the battlefield of Gettysburg, on a golden October morning, the best historian of the battle and of the Civil War, our comrade and friend, the Comte de Paris, himself a veteran volunteer of the war; and by his side the son of one of our veterans, a gallant young recruit, the Duc d' Orleans. We miss the knightly Duc de Chartres, another veteran volunteer drawn from the ranks of the royal house of France; but we have with us the Marquis de Lasterie, descendant of Lafayette. Here in the cemetery of dead heroes, under the shadow of the great Reynolds, are assembled in the same group for the first time since the battle all but one of the living corps commanders who fought here, Slocum, Howard, Sickles, Newton, Doubleday; and the leaders of the divisions, Gregg and Wright. We miss Pleasonton, commander of the cavalry corps, kept away by illness, but we have Butterfield, chief of staff. The men who made history surrounded the historian.

The strongest emotion of the visitor to Gettysburg is the memory of those who here nobly fell in battle—"those who here gave their lives that the nation might live." Volunteers of 1861-2-3, flower of our young manhood, the loved ones of our Northern homes, volunteers without bounty, men gold could not hire, for whom the flag and the Union were worth all else; men who had only a home to live for and a country to die for. And the great leaders, where are they? Meade, commander-in-chief; Reynolds, who fell on the first day; Hancock, on the third; Sedgwick, Warren, Buford, Hunt, Kilpatrick. Nor can we forget Hooker, who reorganized the army and led it almost here, his chosen field, compelling Lee to give battle.

The transition from 1863 to 1890, little more than a quarter of a century, almost confounds the imagination, and makes the reality seem like a dream. Now we are more than sixty millions, all freemen, united, prosperous, tranquil. Then we were separated, mangled by the struggles of a great civil war of unforeseen duration, nearly all Europe against us, every resource of men and treasure strained to the utmost tension, no one able to forecast the boundaries which the end of the conflict would define.

The Army of the Potomac has lost the peninsular campaign; it has lost Pope's campaign, and, although it has won at Antietam, it has lost Burnside's campaign, and Chancellorsville. The situation at home and abroad is grave. The insurrection that burst upon New York a few days after the battle is already imminent; it is visible in June. England and

Napoleon are hostile to the Union, waiting for a suitable pretext to recognize the Southern Confederacy. Public opinion everywhere is much estranged by the Conscription Act of Congress. Resistance is openly threatened. The Proclamation of Emancipation, the organization of colored troops, and kindred measures have alienated large numbers of people. An impression, almost a belief, gains ground that for military, economical, and political reasons the success of the North is doubtful. Such is the general opinion in Europe. It is feared that the enormous cost of the war makes it impossible to prolong the struggle. It is apprehended that, in the absence of volunteers, the losses caused in our armies by desertions, disease, and battles cannot be filled up by bounties or conscriptions; and we have not yet found a commander who inspires at once the government, the people, and the armies with confidence in his ability to lead us to victory.

I would not have seen Gettysburg had Hooker not sent me a message summoning me from New York, where I was slowly recovering from a contusion received at Chancellorsville. He announced the coming battle, asking me to join my command instantly, giving such urgent and flattering reasons that I could not refuse, although my surgeons, Carnochan and Sayres, protested. I reached headquarters at Frederick on the 28th of June, at the hour Hooker was relieved by Meade. Hardie, who was the bearer of the order putting Meade in command, sat by my side from Washington to Frederick, chatting all the way, without revealing a word of his mission. The change in command of the army was no sooner announced— Hooker sacrificed, on the eve of battle, by the action of Halleck—than I heard from Hayden, and others of my personal friends, earnest remonstrances against my serving under Meade. They knew he was hostile, dating from several incidents in the Chancellorsville campaign. I consult Hooker. He says: "You cannot ask to be relieved on the eve of battle; wait at least until after the engagement." This advice coinciding with my inclinations, I resumed command of the Third Army Corps.

Lee crossed the Potomac on his second invasion of the North at the head of the largest and best-equipped army the South had yet put in the field. It believed itself invincible. It had won many signal victories. It was stronger than ever in numbers, equipment, organization, and discipline. It was led by able corps and division commanders. Lieutenant-General Hood says: "Never before or since have I witnessed such intense enthusiasm as prevailed throughout the entire Confederate army. Exulting cheers reechoed all along the line. Our forces marched undisturbed to Chambersburg. I found General Lee in the same Bouyant spirits which pervaded his magnificent army. After the ordinary salutations he exclaimed: 'Ah, General, the enemy is a long time finding us. If he does not succeed soon, we must go in search of him."

Hooker and the Army of the Potomac were not as far off as Lee and his lieutenant supposed. The campaigns of Chancellorsville and Gettysburg are monuments of his strategical skill. Lee's cavalry, under Stuart, were on a long raid and failed to discover Hooker crossing the Potomac at Edward's Ferry. Pleasonton and his cavalry gave us eyes to see Lee's marches and movements, while they blindfolded Lee so that he could not see ours until Hooker was on his rear and flank challenging him to battle.

Lee commands a halt in front of Harrisburg, on the Susquehanna. What is the matter? His communications are threatened. His retreat may become impossible. He must give or accept battle. He directs the concentration of all his forces at Gettysburg. This was Hooker's revenge for Chancellorsville. Ewell had reconnoitered that position a few days before. It was admirable for the invading army, because it afforded facilities for advance or retreat. And if Lee is quick in his concentration, he may choose a battleground as advantageous to him as Fredericksburg. And so it might have been, if bold and sagacious Buford had not stood in the way with a division of cavalry the counterpart of himself.

The battle of Oak Ridge, on July 1, was a surprise to both armies. It, however, gave to Howard the choice of position at Gettysburg, and was worth all it cost, forcing Lee to offensive tactics. General Lee says: "The enemy occupied the point which General Ewell designed to seize. The strong position which the enemy had assumed could not be attacked without danger of exposing the four divisions present, already weakened and exhausted by a long and bloody struggle, to overwhelming numbers of fresh troops." These fresh troops were Birney's division of Sickle's corps and a division of Slocum's corps, the corps commanders both present. Well might Lee speak of his four divisions as "weakened and exhausted by a long and bloody struggle." The great fight of Robinson's division and the First Corps is an illustration of the terrible conflict at Oak Ridge. Out of 2,500 men on the field, Robinson lost 1,600 in killed and wounded. Hotly engaged for four hours on a July day against overwhelming numbers, repulsing repeated attacks of the enemy, capturing three flags and a very large number of prisoners, they were the last to leave the field. Says Robinson in a letter to Meade, soon after the battle: "We have been proud of our efforts on that day and hope that they will be recognized. It is but natural we should feel disappointed that we are not once referred to in the report of the commanding general."

Lee expected to make his concentration at Gettysburg unopposed. Meade expected to concentrate on his chosen line of Pipe Creek without interference. Strange, but not impossible, that two mighty armies, eager for combat, in near proximity to each other, like two giants groping in the dark, can march and maneuver without the presence of one being known to the other.

At Oak Ridge the enemy had four divisions of infantry, Heth's, Pender's, Rodes's, and Early's—seventeen brigades; and sixteen batteries of artillery—the battalions of Pegram, McIntosh, Carter, and Jones. We had the First Corps—seven brigades and five batteries; and the Eleventh Corps—six brigades and five batteries; that is to say, thirteen brigades and ten batteries. The enemy were four brigades stronger in infantry, and they had a few more guns.

General Humphreys—good authority—says Lee had about eighty-five thousand infantry at Gettysburg; that is to say, nine divisions of ninety-five hundred each. In other words, Ewell's four divisions gave him thirty-eight thousand infantry against seventeen thousand five hundred under Reynolds and Howard, with a corresponding superiority over us in artillery.

Reynolds's battle was brought on without orders, perhaps against orders, if Reynolds received, as the other corps commanders received, the circular orders from General Meade issued early in the morning of the 1st of July, which read as follows:

"If the enemy assume the offensive and attack, it is his (General Meade's) intention, after holding them in check long enough to withdraw the trains and other impediments, to withdraw the army from its present position and form a line of battle with the left resting in the neighborhood of Middleburg and the right at Manchester, the general direction being at Pipe Creek. For this purpose, General Reynolds, in command of the left wing, will withdraw the force at present at Gettysburg, two corps (First and Eleventh), by the road to Taneytown and Westminster, and after crossing Pipe Creek, deploy towards Middleburg. The corps at Emmetsburg (Sickle's) will be withdrawn via Mechanicsville to Middleburg."

Reynolds was right in accepting battle as he did, to gain time, as Hancock says, "for the commanding general of the army to come to some decision." Reynolds's battle was necessarily fought, and well fought, by

Buford, Doubleday, Robinson, Wadsworth, Fairchild, Huydekoper, and Barlow, and, after Reynolds fell, by Howard in command.

Accident, so potent in war, overruled the plans of Meade, drifting him towards a position chosen by the enemy; a better battlefield than he had himself chosen, it had for us the advantages of strong defensive lines and excellent communications, and the enemy was there—sure. Slocum, Hancock, Howard, Sickles, and Doubleday urged Meade that night to come to Gettysburg with all his army. He came. And so swift was the concentration of his forces, under the direction of the chief of staff, that on the morning of the 2nd of July his army was in position, except the Sixth Corps, which had a long march from Westminster, thirty miles, and could not reach the field until late in the afternoon.

As these reminiscences are personal, I will dwell a moment on an anxious hour spent at Emmetsburg in the afternoon of the 1st of July, after hearing of the death of Reynolds, and receiving from Howard and Doubleday earnest appeals for support at Gettysburg. My orders from the general commanding were to hold Emmetsburg at all hazards. These orders, of course, were based on the supposition that the enemy's point of concentration would be at or near Emmetsburg, but no enemy was near. Reconnoiscences and scouts for miles around gave no indication of the presence or proximity of a hostile force. The situation of Howard, so pressed by superior numbers, was hard to resist. Why stay here in idle security, in formal obedience to orders? What order would Meade give if he were here in person and read Howard's dispatch? He would say: "Yes, march to Gettysburg." And so say I: "Yes, I will go, and take the risk of approval. It must be said, at least, that the Third Corps marches in the right direction,—toward the enemy." At 3:15 P.M. I wrote to Howard: "The Third Corps will march to Gettysburg immediately." The column is formed; two brigades under Graham and De Trobriand, with two batteries, are left to hold Emmetsburg. We move forward cheerfully, over a rough road, on a sultry afternoon. We arrive at Gettysburg, marching along the enemy's flank, uninterrupted. The welcome of Howard and his men rewarded us. We saw the proofs of their bloody fight, their resolute bearing, awaiting another attack, entrenched in their strong position on Cemetery Ridge. The Third Corps was massed on their left. At 9:30 that night I wrote to General Meade urging the concentration of his forces at Gettysburg, expressing the opinion that "it is a good battlefield for us, although weak on the left flank." Later in the night I received from General Meade an expression of his approval of my march from Emmetsburg against orders, and also instructions to bring up the two brigades and batteries I had left at Emmetsburg under Graham and De Trobriand.

The early morning of July 2 was spent reconnoitering my front on the left, choosing positions, gathering information about the roads, and learning something of the force and dispositions of the enemy. The prolongation of the line of Cemetery Ridge, perhaps the more desirable tactical position for me to occupy, unless overruled by superior considerations, proved upon examination to be an unsatisfactory line because of its marked depression and the swampy character of the ground between Cemetery Ridge and Little Round Top. The most commanding position on the field was Little Round Top and the ridge running from it toward the Emmetsburg road. Moreover, to abandon the Emmetsburg road to the enemy would be unpardonable. The force at my disposition, ten thousand men, was insufficient to hold the lines from Cemetery Ridge to Round Top and defend that height, which was obviously the key to our position. Longstreet had thirteen brigades of infantry. I had six brigades. He had sixty guns. I had thirty. Information from scouts and from Buford's cavalry on my flank indicated the presence of considerable bodies of the enemy's forces on my front, concealed in the woods and maneuvering to envelop our left. The ground was rocky and undulated with ridges; convenient roads through the woods and valleys gave the enemy excellent opportunities for turning our left flank and gaining our rear.

I had pointed out, the night before, in a letter to General Meade, that our left was our assailable point. Careful study of the field during the morning had confirmed my impressions. At 11 o'clock the reconnoissances of General Berdan with his sharpshooters and Colonel Lake with the 4th Maine revealed the formation of the enemy's columns in large masses, preparing to attack. General Tremain and Colonel Moore, my aides-de-camp, rode over to headquarters again and again all through the morning, reporting the situation of things on my front. Impatient of longer delay, more than ever anxious in view of the certainty of an attack from superior numbers, staggered by the announcement that Buford's division of cavalry had been withdrawn from my flank and ordered to escort trains to Westminster, thirty miles away, I went in person to headquarters and asked General Meade to come with me and reconnoiter the left. He was too busy. I asked for General Warren; Warren was busy on the right preparing for an attack by the right wing on Culp's Hill, under Slocum. Butterfield was too busy preparing Meade's orders. Hunt, chief of artillery, was seated near by. I earnestly asked for Hunt, because I needed his advice in placing my own batteries, and others from the reserve which I was sure to require. Hunt was allowed to go with me.

We went over my part of the field together, looked at all the ground, from the swale and swamp between Cemetery Ridge and Round Top, to my proposed line running from Round Top along the ridge to the Emmetsburg road, en echelon to Cemetery Ridge and the line of Hancock's Corps. Hunt liked my chosen line, pointing out, however, that more troops than I had would be necessary to hold it. Hunt and Randolph, my chief of artillery, found excellent positions for my batteries; all was in readiness for my advance except orders from headquarters. Hunt assured me I might look for those orders as soon as he made his report to General Meade, declining himself to take any responsibility, because he was ignorant of the plans of the general commanding, and so much depended upon his determination to stand on the defensive, or to attack, or to maneuver for another position. I waited an hour. No orders came. My troops, eager for combat and anxious to profit by all the advantages of the ground, leveled all the fences within their reach. The movements of the enemy became more and more aggressive. Their assault seemed to have been delayed by a change in the route of their columns, caused, as appears from their official reports, by my discovery of their formation and the advantages they found in enveloping our left by a march through the forest, which had been uncovered by the unfortunate withdrawal of Buford's cavalry from the flank.

Impossible to wait longer without giving the enemy serious advantages in his attack, I advanced my line towards the highest ground in my front, occupying the Emmetsburg road at the very point where Longstreet hoped to cross it unopposed, covering Round Top and menacing the enemy's flank if he attempted to turn our left. He accepted battle on my line. Birney's division extended from the Devil's Den, a great mass of boulder rocks, across the wheat fields and Peach Orchard, towards the Emmetsburg road. Humphrey's division held my right and the Emmetsburg road. It was 3 o'clock. The enemy's lines of battle were developing in enormous strength. The artillery opened fire. I am summoned to headquarters. What can it mean?

(Circular)

"Headquarters Army of the Potomac,

"July 2, '63, 3 P.M.

"The commanding general desires to see you at headquarters. Very respectfully, your obedient servant, Daniel Butterfield." Major General and Chief of Staff.

"Sent to Major-Generals Sedgwick, Sickles, Sykes, Newton, Slocum, Howard, and Hancock."

General Sykes says: "At 3 P.M. General Meade sent for me, and while myself and other commanders were conversing with him the enemy formally opened the battle, and developed his attack on our left. I was at once ordered to throw my whole corps to that point, and hold it at all hazards."

It is evident the commanding general has no appreciation of the gravity of matters on my front. Else why summon me and all the corps commanders to headquarters at such a critical moment? This question is answered by General Meade's telegram to Halleck, general-in-chief, at the same hour, 3 P.M. July 2:

"The army is fatigued. If not attacked, and I can get any positive information of the position of the enemy which will justify me in so doing, I shall attack. If I find it hazardous to do so, or am satisfied the enemy is endeavoring to move to my rear and interpose between me and Washington, I shall fall back to my supplies at Westminster ... I feel fully the responsibility resting upon me, but will endeavor to act with caution."

This telegram from our commanding general shows that at the supreme moment—3 P.M. July 2—when the enemy was advancing to attack, we had no plan of action, no order of battle. For Meade the battle of July 2 is a surprise, like the battle of July 1. Lee knows what he wants to do; his corps commanders know his plans; they know the order of battle; they are executing it.

Unable to reply in writing, I point out to the staff officer who brought the order the attitude and movements of the enemy, and ask him to beg General Meade to excuse me from complying with the order, as my presence is necessary with my command. A second order comes from headquarters, peremptory, immediate. I reluctantly turn over the command to Birney, and proceed to headquarters. General Meade meets me at his door, saying: "You need not dismount, General. I hear the sound of cannon on your front. Return to your command. I will join you there at once."

The sound of my guns breaks up the council. We fight here.

Spurring my horse to the utmost speed, I soon relieve Birney. The battle begins with the quickening fire of the skirmishers. General Meade arrives; thinks my line too much extended; too weak to resist the enemy. "Yes," I reply; "but I can hold him until reinforcements arrive. I will contract my line, or modify it, if you prefer. My men are easily maneuvered under fire." "No," said Meade, "it is too late; I will support you. I will order up the Fifth Corps on your left; call upon Hancock to support your centre and right. If you need more artillery send to the reserve for it."

Leaving me with these instructions, I did not see General Meade again, nor receive any communication from him, during the action. The enemy's attack was pressed with all the vigor and boldness characteristic of Longstreet, Lee's ablest lieutenant. The conception of the enemy's movement was based upon Jackson's assault on our right flank at Chancellorsville. The force employed was about the same. The ground, woods, and roads all favored it; and the loss of Buford's cavalry made it practicable. But the menacing attitude of my corps, in close proximity to Longstreet's column, threatening its flank, compelled every inch of ground to be disputed from the onset. Every inch of ground was disputed along the whole line, from Round Top to the Peach Orchard. Warren, who comes with Meade, goes to Round Top to reconnoiter. Seeing the efforts of the enemy to envelop my left, quickly discerning the importance of Round Top and the enemy's desire to seize it, Warren sends to me for a brigade. I have none to spare, needing every man, and more, on my front. I advise him to send to the Fifth Corps, already on the march toward us. Another message from Warren, saying the heads of column of the Fifth Corps are still distant and may arrive too late. We have seen it was not ordered over from the right until after 3 o'clock. At this moment the gallant and gifted Weed, of Ayre's division, reports in person to me that his brigade is near.

Pressed by Birney for support on my left, pressed by Warren for troops to occupy Round Top, the key of our position, I send Weed to him just in time. The gallant Weed falls mortally wounded on Round Top, and Hazlett, too, was killed as he leaned over the body of the dying Weed to hear his last words. Zook's, Cross's, and Brooke's brigades, of Caldwell's division, of Hancock's corps, arrive and are at once engaged. The full force of the enemy's attack is felt. Zook and Cross and O'Rourke are mortally wounded. Our lines waver, but rally again and again. The same ground is fought over and over. Barksdale, of Mississippi, is mortally wounded in a charge within our lines. The chivalrous Graham, on my centre, falls seriously wounded and is captured by the enemy. The brave Ellis, leading his Orange Blossoms, is killed in the Devil's Den while leading a charge of the 124th New York. Vincent and Willard are killed at the head of their brigades. Bigelow's battery, in front of my corps colors, loses more than half its men and eighty horses. Randolph and Seely are wounded. The Sixth Corps is coming, out strongest corps, and is ordered to support the left. Humphreys, Carr, Brewster, and Sewell, of my corps are engaged. Gallant Crawford, of the Fifth Corps, with a regimental flag in his hand, leads his Pennsylvania Reserves in a charge on the enemy's flank and front and drives him out of reach. This is the same division so brilliantly led by General Meade at Fredericksburg. Humphreys still stands firm on the right. I am wounded. I turn over my command to Birney and am carried to the rear, knowing that victory is ours.

We see from this glance of the battle of July 2 that as soon as our troops on the left equaled those of the enemy the battle was decided in our favor. If this equality had existed at the outset of the conflict, our victory would have been decisive early in the action, and the Sixth Corps, our strongest, would have been available to follow up on our success and deal a decisive blow to the enemy; and if Buford's division of cavalry had remained on the left flank, its cooperation would have given us overwhelming advantages. With two corps, say twenty-five thousand men, holding the left, entrenched in good positions, holding Round Top and commanding the ridges and roads on our left, the repulse of the enemy would have been as disastrous to them as our assault on their lines at Fredericksburg was destructive to us. With the Fifth Corps in reserve on the left, our fight would have been an easier one, but Sykes was not engaged until 5 o'clock.

A signal feature of this battle was the buoyancy of the troops, their readiness to respond to commands, the eagerness of chiefs of battalions, batteries, and brigades to support each other, often without formal orders. The charges and countercharges between sunset and dusk would take pages to describe. The impetuosity of the men and their field leaders in the Second, Third, and Fifth Corps was a priceless factor, without which our victory would not have been achieved. And it is remarkable, as showing the fierceness of the struggle on the 2nd of July, that the losses of the enemy in both Hood's and McLaws's divisions exceeded the losses in killed and wounded in Pickett's division on the following day. The losses on both sides on the second day were greater in killed and wounded than the combined losses on the first and third days of the battle. It is a moderate and safe estimate of the enemy's forces engaged on the second day to place them at thirty thousand infantry and eighty pieces of artillery. Hood's, McLaws's and Anderson's divisions included thirteen brigades of at least twenty-five hundred men each. The artillery of Longstreet's and Hill's corps amounted to one hundred and forty-four guns.

At the close of the battle of the 2nd, after the enemy retired, the disposition of our forces remained as already described, except that a portion of the First Corps was moved to the left of Cemetery Ridge, the Third

Corps under Birney in support; Carr's brigade of the Third Corps, slept on the field, in its position on my right. On the other flank, at Culp's Hill, the enemy had gained a foothold in our works during the absence of a considerable part of the Twelfth Corps, under Williams, which was ordered to our left, but Greene's brigade fought like a division and held the enemy, until Slocum, commanding our right wing, brought back his forces and drove Ewell once more to his position.

We pass over the council of war on the night of the 2nd without comment, since it had no result. We stayed and fought it out at Gettysburg. General Lee persisted in his offensive tactics, against the remonstrance of Longstreet, and notwithstanding that our left had been made so strong as to resist the assaults of thirty thousand men the day before, General Lee rashly attempted to break our lines with eighteen thousand men on the 3rd. It is true he expected the cooperation of Stuart's cavalry on our rear, but our cavalry, Gregg on our right and Kilpatrick on our left, had destroyed that hope, inflicting decisive defeats on Stuart, whose object Pleasonton, Gregg, and Kilpatrick quickly divined.

The great cavalry combat of Gregg we hear described by himself in modest, yet vivid, colors. Scarcely mentioned in the official reports, yet we see it was one of the most brilliant incidents of the Gettysburg campaign. Twelve thousand sabers flashing in the July sun on the open fields beyond our right. The thundering of two hundred cannon echoing from the main army answered Gregg's and Stuart's artillery. The ripening grain withered under the tread of heavy columns—columns of squadrons charging again and again, whilst the reapers of Gregg and Custer gathered a harvest of honor and fame.

Kilpatrick, too, with his division of cavalry, supported our left, besides the Fifth and Sixth Corps and a portion of the First, with the Third in reserve. Kilpatrick's cavalry battle on the 3rd was no less effective on our left, as from this flank also the enemy's cavalry attempted to gain our rear and unite with Longstreet in piercing our left centre. In this fight the gallant Farnsworth fell. "A general on the 29th, on the 30th he baptized his star with blood, and on July 3d, for the honor of his young brigade and the glory of his corps, he gave his life. At the head of his dragoons, at the very muzzles of the enemy's guns, he fell with many mortal wounds." So writes Kilpatrick.

The story of the third day has been so often told in all its dramatic details that it has become a familiar picture of the battle of Gettysburg. It need not be repeated here. We had won the battle. Longstreet pronounced the enemy's last assault hopeless from the beginning. No troops, he said, however valiant, whatever their discipline, could make any serious impression on our left or left centre, the direction of the attack. So profoundly was he impressed with the forlorn and desperate character of the assault that he was unable, he says, to give utterance to the order to Pickett. In reply to Pickett's demand whether he should move, Longstreet could only nod his head in the affirmative. The assault ended, as Longstreet had foreseen, in the annihilation of the advancing columns of the enemy; a useless sacrifice of brave men, sometimes necessary in war, but not required on that day to vindicate the courage and discipline or fortitude of Lee's great army.

The headquarters staff was marked by signal ability. Butterfield had been already distinguished as a commander in the field. In the movement of large columns he had no superior in our armies. Hunt, our chief of artillery, would have won distinction under Napoleon. He was ably supported by Tyler, commanding the reserve artillery. Warren, chief of engineers, was accomplished both in his special corps and as a commander, Pleasonton, chief of the cavalry corps, made his arm superior to that of the enemy in every equal combat. Besides, he was gifted with rare military intuitions. He sent Buford, with our strongest cavalry division, to Gettysburg, when nobody had divined the place chosen by Lee to concentrate his army for battle. He sent Gregg to our right to encounter Stuart and thwart his movement to our rear; on the third day, the day of Pickett's assault, he sent Kilpatrick on our left, where the enemy attempted a similar diversion, but was defeated.

Our army corps were ably commanded. Sedgwick, Reynolds, Slocum, Hancock, Howard, Newton, Doubleday, and Birney were all strong men, each differing from the others in elements of strength, yet forming a group of remarkable power. General Slocum and General Howard were chosen afterwards by General Sherman to command the right and left wings, respectively, of his great army in its famous campaign through Georgia. In the campaign of Gettysburg we lost three corps commanders—Reynolds, killed on the 1st of July; Sickles, wounded on the 2nd; and Hancock on the 3rd.

As Lincoln said to me, "There was glory enough at Gettysburg to go all around, from Meade to the humblest enlisted man in the ranks."

Military men are fond of comparisons between Waterloo and Gettysburg. There are, indeed, several military resemblances, but more contrasts; whilst in moral and political significance these two great battles are as wide apart as the fields themselves. Waterloo put an end to the rule of

Napoleon and the military supremacy of France in Europe, already impaired by the campaign in Russia. Gettysburg upheld the authority of the wise and unselfish Lincoln, and assured the perpetuity of the American Union. Waterloo was the triumph of the reigning monarchs of Europe over the French Revolution. Gettysburg prevented an alliance between the Southern Confederacy and England and France to divide and destroy the United States. Waterloo restored France to the Bourbons. Gettysburg severed the chains from every slave in America, giving force and effect to Lincoln's Proclamation of Emancipation, which before was only an edict.

And here at Gettysburg I hope that the War Department will establish a permanent military post, garrisoned by artillery, and that on this consecrated ground, all of which should belong to the government, the morning and evening gun may forever salute "the men who here gave their lives that the nation might live."

Daniel E. Sickles
Major-General U.S. Army (retired)

Sickles' article is the longest submitted by any of the generals, and it is also the most detailed. This was not necessarily due to any tendencies of Sickles to be a historian. In the nearly three decades that had transpired since the battle had been fought, Sickles had become one of the most controversial leaders to have served on that field. His actions at Gettysburg were the basis for a debate that caused a war of printed words between Sickles and his detractors, most notably among them, General George G. Meade. Meade, and his supporters, publicly criticized Sickles for his actions at Gettysburg, while Sickles endeavored to justify his decision to move his corps, and show that it was the only logical course open to him. He had infuriated Meade and those close to him when he suggested that moving his corps had been a major key to the Union army winning that battle, and that the fight would probably have gone in favor of the Confederates had he not done so. In effect, Sickles had stated that Meade would have lost the battle had it not been for the initiative Sickles had shown. By the time the corps commanders met at Gettysburg, in 1890, the controversy was well known to all who studied the battle. Sickles used this opportunity as yet another public stage on which to present a defense of his conduct on the field. He was now able to do so free from the fear of recrimination from Meade, his greatest critic, as that general had already died.

On the morning of July 1, 1863, Sickles' Corps was at Emmetsburg, ten miles distant from Gettysburg. His orders, from General Meade, were to hold his position there, serving as the left flank of the army. When orders from General Reynolds arrived, directing Sickles to bring his corps forward, with all haste, to support the forces then engaged with the Confederates, Sickles was faced with a dilemma. To his credit, he handled the situation with alacrity and sagacity. Sickles sent word to Meade relating Reynolds' directive and of his plans to leave one brigade from each of his two divisions in Emmetsburg, while he led the other four to Gettysburg assist Reynolds. Unlike Slocum, who vacillated and hesitated, not willing to assume responsibility for acting without orders from his superior, Sickles seems to have been governed by a combative spirit that caused him to march to the sound of the guns. His actions were contrary to the instructions he had received earlier that morning, from Meade. In a circular, from army headquarters, Meade had stated: "From information received, the commanding general is satisfied that the object of the movement of the army in this direction has been accomplished, viz, the relief of Harrisburg, and the prevention of the enemy's intended invasion of Pennsylvania, &c., beyond the Susquehanna. It is no longer his intention to assume the offensive, until the enemy's movement or position renders such an operation certain of success. If the enemy assume the offensive and attack, it is his intention, after holding them in check long enough to withdraw the trains and other impedimenta, to withdraw the army from its position and form a line of battle with the left resting in the neighborhood of Middleburg, and the right at Manchester, the general direction being Pipe Creek." It was these very orders that had caused Slocum's delay, as he felt that bringing on a general engagement, at Gettysburg, was inconsistent with Meade's overall plan of campaign. Sickles, however, took another view of the contradictory orders from Meade and Reynolds. He thought the confusion to be a result of Meade's improvised command system, and his general failure to grasp the situation as events were unfolding. Never a great supporter of Meade, this confusion over orders only served to enhance Sickles' low opinion of the new army commander. Sickles' conviction that Meade was in over his head, and that he was smarter than the army commander, would lead to the actions of the former that proved so pivotal in the battle. Because of the fact that General Sickles did not submit a report of the battle to be included in the Official Records, the account of his participation comes primarily from his testimony before the Committee on the Conduct of the War, and letters he wrote to the New York Herald.

A popular argument concerning Sickles' unauthorized movement of his line is that it allowed the Union army time to concentrate additional forces behind the line of the Third Corps, after it had been pierced by the Confederate attack. In other words, if Sickles had maintained his original position, and Longstreet's attack had punctured his line there, it could have resulted in the Rebels taking control of the Baltimore Pike, and severing the Union army before Meade could respond to the crisis. There are two inconsistencies that are immediately evident in this line of reasoning. First, once the Union forces had been hammered back to the position originally to have been held by the Third Corps, the Confederates were unable to push them any further. This line, as laid out by General Meade, proved to be a more formidable position, and Confederate efforts were unable to dislodge the now battered and weary defenders from it. Sickles' move had taken his line beyond its own artillery support, and had left his corps in a vulnerable position on the field, with both of its flanks open and exposed. The artillery, collected by General Henry Hunt, had been a primary factor in blunting the Confederate assault on July 2, and it is easy to understand why Meade was angry over Sickles' decision to vacate his stronger, assigned line, which was covered by Union artillery, in favor of the advanced and tenuous line that he moved his corps to.

The second inconsistency to Sickles' argument is that, because of the placement of his advanced line, he gave Meade time to shuttle reinforcements onto the field to stop the Confederate attack. The fact of the matter is that Sickles' movements did nothing but exacerbate the situation on the Federal line. Meade's forces enjoyed interior lines during the battle of Gettysburg. The configuration of the famous "fish hook" line meant that Meade could easily move units to critical points, with relative speed, whereas the Confederates, spread out in external lines, had to march their units much further to counter any movements of the Federals. Meade would have been able to easily shift his forces to the point of attack regardless of whether Sickles' line had been where it was supposed to be, or where it ended up. Sickles' argument that his move facilitated Meade's being more able to mass his forces in front of Longstreet's attack is entirely without merit. What the move did facilitate was a situation where all of the Union reinforcements were compelled to go into the fight in the open field, without the benefit of their flanks being anchored to other portions of the Federal army. Units were thrown into the maelstrom of battle piecemeal, without the protection of a prepared line, and without the support of the artillery batteries that had been placed in positions to cover that line. His movement also uncovered Little Round Top, which was recognized by both sides as being a key to the battlefield. When Sickles moved his corps forward, there was no provision made for defending the height, and no men were left behind to occupy it.

Whether or not Sickles truly felt that his proposed line was superior to the one his corps had been assigned, or whether he was merely exhibiting a defiant attitude toward a commander he felt to be inferior to himself, can never be known. What is known is that the movement of his corps was certainly without Meade's consent or permission. Sickles had made several requests to move his line, and even rode to Meade's headquarters to seek permission. Meade was busy planning for the defense of his right flank, and was not prepared to approve or deny Sickles' request. Instead, he sent Chief of Artillery, General Henry Hunt, to examine the ground and make a recommendation. Hunt agreed that the forward position offered some benefits, but noted that a move to that position would make it necessary to place the V Corps on line, in the gap that would be created between Sickles' and Hancock's Corps. Meade had designated the V Corps to serve as the army reserve, and Hunt stated that any change in this designation would have to come directly from the army commander. During the late morning, Sickles ordered Colonel Hiram Berdan's Sharpshooters, along with a Maine regiment, to probe the southern portion of Seminary Ridge and ascertain if it was held, in force, by the enemy. When Berdan's force reached Pitzer's Woods, it came under heavy fire from the Confederates, confirming the fact that the enemy was present, in force. Sickles decided that the Confederate presence in Pitzer's Woods posed a threat to his left flank and decided to send his divisions forward, with or without Meade's approval. At 1:00 P.M., with banners flying, the ten thousand men of his corps marched forward, in line of battle, to occupy the new line. The move uncovered the Round Tops, created a gap between the II and III Corps, and left both flanks of the III Corps exposed and in the air.[2]

When Meade was finally made aware of it, his reaction was highly uncharacteristic, according to observers. Meade was nick named "Old Snapping Turtle" by many of his subordinate officers because of his abrupt and snappish manner. An observer noted that the commanding general was so dumbstruck by what he saw when he examined Sickles' line that he could not even snap. As he peered over the Third Corps lines, and at the Confederate forces that were even then driving back Sickles' pickets, he could only say: "General, I am afraid you are too far out." Sickles argued that his new position was stronger than the one he had been assigned, reluctantly stated "I will withdraw if you wish, sir." "I think it is too late," Meade replied, as the report of a nearby cannon frightened his horse, causing it to become unmanageable. "The enemy will not allow you. If you need more artillery, call on the reserve. The Fifth Corps—and a division of Hancock's will support you." That is all Meade got to say before his terrified steed went racing away with him. It took the Federal commander several seconds to get the animal calmed down, and when he did so, he galloped off to order up the support he had promised Sickles.[2]

Meade was right, the Confederates were not going to allow Sickles to withdraw his corps. General Lee's battle plans for the day were assail the Union left flank, precisely where Sickles out of position troops were drawn up. What followed was the bloodbath associated with Devil's Den, the Wheat Field, the Peach Orchard, and Little Round Top, and General John Bell Hood's and General Lafayette McLaws' divisions of Longstreet's corps swarmed over the advanced Third Corps line. Meade made good on his promise of support. He not only sent the Fifth Corps and portions of the Second, he also stripped the defenses on Culp's Hill in order to be able to shift a large portion of Slocum's Twelfth Corps to Sickles' sector, to try to stem the Rebel onslaught that threatened to shatter his left wing. In the end, the Confederate assault lost its cohesion, as Longstreet's exhausted men finally wore out against the constant stream of reinforcements Meade was throwing into the battle. The Union line had been forced to give ground, and had been pushed back, but it had not broken. Amazingly, the position held by the Federals when they finally threw back the Confederate attackers was roughly along the same line that Meade had laid out for Sickles' Corps to occupy in the first place. As one Union commander put it, the line had been hammered back to a position that the Confederates could not take.

The cost had been appalling. Sixty-five percent of the total Union losses in the three-day battle were suffered during the fighting on July 2, in front of the Third Corps line. Sickles himself was severely wounded, and had to have his right leg amputated. Four Union brigade commanders had been killed: Stephen H. Weed, George L. Willard, Samuel K. Zook, and Strong Vincent. General Gouverneur K. Warren, the savior of Little Round Top, was also wounded. The attacking Confederates fared little better. General John Bell Hood was severely wounded, and would also require an amputation. Dorsey Pender, another Southern division commander, was mortally wounded, while brigade commanders William Barksdale and Paul Semmes were killed. The United States Congress would later award Sickles the Medal of Honor for his service at Gettysburg, an act that would only add to the controversy between him and his commander on that field. Congress had voted its thanks to General Meade, for the winning of the battle, but it had bestowed the nation's highest military award upon Sickles, giving those who championed either man license to advocate for one against the other.[3]

Following the battle, Sickles took every available opportunity to defend *his actions at Gettysburg, and to cast aspersions upon Meade. Is testimony before the Joint Committee on the Conduct of the War, he left the impression that Meade had almost left him to his fate on July 2, when he stated the fighting was "an engagement in which only two corps of our forces took part." The truth is that in addition to his own 3rd Corps, Meade had sent Sickles aide from the 2nd, 5th, and 12th Corps, committing a major portion of his available force to the engagement. During the same testimony, Sickles unleashed a scathing criticism when he was asked if it would have been a hazard to attack Lee's army before it made good its escape back into Maryland. Sickles caustically avowed "No, sir. If we could whip them at Gettysburg, as we did, we could much more easily whip a running and demoralized army, seeking a retreat which was cut off by a swollen river; and if they could march after being whipped, we certainly could march after winning a battle."*[4]

The attacks against Meade's handling of the army were ongoing and merciless. At every opportunity, Sickles declared that his actions at Gettysburg had saved the army and won the battle. He painted Meade as being indecisive, on that field, and tried to give the impression that, because of Sickles' actions, Meade had won at Gettysburg in spite of himself. When opportunities were not readily available to Sickles, he used his prior experience, gained with Tammany Hall, to create them. On March 12, 1864, the New York Herald *ran an open letter to the editor from an author known only as Historicus. Though Historicus was generally regarded to be Dan Sickles, definitive proof of that fact could not be obtained. In the letter, Meade is roundly criticized for virtually every decision he made on the field, while the actions of Sickles and his corps are lauded in almost mythical fashion. At one point, Historicus accuses Meade of trying to cover for his own mistakes by deceiving his superiors and the public in his reporting of his actions. "Without meaning to do injustice to General Meade, it must be admitted that his report of this great battle is at such variance with all the statements which have appeared in the press, that it is due not only to history, but to the indomitable prowess of our heroic army, that every fact sustained by concurrent testimony should be given in order to fully establish documentary evidence to support the facts furnished."*[5]

When Abraham Lincoln had told Sickles that there was "enough glory at Gettysburg to go all around," as Sickles states in his article, it was an effort, on the part of the President, at conciliation. Though Sickles does not mention it, Lincoln's statement was intended to mediate the controversy that was already raging between Meade and Sickles. It was his way of saying that the feud between the two generals was unnecessary and should be dropped. Meade had filed a complaint with the War Department, following the article in the New

York Herald, *seeking protection for his reputation. In the response, from General Henry Halleck, he was advised not to enter into a public controversy, as that would be playing right into Sickles' hands. All who read the article agreed that it was either written, or dictated, by him, but that it would be impossible to prove it. Halleck's advice was to simply ignore the attacks.*

By the time the Union commanders met once more on the fields of Gettysburg, in 1890, George G. Meade had died, and was no longer able to refute any derogatory statements Sickles made about his conduct in the battle. Meade was a fallen hero, acknowledged by most of the population as being the victor at Gettysburg, and attacking his conduct could prove to be a tricky thing. In Sickles' article, he never directly accuses his old commander of any misdeeds. Instead, he focuses on putting his own service, and that of his corps, in the best light possible, using subtlety and innuendo to make his case against Meade.

Following Gettysburg, and recuperation from his wounds, Sickles was commissioned, by President Lincoln, to make a tour of Union-held territory in the South, to evaluate the effects of amnesty proposals, the progress of Negro emancipation, and reconstruction. He then completed a diplomatic mission to Colombia, before serving as military governor of South Carolina, at the close of the war. In 1869, he was retired from the army with the rank of major general of regulars. That same year, President Grant appointed him minister to Spain. In 1893, Sickles was elected to the United States Congress. For many years, he served as chairman of the New York State Monuments Commission, charged with placing monuments to New York troops on the various battlefields of the war. Daniel Sickles died, at his home in New York, on May 3, 1914, and was buried in Arlington National Cemetery.[6]

General David Gregg, USA

David McMurtrie Gregg was born in Huntington, Pennsylvania, on April 10, 1833. After completing the course of studies from what is now Bucknell University, he attended West Point, graduating from the academy in 1855. Gregg was serving in California when the war broke out. As soon as circumstances permitted, he came back east, where he was commissioned colonel of the 8th Pennsylvania Cavalry in January of 1862. Gregg had influential support in the Pennsylvania state government, as Andrew Curtin, the wartime governor, was his first cousin. He performed well during the Peninsula Campaign and at Antietam, and was promoted to the rank of brigadier general in November of 1862. During General George Stoneman's raid on Richmond, and in the Chancellorsville Campaign, Gregg commanded a division of cavalry. At Gettysburg, Gregg's division was assigned to cover the extreme right of the Union line, and was called upon to halt the advance of J.E.B. Stuart's troopers and protect the threatened wing. Although General Alfred Pleasonton was in command of the cavalry corps at Gettysburg, and was responsible for the overall performance of the mounted troops, Gregg is generally credited with the victory over Stuart's horsemen.[1] Even for serious Civil War buffs, the history of the mounted fight at East Cavalry Battlefield is one of the lesser-known events of both the battle of Gettysburg and the war. It was overshadowed by the grand martial spectacle of Pickett's Charge at the time that it took place, and over the ensuing years. For those generals who commanded troops on the fields of Gettysburg, the importance of Gregg's victory has never been in question, as attested to by the esteem with which the other corps commanders held Gregg.

When those two giants of the War of the Rebellion, the Armies of the Potomac and of Northern Virginia, had determined, by invitation of the latter, to seek a new field of combat far removed from the desolated plains of Virginia, that of Gettysburg was well chosen. Its commanding eminences, with the undulating vale between, all under cultivation, with here and there open groves of goodly trees, gave to the infantry and artillery of the combatants all that could be desired for effective attack and defense. Off on the flanks were fair and wide fields for mounted cavalry by thousands to mingle in wild melee, where pistol and saber did their keenest work, and light batteries scattered canister most grievously in the faces of their would-be-captors.

A field which made it possible for a great battle to be fought to the finish, in which each of the three arms of service was properly employed in its own sphere, and thus rendered its most effective service. There were attacks sublime in execution even to the point of their failure, which only occurred because success was impossible. Resistance was heroic. Surprises there were none, but there were many mighty rushes.

On one of the bright days of October last, on this famous field were assembled some eight generals and a smaller number of officers of lesser rank, all having served in the Union army in the battle of Gettysburg. Of the general officers, five had been corps commanders, one the chief of staff, and the remaining two division commanders of infantry and cavalry respectively. They were in attendance upon the distinguished historian of the War of the Rebellion, the Count of Paris, with whom all had served on the peninsular campaign.

The same sky was above. Round Top, Culp's Hill, and Brinkerhoff Ridge, the village with the seminary and cemetery, were all there. The stage was the same, but where were the actors? Where the great masses of men that were clad in blue and in gray? Could there be a reassembling of the mighty armies that contested this field twenty-seven years ago, those that could appear in the flesh would be outnumbered by the ghostly representatives of the dead. Nor have these assembled officers escaped the change that time works. When the battle was fought, the oldest of them had not more than reached the full majority of manhood; and now the youngest could only claim to be in the old age of youth or the youth of old age.

It was a pleasant meeting. There were a kindness of greeting and heartiness of grasp that plainly showed how glad these old sailors were to meet again, some not having met since the close of the war. As each stood upon the portion of the field where his command engaged the enemy, his story was briefly told. Indeed, it was scarcely more than pointing out lines and positions. The historian was not here so much to learn as to verify. A question asked, he was quick to be the narrator.

The entire field having been gone over, the party separated, all feeling that the day had been pleasantly and profitably spent. The old battlefield has dotted over it along the entire Union line monuments both beautiful and chaste, but the work of adornment is incomplete. On some commanding point near the centre of the line there should rise a colossal monument to the memory of the commander of the Army of the Potomac, George Gordon Meade. It should be built of material as pure as his character and as enduring as his fame.

In front of it, and just beyond the reach of its tallest shadow, there should be another to his able lieutenant, Winfield Scott Hancock, who on this and a score of other fields showed that his first commander had not erred in styling him "superb."

D. Mm. Gregg

General Gregg's account of the reunion of the Union commanders is quite reflective, but not very informative. It may be that he felt it inappropriate for him to leave a history of his activities as he was the only officer, other than Butterfield, the army chief of staff, who had not commanded a corps in the fight. It's possible that he was hesitant to include his memories among those of the men who had been his superiors. Whatever the cause, Gregg's documentation of the day was of an emotional bent, memorializing the field and a few of the officers whom he admired, namely Meade and Hancock. Though his own efforts upon that field had been substantial, Gregg left others to sing his praises, taking no credit to himself for any great deeds or momentous decisions. The praise given him by the other surviving commanders, however, allows both the casual observer, and the historian, a glimpse of the modesty and character of Gregg.

Gregg was still relatively new to division command at the time of the battle of Gettysburg. He was even more inexperienced in independent command, which is the position he would find himself in as he faced J.E.B. Stuart's gray-clad horsemen in the ridges and valleys east of Cemetery Ridge on the afternoon of July 3. Pleasonton, the overall commander of the cavalry corps, was with Major General Judson Kilpatrick's division, forming the far left of the Federal line, in the vicinity of Big Round Top, intent upon making an attack on the Confederate right flank. Gregg, with his division, was positioned to guard the Union right flank, in the vicinity of Culp's Hill. Gregg's line con-

nected with that of the infantry, on Wolf's Hill, and extended to the right, where it covered the Hanover and Low Dutch Roads. General George Armstrong Custer's brigade formed the right flank of Gregg's line, but he had received orders to return to his own division, joining Kilpatrick on the Union left. Custer had been pulled out of line, and was preparing to obey his orders when a large force of Confederate cavalry was sighted, prompting Gregg to request him delaying the execution of his movement until the situation in Gregg's front had been fully developed. Custer, always brooding for a fight, was only too happy to agree.

What Gregg's troopers had observed was General J.E.B. Stuart's cavalry attempting to ride around the Union flank and assume a position in the Federal rear. General Lee had ordered Stuart's column to take part in what was intended to be a three-pronged attack on the Union line. Major General George E. Pickett was to command the main infantry assault, directed against the Union center. Lieutenant General Richard Ewell was to coordinate a demonstration against the Union right, on Culp's Hill, to prevent Meade from being able to reinforce his center against Pickett's attack. General Stuart was ordered to attack the Union rear, to create a further diversion in Pickett's favor, and to maximize the disorganization that would follow a successful penetration of the Union line. But Lee's plan of attack started to unravel almost from the start. Ewell had prematurely launched his attack, which had fizzled out before Pickett's battle lines surged forward. Stuart's column had now been spotted, before getting into position, and Gregg's cavalry stood ready to block their path. About 2:00 P.M., Colonel John B. McIntosh dismounted his 1st New Jersey Cavalry and sent the men forward as skirmishers. As the Confederate position began to be developed, Southern artillery opened on the Union troopers, which drew the immediate response of the Union guns. McIntosh ordered the 3rd Pennsylvania Cavalry forward, in support of the 1st New Jersey. McIntosh soon discovered that the Confederate force was too strong for him to deal with, and he sent word to Gregg requesting that Brigadier General Irvin Gregg's Brigade be forwarded to his support. Gregg's Brigade was far to the rear, prompting General David Gregg to request assistance from Custer. General Gregg appeared on the field at approximately the same time as Custer's command, at which time he took command of the engagement. By this time, the 1st New Jersey and 3rd Pennsylvania began to run short of ammunition, and Custer sent the 5th Michigan to relieve them. The New Jersey and Pennsylvania men attempted to withdraw, but were so closely pressed by the Confederates that they were forced to face about and resume the fighting. The 5th Michigan was soon running short on ammunition, as well, and the entire

Union line began to give way. General Fitzhugh Lee, seeing this, threw forward the 1st Virginia Cavalry to attack the Union right and center. The 7th Michigan Cavalry was ordered to counterattack, advancing in a close-packed column of squadrons. Stuart pressed his attack by adding the 1st North Carolina Cavalry and the Jeff Davis Legion to the 1st Virginia's assault, overpowering the 7th Michigan and forcing it to withdraw. Though the Confederates made a gallant attack, they were eventually compelled fall back by Union artillery and flank fire from the Federal line.

Stuart formed the remainder of Hampton's and Lee's brigades and threw them forward, toward the Spangler House, in an effort to decide the engagement, once and for all. The Rebel horse rode forward in close column, driving the Federal skirmishers before them. Union artillery concentrated on the gray-clad troopers, tearing huge holes in their formation, but on they came, in an almost irresistible wave. General Gregg ordered the 1st Michigan Cavalry to make a counter-charge, and Custer placed himself at the head of the closely packed columns. In an instant, they were dashing off toward the enemy. The opposing horsemen rapidly closed on each other, with an ever increasing gait, until they came together in a violent crash that caused horses to be thrown end over end, their riders being crushed beneath them. Colonel McIntosh gathered what loose men he could find, and with his headquarters staff, charged into the melee. The engagement was now at a critical stage. Portions of the 1st New Jersey and 3rd Pennsylvania surged forward, without orders, to attack the Confederate flank, causing Custer to gain an advantage at the front of the enemy column. Casualties continued to mount, including General Wade Hampton, as the Rebel assault began to lose its impetus. After more hard fighting, at about 5:00 P.M., the Confederates were forced to withdraw, and the battle fizzled into sporadic artillery and skirmish fire. The danger to the Federal rear had been averted, and J.E.B. Stuart's cavalry had been issued a rare defeat.[2]

General Gregg received the lion's share of the credit for the cavalry victory, while George Armstrong Custer became an immediate hero for the charge of the 1st Michigan. In reality, Gregg had little to do with the fighting, and his most important contribution was acquiring Custer's assistance in the fight. McIntosh had established the Union line, and initiated the battle. Gregg ordered the 1st Michigan to counter the charge of Hampton's and Lee's men, but the issue was still very much in doubt when the 1st New Jersey and 3rd Pennsylvania assailed the Rebel flank. This action was undertaken not only without, but against Gregg's direct orders. Both regiments had been given orders to hold their position. Captain William Miller, of the 3rd Pennsylva-

nia Cavalry, showed the disobedience to Gregg's orders when he turned to a subordinate and said "I have been ordered to hold this position, but, if you will back me up in case I am court-martialed for disobedience, I will order a charge."[3] Gregg could no more take credit for the spontaneous flank assault that turned the tide of battle than could Grant in the charge of the Army of the Cumberland up Missionary Ridge. He was a spectator to the events that were transpiring, not the person responsible for creating them. Custer and McIntosh were the real heroes of the battle. The former was propelled to everlasting fame. The latter was relegated to relative obscurity.

Unlike Sickles, Gregg never took credit for the Union victory on his part of the field. Indeed, he shied away from any accolades that came his way, downplaying any importance he had contributed toward the defeat of Lee's army. The manner in which Gregg conducted himself is a credit to his integrity and character.

Following Gettysburg, Gregg distinguished himself in Grant's Overland Campaign of 1864, in command of the 2nd Division of the Cavalry Corps. On February 3, 1865, he inexplicably resigned his commission in both the regular and volunteer service and quit the army. The official records shed no light upon the reason for Gregg's decision, and both Gregg and his superiors remained silent as to the cause, creating a mystery that remains to this day. In 1907, he published "The Second Cavalry Division of the Army of the Potomac in the Gettysburg Campaign."[4] Gregg retired to a farm near Milford, Delaware, where he quietly passed away his life until being appointed United States consul to Prague, by President Grant, in 1874. After a brief stint as consul, he moved to Reading, Pennsylvania, where he resided until his death on August 7, 1916. David McMurtrie Gregg was buried in the Charles Evans Cemetery.

General John Newton, USA

John Newton was born in Norfolk, Virginia, on August 25, 1822. After graduating second in his class at West Point, in 1842, he was assigned to the Corps of Engineers. From then until the outbreak of hostilities, he was almost exclusively employed in engineer service, the only exception being a brief field command during the Mormon Expedition in 1858. In September of 1861, Newton was commissioned a brigadier general of volunteers, and was assigned to the construction of the defenses of Washington. He commanded a brigade in General Slocum's Division of the Sixth Corps during the Peninsula Campaign and at Antietam before being promoted to division command at Fredericksburg. Newton was one of the most prominent of the officers to denounce Ambrose Burnside's fitness for command to President Lincoln following that battle. When Burnside learned of Newton's actions, he included him on a list of seven general officers he wished to be relieved from the service as a condition for his own continuance in command of the Army of the Potomac. Lincoln's reaction was to relieve Burnside instead. Though Newton was retained in the army, his participation in the efforts to have Burnside removed tainted him somewhat with the Joint Committee on the Conduct of the War, and though he had previously been nominated for promotion to the rank of major general, Congress refused to confirm his appointment until March 30, 1863. Newton's command was conspicuous in charging Marye's Heights during the Chancellorsville Campaign, earning him a reputation as a first-rate division commander. Because of this reputation, along with Meade's lack of confidence in Abner Doubleday. Newton was selected by the army commander to assume command of the First Corps, following the death of John Reynolds, even though Newton was from another corps.[1]

The recent visit to the field of Gettysburg in company with the Comte de Paris, the Duc d'Orleans, and the gentlemen who accompanied them to this country, was an interesting event, whether regarded in the light of bringing the distinguished historian of our Civil War face to face with the military features of that great battlefield, or of affording a few of the survivors of the battle, who escorted the party, the opportunity of renewing their memories of the deadly and gigantic struggle, which was a turning-point in the fortunes of the Union and of the Confederacy.

Thanks to the liberality of the governments, national and State, the individual share which each organization, on the Union side at least, took in the battle is recorded in words and in many cases in stone monuments, and adequate information has also been collected in regard to the Confederate forces; so that all that is required, beyond what has been done and is now in progress, is the historian who is capable, from the immense magazine of facts placed at his disposal, to group these scientifically in the relation of cause to effect, and to correct history, may be, by assigning anew to the prominent leaders on either side their just measure of praise or censure.

I do not think it possible to have gone the rounds of that field, listening to the simple, and in the main accurate, accounts of the incidents of the contest from the lips of the guides, without being profoundly moved.

Beginning with the action of the first day, we see the First and the Eleventh Corps displayed in an arc of a circle, covering the roads from Chambersburg and York, respectively, to Gettysburg. The Third Confederate Corps, Lieutenant General A.P. Hill, from Chambersburg attack the First Corps on the Seminary Ridge, and the Second Confederate Corps, Lieutenant General R.S. Ewell, from York attack the position of the Eleventh Corps. The contest, with unequal numbers against the First Corps, wages fiercely for hours, until after the lines of the Eleventh Corps were forced by the enemy. This exposed the line of retreat of the First Corps, and numbers were captured subsequently in the attempt to fall back through Gettysburg to the Cemetery Ridge. In this affair that splendid soldier General Reynolds, commanding the Union troops, fell early in the day.

The fault, if any, of the First Corps was in the obstinacy of their resistance, and in bravely prolonging the fight after their right flank and rear had become exposed. Who is responsible for the failure to give the order to fall back in season, it is not proposed to discuss in this article.

The position of the Eleventh Corps was, in a military sense, a nearly smooth plain, which afforded the opportunity for a magnificent display of artillery. A competent force of guns here would have checked Ewell, or at least have seriously delayed him, and the disaster to the First Corps from having its flank and rear turned would have been prevented.

Another inquiry pertinent to the occasion is why the Union forces, which operated on interior lines with respect to the enemy, should in this first important action have appeared on the field with inferior forces. This in itself was a great blunder.

The remnants of the First Corps and the Eleventh Corps took position on the Cemetery Ridge, where they were early reinforced by the Twelfth Corps, which occupied Culp's Hill and formed the extreme right of the Army of the Potomac during this and the subsequent days.

General Lee, after having a reconnaissance made of the new position of the Union forces on Cemetery Ridge, declined a further attack that day, although with the superior Confederate force upon the field the chances of success under the circumstances, by a flank movement to the right, would have been good. As a result of the battle of the first day (July 1), the First Corps was reduced to about 3,300 men, and one of the divisions of the corps to 900 men. On the second day a new Vermont brigade was assigned to the Third Division, making the total of the corps between 6,000 and 7,000 men. The Eleventh Corps suffered, but not so severely.

Just here, to prevent misconception, it is necessary to state that the term "corps" as applied to organizations in the Union army was often a misnomer, as some of the corps might in respect to numbers be properly called divisions. The Confederate corps deserved the name.

Until some statistician devotes himself to an elaborate analysis of the battle returns of the Union and Confederate armies, it is impossible in most cases to ascertain the relative strength of either in their engagements; for while the Confederates counted the men in line of battle, the Union authorities stupidly relied upon the muster returns for the strength of their armies. Consequently it was seldom possible to ascertain, even approximately, the actual number present in battle. There were other causes of a selfish nature which sometimes swelled on paper the number in regiments.

On the night of the 1st of July Ewell's corps was in Gettysburg, with the left threatening Culp's Hill; Hill's corps occupied the Seminary Ridge. Two divisions of Longstreet's were four miles from Gettysburg; the other division, Pickett's, was absent and not available for services on the second day.

On the Union side the Twelfth Corps occupied the extreme right at Culp's Hill; next came Wadsworth's division of the First Corps; then the Eleventh Corps on Cemetery Ridge; on their left Robinson's division of the First Corps. The portion of the Third Corps that had come up occupied the extreme left of Meade's forces present on the field.

A long space from the left of the Third Corps to and including the Round Top was entirely unguarded, and this fact, as well as the easy nature of the ground, invited an attack here from the enemy.

The testimony is direct and not to be questioned that Longstreet was ordered by General Lee to attack early in the morning of July 2 with two divisions of his corps, supported by Anderson's division of Hill's corps, and turn the Union left before reinforcements, which were the Second, Fifth, and Sixth Corps and a portion of the Third, should arrive. As soon as Longstreet's guns opened, Ewell was to assail our right and Hill to lend such assistance to both as the case might demand.

A vigorous and concerted attack of this nature could scarcely, in the absence of more than half of the Army of the Potomac, have failed of success by cutting that army in two, and thus have caused a disaster which it is unpleasant even now to contemplate. At all events, even if interrupted in complete success by the arrival of the Second Corps, which took place about 7 A.M., still the Confederates could have seized the Round Top, which alone would have rendered the position of the Union army untenable.

Longstreet did not attack, and his reasons for abstaining have never seen the light.

On the other hand, the serious nature of the mistake that was made in permitting a dispersion of the Union forces at the critical moment of the campaign is thus brought home to the mind of every one.

After the arrival of the Second Corps, which took up the position occupied by the Third Corps, the latter advanced to the front beyond the general line, and occupied the place which has become historic as the Peach Orchard. This spot, the Devil's Den, the rocky slopes leading to the summit, and the Round Top itself, became on that eventful afternoon the theatre of a bloody and memorable contest between the Third Corps and portions of the other corps on one side and Longstreet's forces on the other. Longstreet did not attack until 4 P.M., and up to that moment, and even for some time beyond it, he might have seized the Round Top, for the attention of the Union commander does not appear to have been called to its importance until a late hour of the day.

Notwithstanding the bloody results of the day to the Union forces, who fought under the peculiar disadvantage of having to meet the initiative of the enemy without a well-defined plan of their own, the end was, on the whole, favorable, as, after two days of apparent reverses, they found themselves hammered into a good position.

I had the opportunity to express this idea in the way of congratulation to General Meade at nightfall of the 2nd of July, when the battle of the day was over.

The entrenched lines of the Twelfth Corps on the right were on this afternoon considerably stripped of troops, and Johnson's division of Ewell's corps took advantage of this fact to occupy a portion. To anticipate events a little, on the morning of the 3rd of July, at a very early hour, Johnson was attacked, and after a fierce struggle was forced to leave, and the Twelfth Corps resumed full possession of its first position.

The visit paid to the little old building which was General Meade's headquarters during the battle revived recollections of the council of war held on the night of the 2nd of July, which has been so variously represented that a simple statement of its proceedings is in order here. After calling from each corps commander for a field return of the number of his troops, the discussion turned on the probabilities of the morrow. All agreed, so far as I remember, that the position in itself was a good one, but I suggested the possibility of an attempt to turn our left, which could be done with a whole corps secretly at night and without breaking or weakening too much the Confederate lines; that we ought to look to it by having a force there to prevent such a demonstration. General Meade said that Lee would attack the next day on the easy ground between Cemetery and Round Top. I replied that I thought General Lee too good a soldier to do that, as he would infallibly be badly whipped. We were both correct, it seems; General Lee did attack, and at the same time he was badly whipped. For the rest, the council unanimously voted to fight it out on the position we held. A force also was sent to watch for any attempt to turn the left flank.

Early on the morning of the 3rd of July, about daybreak, a terrific fire of musketry at the position of the Twelfth Corps gave notice that the contest with Johnson's Confederate division had begun.

The Third Division of the First had the evening before taken post on the left of the Second Corps, and on the morning of the 3d I found that our line thence to the Round Top was very incomplete. Reporting the fact to General Meade, I was directed to get troops from the Sixth Corps, and batteries from the reserve artillery to fill out the empty spaces. By my official report it was about noon before this was completed. Longstreet meanwhile had been ordered to attack early; he had at his disposal Pickett's, Hood's, and McLaws' division of his corps, and, later, Heth's and Pender's division of the same corps; this attack was to be supported with artillery.

The attack was not made early or with all the force that was available; neither was it supported by artillery, because that arm had beforehand exhausted, it is said, its ammunition. This defect was not made known to General Lee before the attack was made.

It is a matter of speculation what would have been the result if the attack had been made in full force, supported by artillery, early in the day, before our lines on the left to the Round Top had been consolidated.

It has been the occasion of unfavorable criticism of General Meade that, on the repulse of the final charge, he did not take aggressive action. I think, however, a candid consideration of all circumstances will show that little benefit could have followed such a movement.

The same might be said of an attempt to press the Confederates in their retreat to the Potomac. In the broken and wooded country traversed by them numberless positions for defense offered themselves, and the assailants would have suffered out of all proportions to the defenders. Finally, the proposed attack on the Confederate lines at Williamsport was pronounced folly by the most experienced officers of the Army of the Potomac.

I have not attempted criticism, except of the scattered condition of our army on the first and second days, but I give facts sufficient to attract the attention of historians and thereby to lead to a full investigation and thorough analysis of this battle.

John Newton
Commanding First Corps, 2d and 3d July, 1863

General Newton writes an informative and straightforward account of the battle, though a great deal of what he writes about took place under Abner Doubleday's direction, and not his own. He also steps outside of the telling of his own activities, or those of himself, more than any of the other commanders, giving an overview of the entire battle as well as the resulting Confederate retreat. In some ways, this would seem to be appropriate, and Newton assumed command of the First Corps after it had done most of its fighting at Gettysburg, reducing him to more of an observer than a participant.

Newton's article is largely in the words of a spectator, not a participant in the battle. His condemnation of the conduct of the 1st Corps on July 1 seems harsh and unfair, especially since it comes from an officer who was not even on the field during the fighting. His comments about the "failure" and "fault" regarding the lack of orders to withdraw the Corps seem to be an ill-disguised affront to General Doubleday and his conduct of the battle. The fact is that Doubleday's heroic stand, as much as any other factor, made it possible for the Union to win at Gettysburg. If the 1st Corps had not made this desperate stand, against overwhelming odds, it is likely that Lee's army would have held the high ground when the rest of Meade's army concentrated at Gettysburg. Doubleday's men were so heavily engaged that they could not have withdrawn without being closely pressed by the enemy. This was indeed the case when the corps was finally obliged to fall back, as the victorious Confederates pursued the 1st Corps men through the streets of Gettysburg. The prolonged stand of the 1st Corps had, however, bought time for Howard to establish a new defensive line on Cemetery Ridge, giving the retreating men a new position to rally upon. If, as Newton suggests, the 1st Corps had shown good judgment and vacated its position, instead of sacrificing itself to the constant blows of the enemy, it is probable that the Confederates would have swept it beyond the high ground of Cemetery Ridge, and captured the most important ground on the field. Possibly Newton was attempting to justify his appointment to command of the 1st Corps, replacing Doubleday, an officer who seems to have performed credibly in that capacity. It is certain that his comments would not have been warmly received by the previous members of that corps, who resented his appointment over them on the battlefield, and surely would have taken slight to his remarks concerning their heroic sacrifice that bought time for the army to be concentrated. The 1st Corps had fought its heart out, at Gettysburg, and had shown a grit and determination that may have been equaled, but was surely not surpassed in the annals of the war. Of the 10,022 men who went into that fight, more than 60 percent fell as casualties.[2]

Newton incorrectly states that General Lee, after examining the Union position on Cemetery Hill, declined to continue his offensive strikes. The implication is that Lee found the position to be too formidable to assault without sustaining undue casualties. It is incredible that, twenty-seven years after the end of the battle, Newton could not have known that General Lee had indeed given R.S. Ewell discretionary orders to seize the heights held by the Federals forces on the evening of July 1. At that time, the Federal position was lightly held, and most probably could have been brushed aside by the Confederates. Ewell had been ordered to take the heights, "if practicable." Lee had intended that an assault be made, but Ewell interpreted his orders to mean that the assault was to be made at his discretion. With all of the severe fighting that had already taken place on July 1, Ewell chose not to press the advantage gained in the gathering twilight, thus squandering one of the best opportunities for the Confederates to decide the great battle in favor of Southern arms.

Newton's comments regarding Meade and Sickles are also insightful. His statement concerning Little Round Top that "the attention of the Union commander does not appear to have been called to its importance until a late hour of the day," and his assertion that the Union army was "hammered into a good position," seems supportive of Sickles and critical of Meade. But then, Newton was not a stranger to criticizing his superiors. Following the battle of Fredericksburg, he had been a leading opponent of General Burnside, contacting President Lincoln directly to voice concerns over his commander's decisions and competency to command.[3]

Newton asserts "a vigorous and concerted attack" by Longstreet, on the morning of July 2 "could scarcely, in the absence of more than half of the Army of the Potomac, have failed of success by cutting the army in two." Indeed, the Confederates had held a numerical advantage as of the evening of July 1, but all that had changed by the morning of July 2. By daylight, there were 68,000 Federal troops on the field, as opposed to 60,000 Confederates. Union divisions continued to arrive throughout the morning and afternoon, with 29,000 more troops reaching the field by 4:00 P.M. Newton's assertion that only half the army was on the field on the morning of July 2 is incorrect, as is his assumption that the Confederates had the numbers available to overwhelm the Federals.[4]

In referring to the savage fighting of the second day of the battle, Newton says "Notwithstanding the bloody results of the day to the Union forces, who fought under the peculiar disadvantage of having to meet the initiative of the enemy without a well-defined plan of their own, the end was, on the whole, favorable, as, after two days of apparent reverses, they found themselves hammered into a good position." Newton, it would seem, completely exonerates Sickles for the part his unauthorized and ill-advised movement of his corps had played in events that took place on July 2. It also suggests that Meade had no clear plan of operation, and would give the reader the idea that the Federal commander was unsure of what to do in the impending crisis. The fact is that Meade's actions were consistent with his decision to assume a defensive posture toward the Confederates, defending a strong position and looking for an opportunity to deliver a counterpunch if the situation presented itself. The movement of Sickles' corps initiated the fighting that day along a line that

Meade was not prepared to defend, forcing him to divert reinforcements from other portions of the field to guard against a break-through by the Rebels. Newton does not state that, after a day of bloody conflict, the position the Union army had been "hammered into" was the very line Meade had originally selected for the III Corps to hold.

For all his apparent criticisms of Meade's handling of the battle, Newton does come to his support concerning criticism over the Federal commander's failure to launch a counter-attack following the repulse of Pickett's Charge. He also defends Meade's decision not to assault the Confederate position at Williamsport, Maryland, during the Rebel retreat from Gettysburg, stating that a majority of the "most experienced officers of the Army of the Potomac" were against such a move.

Following Gettysburg, when the 1st Corps was broken up, and the men assigned to the remaining corps in the army, Newton was transferred to the Western Theater to serve under General Sherman. During the Atlanta Campaign, he commanded a division in General Oliver O. Howard's IV Corps, serving with distinction. Following the fall of Atlanta, Newton was assigned to command of the District of West Florida, a post he would hold until the conclusion of hostilities. After the Civil War, Newton served in the Corps of Engineers, becoming Chief of Engineers, with the rank of brigadier general in 1884. He retired from the army in 1886, just four years prior to the gathering of corps commanders at Gettysburg. General John Newton died at his home, in New York, on May 1, 1895, and was buried at West Point.[5]

General Daniel Butterfield, USA

Daniel Butterfield was born on October 31, 1831 in Utica, New York. After his graduation from Union College, at the age of eighteen, he studied law before becoming the superintendent of the eastern division of the American Express Company. On April 16, 1861, Butterfield enlisted as a sergeant in the Washington, D.C., Clay Guards, and on May 12, he was commissioned as colonel of the 12th New York Militia. He served under General Robert Patterson, in the Shenandoah Valley. On September 7, 1861, Butterfield was commissioned a brigadier general of volunteers and assigned to command a brigade in George Morrell's Division of the Fifth Corps. He served in the Peninsula Campaign, being wounded at Gaines' Mill, where he won the Congressional Medal of Honor He commanded his brigade at 2nd Manassas and Antietam before succeeding Morrell in command of the division on October 30, 1862. When General Fitz John Porter was removed from command of the Fifth Corps, Butterfield was selected to replace him, and he led the corps during the Fredericksburg Campaign, being promoted to the rank of major general on November 29, 1862. He was chosen to be chief of staff of the army when Joe Hooker replaced Burnside in army command, and was responsible for designing the corps identification badges for the army. Butterfield continued to perform the duties of chief of staff after George G. Meade replaced Hooker, and received his second wound of the war at Gettysburg.[1]

The successful reunion of the surviving corps commanders at Gettysburg to meet the Comte de Paris—save only the thorough soldier Gibbon, of the Second Corps, stationed so far away on the Pacific as to cause no effort for his presence through the uncertainty of our date, and the able cavalry commander Pleasonton, an invalid and unable to respond to the call—left nothing other than their absence to regret.

Time was cut short from the Gettysburg programme by the most interesting tour of the previous day, which covered the battle-grounds of

Harper's Ferry, Bolivar Heights, and Antietam, with a charming trip to the Mountain House. None of us will forget the vivid picture of the battle of Antietam so clearly drawn and pointed out from the Confederate side by Colonel Kyd Douglas. The mountain view repaid us for the loss of two hours of that afternoon intended for Gregg's cavalry fight. But we were fortunate enough to get that next day.

The well-known and competent guide, Long, who has a correct knowledge of all roads, lines, and positions of organizations of both armies in the battle, was placed with the driver of the first carriage to show the route selected. This carriage contained always the Comte de Paris, the Duc d'Orleans, his son, and the corps commander of the particular line or position where we were, changing as required. An order of the day had been prepared, and, by the courtesy of the railway staff of General Orland Smith, copied and distributed. Each commander was thus prepared in advance for the journey over his lines. Colonel de Parseval, the Duc d'Uzes, and Captain Treat rode near the leading carriage, and thus we were well organized for the tour of the battlefield.

The programme was as thoroughly adhered to and complied with by all present, through the force of soldierly habit, the evident necessity for our purpose, and the character of the assemblage, as if a military order from a supreme commander. Recognition of this feature is a double satisfaction in that it is a pleasure and a duty.

All went smoothly. Surprises were not looked for, but they came— of exceeding interest to most of us; to none more that the writer.

Howard's and Doubleday's descriptions of the first day's battle and the movements of glorious Buford's cavalry and the First and Eleventh Corps gave a clearer understanding of the extent of the lines, the work done, and the ability shown on that day, with the unfavorable conditions existing on our side, which were never so clearly understood and appreciated before by many of those present.

The guide's face showed profound astonishment when the Count pointed out, before they were indicated to him, positions and localities he had never seen. For the first time on the field, previous study of the battle and the War Department maps had made him as familiar with it as if he had fought the battle.

In the first half-hour the Count ventured to correct an accidental error as to a locality indicated by one of our number; and the Count was right. It was simply marvelous to us all, this faculty and knowledge of our gallant comrade and historian.

The current of affairs going smoothly gave moments for thought and recall of incidents, between the clear and cold analytical statements (if one might use the expression) of the corps commanders as to their lines, positions, and movements, and those of the enemy. The guide furnished occasionally, when requested—with more poetic license of description than a military report ordinarily carries,—a glowing word-picture of the battle's phases, replete with details as to the location of troops and commands engaged on both sides. By this we first knew what was told to the world of visitors to the field. It was a surprise again to find so much accuracy in the recital as to position and commands. Many things were not told. How could they be? They were not known.

Overlooking the field, and hearing a side discussion as to the opening of the battle, recalled the incident of General Hooker's words in laying down a map of Pennsylvania and Maryland early in June. By the light of subsequent events it seemed a marvelous inspiration or intuition.

"They are worrying at Washington and throughout the North," said he, "fearing we shall permit Lee's army to get across the Potomac. If he would not cross otherwise, I would lay bridges for him and give him a safe pass across the river. But he will cross, and we must endeavor to guide his march there."

Suiting the action to his words, he pointed on the map to the Williamsport crossing, and, his finger along the west side of the South Mountain Range, stopped at the point where the shading indicated a break or pass, saying:

"He will go on this route, and we will fight the battle here, and, before we fight it, concentrate troops enough from all available sources to prevent Lee's return. If he gets away with his army, the country can have my head for a football, and will be entitled to it."

The battle point indicated was Gettysburg!

Subsequently to this conversation an order to proceed to Washington and Baltimore, securing 15,000 troops from Heintzelman's command at the capital and Schenck's in Maryland, and place them near the passes of the South Mountain, failed through General Halleck's declaration to President Lincoln, in my presence, that such a withdrawal would endanger Washington. Schenck freely offered what could be assembled and spared from his command. The result was a Maryland brigade only. The 7th New York (city) National Guard was offered, and many of them were anxious to go. But it was decided to leave them in Baltimore.

The refusal by Halleck of this column strengthened Hooker's feeling that there was a want of proper support at headquarters, and culminated with the Harper's Ferry incident of the like refusal of French's 10,000 and Hooker's request to be relieved. He said there was too much at stake to permit any personal feeling, and he felt it his duty to ask to be relieved, and the command given to some one who would receive all support.

In a private conversation with President Lincoln at the camp at headquarters, after Chancellorsville, Hooker had indicated to the President his unbounded confidence in Reynolds and Meade as capable commanders for that or any army.

But three days in advance of the impending and intended battle, one of the most self-contained, conservative, quiet, and at the same time gallant, soldiers of the Army of the Potomac was called out of bed before daylight—an utter surprise to himself—and placed in command of the army. So quiet and unobtrusive were the ways of General Meade that he was in some parts of the army almost personally unknown. All knew of his gallant fight at Fredericksburg. He thought to assemble the army at Frederick, and have a review, to see and know and be known by those portions of the army with which he was not familiar. Upon receiving an explanation of the entire situation, he assented to the continued march of our columns prepared for the next day, and the programme of Hooker's movement after French's column was refused him was carried out unchanged until Reynolds reached Gettysburg and met the enemy. Hooker was to send French, under the command of Slocum, with the Twelfth Corps upon Lee's line of communications. This was abandoned when French's troops were denied him.

But we are not to fight the battle over again in this article. It would take more than a number of The Review to place in the record much that would be of interest. More will be interested, perhaps, in the impressions and reminiscences. So many years after, men then unborn are now living and important factors in the body politic. It would seem hardly possible that they could realize what Gettysburg meant without the personal experiences of the time.

The absolute self-possession and quiet demeanor of the corps commanders present at this (in war history) unique assemblage so many years after the battle, though marked, was not as strongly marked as the same characteristic of all during the three day's fighting. It strongly and forcibly recalled it.

Typical of this, it brought back Meade sitting quietly on the little grass plot at the residence of the headquarters house, in the midst of the battle; shells bursting constantly every few minutes and officers' horses disabled; surrounded by a small group of staff officers attached to headquarters; telling, as quietly as if at a quiet home in a peaceful glen, an interesting experience and incident of his career as a young officer. Generals Sharpe, the loved Seth Williams, Perkins, and others were of this group. The world might naturally suppose that, with the immense responsibility so suddenly placed upon him unsought and unexpected, Meade might have been a trifle nervous or excited. If he was, he never betrayed it. This self-possession and absolute coolness, so marked throughout that battle on the part not only of the principal commanders, but of most of the subordinates, was more strong and pronounced, to so express it, than in any of a source of battles of personal recollections and experience.

Slocum was much more quiet and collected on the night of the council of war (after the second day's battle) when, reclining with almost absolute nonchalance, he answered, as his vote on the proposition of a change of our position, "Stay and fight it out," than he was when listening to the words of Howard, Doubleday, Gregg, and the others so many years after. He did not tell us why the proposal to which he assented, and for which he held his command ready, to follow up the repulse of Pickett's assault, was not accepted or approved.

We never thought to ask him of the truth of the story current of the oldest living and one of the bravest of Gettysburg's veterans, General Greene, beloved by us all—that in the midst of the darkness and night of the second day he stood almost within the enemy's lines under orders to retake his former position, and ordered his command, although they were a long way out of reach of his voice, as though present, with the successful purpose of retarding the enemy's movement until his own men could get there.

Howard seemed more calm and unmoved on the second day's fight, when he came to the headquarters council called, but not held, for a joint understanding of the proposed movement, and announced the battle opening on his front, than he was sitting on the rocks at Little Round Top, listening to the story we asked the guide to tell as he told it to battlefield visitors. From the first-mentioned encounter Sickles was carried away minus a leg, but with lasting honor. He gained another crown of honor on our visit, in the thought of some of us, since he never mentioned his initiative and strong demand repeated to headquarters for the occupation of that position which caused Warren to be sent where his statue now stands.

Dear General Wright, gallant, quiet, modest to the extreme, was far less demonstrative in manner, language, and mood (not in force) so many years ago than he was when his quiet yet decided manner gave about the only corrective suggestion made during the day to the guide's story of any movements.

Newton's genial and calm temperament seemed, if anything, no less marked that when he said to Meade, to the latter's apparent disgust, on the evening of the second day's battle:

"General Meade, I think you ought to feel much gratified with to-day's results."

"In the name of common sense, Newton, why?" was the inquiry in reply.

"Why," said Newton, with his pleasant expression and smile, "they have hammered us into a solid position they cannot whip us out of."

Doubleday's strength was sorely tested, invalid as he is, in the severe assent to the belfry of the seminary. His clear and lucid description of Buford's work and his own on the first day of the fight, before and after Reynold's death, and his explanations of the splendid coup of Robinson, with Wadsworth's and Fairchild's work, were interrupted and broken, but not impaired, by inability quickly to regain breath and strength after climbing such a height. He was much more quiet and composed during the battle days.

Gregg, with his courteous, high-bred manner, briefly described in the clearest was his brilliant cavalry fight. One would hardly have thought he was a participant, so modestly and tranquilly he spoke. He seemed not a day older nor a whit changed in any respect (save being in mufti) from the beau sabreur and quiet gentleman who always rode so tranquilly at the head of his command in or out of the fight.

At the visit to headquarters the scene and discussions of the council of war on the night of the second day's battle were recalled. The recollections by all after so many years were in entire accord, with the slight exception that one commander thought Meade used the language, in expressing his opinion, that "Gettysburg was no place to fight a battle," instead of "Gettysburg is no place to fight a battle." The trifling difference was not worth discussion, since all agreed so closely.

There were recollections, musings, regrets, on that day, not alone by the writer, but, I think, more or less by all. They would fill a volume, and would be of interest to survivors of the field.

There was a strong regret that the good people of Philadelphia or

Pennsylvania had not placed the equestrian statue of Meade on that field, where it belongs, rather than in Fairmont Park. It was Meade's victory, as it would have been his defeat had it terminated in the enemy's favor. Everybody who goes there, and who will go, will always wish to see the commander as he was. Perhaps Pennsylvania will yet do it. What a group it would be to place in the field where the wooden observatory is, opposite the cemetery! Equestrian statues, life-size, of Meade, Reynolds, Hancock, Sedgwick, Wadsworth, Buford, Humphreys, Sykes, Birney, and others gone, as they were in life in that battle, and the gallant commanders yet living who will follow them to a future crown!

Whatever we may have thought in years agone, with less reflection and no knowledge of present results, speculation as to what might have occurred is but speculation. We know what the Army of the Potomac did at Malvern Hill after previous defeats, and we realize that our opponents were not to be undervalued for courage or tenacity. They proved it in our fighting days, as did their ancestry side by side with ours in the days of '76, at Yorktown, Saratoga, and the other fields of the Revolution. That they believed they were right, while we fought because we thought we knew they were wrong, passes unchallenged into history.

We cannot blame the prudence and conservative judgment that led Meade not to stake what, in case of failure, might perhaps have caused a fatal result to our Union. His great responsibility did not descend below the commander or to those of us who would have had it been otherwise.

Some of us believe that it was a good Providence that endowed him with caution, if the consciousness of his grave responsibility did not of itself do it. We believe that his unquestioned bravery in obeying orders carried with it a saving and prudent judgment when he personally commanded; that it was better for the country, for all sides that the fighting was not pushed for the conclusion and results we then thought and still think might have been possible, and that we can be profoundly grateful for the results as they stand to-day.

It is not to be wondered at that there are many honestly mistaken as to the real effect and results of their own work in this battle, tactically of accident, strategically of purpose.

Many subordinate commanders to this day think their own action won the battle, which would have been lost but for the combined work of all. It will never cease to be a regret to every true soldier that the full and just mode of recognition has not been given to all who deserved so much on that field.

There is no reason why the Illinois cavalrymen should not have honestly supposed he was right when he marked the spot where he believed he fired the first shot of the battle about 7 A.M. July 1. He was ignorant of the fact that one of the 6th New York Cavalry had opened the fire some hours before daylight. Although ordered not to fire at night, he reasoned that his orders not to fire during the night ended with daybreak, and he fired into the fog at the sound of the enemy's cavalry close to his picket post, though he could not see them—a lucky shot, in that it halted the advance of the enemy for the time. They could not see him. It added time for concentration.

It would be of the greatest interest to know if the great and glorious soldier, Reynolds, who was fully apprised of Hooker's views and purposes, had in his mind the actual battlefield on the second and third days, and moved in front of it on that morning to give time for and cover the necessary concentration of our army, which he knew we could make by our distances as soon as, if not sooner than, Lee's entire army could. The battle-field memorial association will, we hope, some day, get light on many such points of interest. They have done and are doing excellent work.

It is not worthwhile to speculate upon a proposition to which there can never be an answer or positive solution. We could not rewrite the history of Europe if Wellington had been defeated at Waterloo, nor the result if we had failed at Gettysburg. Hence it is only speculation and opinion, with no certainty, as to what would have occurred had Lee adhered to the stated forecast of his campaign that it should be "strategically offensive" and "tactically defensive," leaving us to be the attacking party. We must always be grateful that Lee changed this. So theories or speculations as to the result had Hooker retained command are idle, as well as what would have occurred had Slocum been permitted to enter upon the pursuit after Pickett's repulse, backed by a division of the Sixth Corps, as he was ready to do.

Nor need we speculate on the results if Sickle's position on the second day had not prevented Longstreet's junction with the force sent to our rear for that purpose of any withdrawal from our position, or on what result would have occurred if the magnetic, forceful, and impetuous Stonewall Jackson had been there commanding the force cooperating with Longstreet. We may on both sides cherish theories of results, but they are vain and idle. There are dangers before us now from virtually the same causes that brought on the War of the Rebellion—avarice, greed, and selfishness—that we may rather speculate upon with the hope to counteract.

We may, and we should be, profoundly thankful that results are as they now exist; more than grateful to the splendid, brave old Army of the Potomac, down to the last soldier on its fighting rolls, before, and at, and after the days of Gettysburg. It never proved more thoroughly or strongly its great discipline, organization, patriotism, and endurance that in those eventful days. Its memory and its luster will never grow dim with us, and will always reflect with added brilliancy the glories of the armies of the West, of the Tennessee, the Cumberland (its glorious western counterpart), and the Ohio. This light and luster in all the armies came from the same source—the soldier in the ranks. He was always of good material, and ever showed it when trained and led by competent officers—sometimes without such leadership.

How appropriate here the words of our greatest soldier, Grant! How true!

"My sympathies are with every movement which aims to acknowledge our indebtedness to the private soldier—the countless, nameless, often disregarded, heroes of the musket and bayonet, to whose true patriotism, patient endurance, and fiery courage on the day of danger we who are generals owe victory, and the country will yet owe its salvation."

Gettysburg, so often called the "soldiers' battle," appreciatively bears monuments from their states on the lines where they fought. We ought to place there monuments to mark the lines of our opponents, now, we trust, forever our fellow citizens. The display of their great courage emphasizes that of our own brave men.

Daniel Butterfield

General Butterfield, the organizer of the reunion of commanders, wrote an article that was second only to Sickles' for the controversial nature of its content. He had served as chief of staff for General Hooker, prior to Meade's assumption of command, and was still quite loyal to his old boss at the time of the battle of Gettysburg. For his part, Meade did not have time to reorganize the army, or to place individuals he trusted in important command positions prior to the commencement of the battle, and was forced to work, as best he could, with Hooker's old staff. New to his command responsibilities, and facing the possibility of having to fight one of the greatest battles of the war, Meade was also confronted with a staff that was somewhat resentful over his replacing Hooker.

Though Butterfield's article opens with praise for Meade's qualities as an officer, and appreciation for the difficult situation in which he had been placed by being assigned to army command on the eve of the decisive battle of the campaign, he is profuse in forwarding Joe Hooker as being the real brains of the two. He relates how Hooker, with prophetic intuition, pointed to Gettysburg on a map when discussing the campaign, and declared that the decisive battle of the campaign would be fought there. In so doing, Butterfield is passively stating that Hooker, and not Meade, selected the site of the battle, and is due credit for the outcome. It must be remembered that Meade had drawn up his plans based on fighting the enemy at Pipe Creek, Maryland, and was forced to change his plans due to circumstances in the field. In essence, what Butterfield is saying is that Hooker had chosen the right place for the battle, and Meade had been forced to fight there against his wishes. To be sure, Meade had indeed planned to fight the battle south of Gettysburg, along his proposed Pipe Creek line, but it can not be questioned that it was he who also changed that plan and decided to fight at Gettysburg, instead. Neither Meade nor Lee had intended to fight at Gettysburg, but when the armies came in contact there, it was the measured decision of both to fight it out on the lines their respective forces occupied on those fields. Either commander could have broken off the engagement and sought other ground on which to fight. In Lee's case, General Longstreet was advocating just such a move. Longstreet advised that the Confederates break off the battle, after the first day, relocate their army to a position between Meade's army and Washington, and force the Federals to attack them. Lee's response was that the armies were already there, and he must attack the enemy. Meade's decision was based on the same premise as was Lee's, but it was no less his own choice. Butterfield's statements insinuate that Meade had no control over the situation, and was forced into playing out the hand that was dealt him. If that was so, how does one explain the council of war held by Meade after the second day's fighting at Gettysburg? If Meade was, against his own will or better judgment, being compelled to fight at Gettysburg, then why was the topic of discussion on July 2 whether or not the army should hold its positions or retire? Meade chose to fight at Gettysburg, after the initial clash of July 1, because the ground and the Federal position lent itself to giving a possible repulse to the enemy.

Butterfield's comments regarding Meade's deportment, during the battle, appear to refute Newton's contention that the Union army fought the battle without a definite plan, and, by association, without firm leadership from its commander. Butterfield depicts Meade as being in full control of the situation, exuding a calm resolution in his interactions with his subordinates that *was mirrored by all of the leading commanders on that field. His assessment of Meade's personal conduct during the battle leads one to believe that the army was, at all times, under the control of a competent and confident leader, and further dispels Newton's insinuations that the army was left to fight it out on its own, without firm and decisive leadership. To be sure, Butterfield is generous in his comments toward all of the top generals who served at Gettysburg, including General Sickles, and it may be felt that he was merely being magnanimous in extolling Meade, a since fallen comrade and commander. In his general statements, this may be true. However, the specific statements Butterfield makes about Meade's interaction with his officers, his coolness as the battle raged all around him, and his constant state of calm determination leave a lasting impression of Meade, the commander, that transcends mere flattery or exaltation.*

In discussing the council of war, held at Meade's headquarters, on the night of July 2, Butterfield comments that Meade stated "Gettysburg is no place to fight a battle." This is confusing, given the fact that he has previously extolled his virtues as a soldier and a commander. On the surface, it would seem that Butterfield is agreeing with Newton that Meade was not in control of events, and was merely reacting to the current situation. It is this writer's belief that these comments were not intended to cast aspersions on Meade's command. Instead, they were to justify Butterfield's previously stated contention that Hooker was the true architect of the victory. According to Butterfield, Hooker had correctly assessed the location of the decisive battle, and had put in motion all of the events that led to its consummation. By stating Meade's lack of confidence in the position at Gettysburg, Butterfield is providing final vindication to both Hooker and his plan of campaign. He is also giving credence to what had, by that time, become a belief with some that Meade had intended to retreat from the field on the afternoon of July 2. The basis for this belief can be traced to a statement, made by General Pleasonton in October of 1865, that Meade had ordered the cavalry to be ready to cover a retreat. Pleasonton said that the order was received at 5:00 P.M., before Sickles' line was forced to give way. This statement was picked up by the press and used in an effort to show that Meade's intentions were to retreat from Gettysburg. In reality, the orders Pleasonton said he received were wholly uncorroborated by the official reports, as well as by Pleasonton's own testimony before the Joint Committee on the Conduct of the War, in March of 1864. During that testimony, Pleasonton was asked if he had knowledge of Meade "ever having had any idea of retreating from Gettysburg." Pleasonton replied that he "did not remember" any such event. In response to the allegations leveled against him over his alleged plans to retreat, Meade stated "I deny under the full solemnity of my oath, and in the firm conviction that the day will come when the secrets of all men shall be known—I utterly deny ever having intended or thought, for one instant, to withdraw that army, unless the military contingencies, which the future should develop during the course of the day, might render it a matter of necessity that the army should be withdrawn." Meade had no intention of surrendering the field to the Confederates unless compelled to do so by a defeat of his own army that rendered the positions it then held untenable.[2]

Butterfield's numerous comments regarding the need for monuments at Gettysburg would eventually see fulfillment, as the leading combatants were honored with statues commemorating the part they played in the greatest battle to take place on the North American Continent. The reverence with which he held these Pennsylvania hills and fields can be seen, not only in the words of his article, but also in his efforts to organize this first reunion of commanders. The student of the battle owes him a debt of gratitude for gathering together this honored assemblage, and for the subsequent insight gained through their reminiscence of their actions during those first three days of July, 1863.

Following Gettysburg, and after he had recovered from the wound received there, Butterfield was reunited with Hooker when that officer assumed command of the XI and XII Corps at Chattanooga. During the Atlanta Campaign, he commanded a division in the XX Corps, before leaving the service due to illness. Butterfield would see no further service during the war. As with Doubleday, Sickles, and Newton, he would witness the end of the war from a position of relative inactivity. Butterfield resigned his commission in the army in 1870. His post-bellum life was a series of successes in the business and political arenas, and he served in several capacities for his friend, U.S. Grant. Butterfield is perhaps best known for his musical accomplishments, however. An ardent fan of bugle calls, he had written several of his own for army use, including "Taps." Daniel Butterfield died at his summer home, in Cold Spring, New York, on July 17, 1901. He was buried at West Point.[3]

Major General John Gibbon, USA

John Gibbon was born in Philadelphia, Pennsylvania, on April 20, 1827. As a small boy he moved to North Carolina, and it was from that state that he was appointed to the United States Military Academy at West Point. Following his graduation from West Point, in 1847, Gibbon saw service in the war with Mexico, and was later assigned to Florida, where he campaigned against the Seminoles. For five years, he served as an instructor of artillery tactics, at West Point, and 1861 found him a captain in the 4th United States Artillery. Though his wife was from Baltimore, and three of his brothers joined the Confederate army, Gibbon remained in the Union army, serving as chief of artillery for General Irvin McDowell's Division. On May 2, 1862, he was promoted to the rank of brigadier general and given command of the "Iron Brigade." With that unit, he participated in the battles at 2nd Manassas and Antietam. In November of 1862, Gibbon was promoted to command of the 2nd Division of John Reynold's I Corps, which he led at Fredericksburg, where he was severely wounded. Upon his return to duty, he was assigned to command of the 2nd Division in Winfield S. Hancock's II Corps, in which position he served in the battle of Gettysburg, where he was again wounded.[1]

It is said of General Taylor that he, on one occasion, after listening to several stories told of the battle of Buena Vista, remarked that he sometimes wondered whether he himself was present at that battle, so marked was the contrast between what he heard of it and what he had seen and heard at the battle.

I have been much interested in reading the several contributions in the March number of *The North American Review* on the battle of Gettysburg, and fear that Meade, could he read them, might be reminded of General Taylor's remark. He would certainly be reminded of the fact that fighting a battle is one thing, and fighting it afterwards on paper is a very different thing.

I once sat for several hours a day, for some days, in the studio of an artist whilst he was painting a picture of the battle of Gettysburg, chatting with him as he painted, and telling him what I knew of the battle, and referring him to others who could tell him more of the particular phase of the battle which he had chosen as the scene to be painted. In the course of these talks it came out that all the statements the artist had received did not agree, and in some of them the facts were so glaringly perverted, with the selfish object of exaggerating the services of particular individuals and commands, that I made the remark that the artist, in his endeavors to get at the truth, so as to present a faithful picture of the battle, must, from the varying statements made to him by the different participants, have formed a very poor idea in regard to the character of military men, their spirit of fairness, their little petty jealousies, and their ambitions. To my surprise he said "No"; on the contrary, he was generally impressed with their spirit of fairness and desire to give what they thought to be facts. If this was the conclusion of an impartial investigator, who desired simply to get at the facts for the purpose of representing them on canvas, it is to be hoped that an impartial public will look at the subject in the same way when the narrators confine themselves to facts viewed as they received them.

When, however, they drop the statements of facts, and resort to speculation as to what might, could, would, or should have taken place, if all the facts now known had been as clearly known at the time, or if the conditions had been different from what they were, it is possible that an impartial public may not be as charitable as the artist.

The efforts to belittle General Meade's services in the battle of Gettysburg have been persistent, and are shown in a very marked manner in some of these papers. His best friends do not claim for General Meade any very remarkable maneuvers on the field of battle itself, but they do claim that he varied his plan of campaign to suit the circumstances of the case; that three days after taking command of the army he concentrated his force at Gettysburg, placed it in position, and fought the battle to a successful issue under some considerable disadvantages.

There are those who will be disposed to question the assertion that "Hooker had no superior in maneuvering a large army"; and the campaign of Chancellorsville is generally regarded amongst military men as anything but a monument of "his strategical skill." How Gettysburg can be regarded as another monument of Hooker's strategical skill, it is difficult to understand. Even if he had, with the foresight of a prophet, designated Gettysburg as the scene of the coming conflict, he does not stand alone in that prediction; and certainly he had nothing whatever to do with placing the army there; Meade had, and not only placed it there, but kept it there. Meade's maneuver of his army before the battle cannot be belittled by the introduction of Hooker's name in a resolution of Congress, or in a narrative, any more than can his services during the battle be underrated by claiming the meritorious parts of it for subordinates.

Whether "accident overruled the plans of Meade" and did drift him towards "a better battlefield than he had himself chosen," is a proposition which can never be established, since the battlefield once proposed by Meade was never fought on, and the battlefield of Gettysburg was. Once he decided to give up his proposed battle-ground and accept that of Gettysburg, at the recommendation of one in whose military judgment he placed great confidence, and who had been sent to the front to decide that very question, Meade lost no time in concentrating his army there. "And so swift was the concentration of his forces there, under the direction of his chief of staff, that on the morning of the 2nd of July his army was in position," etc. Under whose direction would he naturally make it but that of his chief of staff or his adjutant general? Both are sometimes used; sometimes other officers; and sometimes the commanding general of an army does it verbally. As a commander at the time of one of the component parts of that army (the Second Corps), I can testify that the order to move to Gettysburg was received from General Meade's own lips before the receipt of Hancock's report from the front, and it was repeated in the same way at my camp after midnight as General Meade rode that night towards the field of Gettysburg.

The chief of staff, therefore, cannot claim all the merit for this "swift concentration." The same chief of staff acted for Hooker when he was building the "monument of his strategical skill" at Chancellorsville. It might be pertinent to ask, Was the chief of staff entitled to the credit of the "strategical skill" in that case? and did the chief of staff, or General Hooker, display "strategical skill" when, two columns of our troops having emerged from the Wilderness and pushing on towards Fredericksburg, without any enemy in sight, they were ordered back to that tangled Wilderness which proved so disastrous to our arms?

The question in regard to the movements of the Third Corps at Gettysburg is revived in these papers. Whatever can be said in favor of the forward movement of that corps on the 2nd of July, the facts remain that it was placed in a position to which it was not ordered by General Meade;

that it was attacked in that position by the enemy and, in spite of the rein-forcements sent to it forced back with heavy loss to the position General Meade originally designed it to occupy—one of the positions which General Newton refers to as those into which we were hammered, and out of which the enemy could and did not whip us. That the corps and the troops with it did good fighting no one can ever justly deny. Whether it can be said of those operations that victory remained with us, depends a good deal upon what we mean by "victory." It is not usual to claim victory for the troops who are driven from the ground, leaving their dead and wounded behind; otherwise the First and Eleventh Corps might claim a victory after their hard fight against superior forces on the 1st of July. If by "victory remaining with us" is meant that the Army of the Potomac maintained possession of its main line of battle, the statement is correct; but of that fact the commander of the Third Corps was not aware at the time he was carried from the field; and towards the maintenance of that main line General Meade himself contributed by leading forward in per-son reinforcements to the threatened line after the disaster to the Third Corps.

General Sickles says "that as soon as our troops on the left (the Third Corps and its supports) equaled those of the enemy the battle was decided in our favor." How decided in our favor? By those troops being driven from the advanced position they occupied? "If," he continues, "this equal-ity had existed as the outset of the conflict, our victory would have been more decisive early in the action, and the Sixth Corps," etc; "and if Buford's division of cavalry had remained on the left flank," etc. All of which sounds very much like saying if the writer had been in command, instead of Gen-eral Meade, results would have been more satisfactory. This is another one of those questions which can never be decided, and even the future his-torian will probably ignore it and describe the features of the battle with Meade in command, and state the circumstances as they actually existed; mindful of the fact that Gettysburg is not the only great battle in the his-tory of the world, nor even in the history of our own country, with regard to which attempts have been made to underrate the services of the com-mander and overrate those of some subordinates.

I do not understand what General Sickles means by saying "at the close of the battle of the 2d, after the enemy retired, the disposition of our forces remained as already described," for certainly no description in his article preceding that remark can apply to any portion of his command. He says: "We pass over the council of war on the night of the 2d without comment, since it had no result." This is a somewhat remarkable statement, since General Meade's enemies have openly and persistently asserted that he wanted to retreat; in fact, had given orders to retreat, and would have retreated but for the "result" of that council. The statement made by General Sickles, who was not present at the council, is not at all in accord with that of General Newton, who was. General Newton says: "The council unanimously voted to fight it out on the position we held." Surely this cannot be called "no result."

General Newton, in commenting on the council says: "All agreed, so far as I remember, that the position in itself was a good one, but I suggested the possibility of an attempt to turn our left," etc. This recollection agrees substantially with my own, and General Newton was the only one in the council whom I heard make any objection to the position. That he did make some objection is made all the more distinct in my memory from the fact that he was the only engineer officer in the council (Warren being asleep on the floor). His objection, therefore, came with especial force, and for a little while conversation on that point between General Newton and myself occupied the attention of the members. The objection to the position that it could be turned on the left was made by General Hancock in his first report sent from the front to General Meade on the 1st of July, and was, I presume, the cause of Hancock sending me orders to halt the Second Corps short of the battlefield that night, from which place General Meade soon after midnight ordered me forward, as above stated. There could, at that time, have been no doubt in General Meade's mind about Gettysburg being a place in which to fight a battle.

Too much stress has been laid upon the unanimity with which those present at this October meeting agreed in attributing to General Meade a certain form of expression that it will not be out of place to put side by side the names of the corps commanders who were present at the council of war on July 2d and the name of those present twenty-seven years after, who determined, with so much unanimity, that General Meade was held to the battlefield only by the votes of his subordinates.

Even were the three present "in entire accord" regarding General Meade's assertion, two of the number must have changed their opinions on the subject since they first expressed themselves.

But in any event it will be the province of the future historian to weigh in the balance the testimony of three members given twenty-seven years after the battle with that of seven out of the nine officers comprising the council of war placed on record soon after the battle. From the balance must necessarily be excluded the testimony of two present at the meeting in October, 1890, since they were not present at General Meade's council. The other officer (General Butterfield) present at the council and at the meeting twenty-seven years afterwards, it has been publicly asserted, was the one who, as General Meade's chief of staff, wrote out the order for the army to retreat from Gettysburg, and it was stated in newspapers soon after the battle that a corps commander had this order in his pocket when he ordered an advance of his corps. It was intimated also that he ordered the corps forward for the very purpose of bringing on a fight, and preventing a retreat. This allusion was, of course, to General Sickles and the Third Corps. What truth there was in the newspaper reports I have no means of knowing. It is, however, a remarkable fact that no copy of that order has ever been produced, not even the copy alluded to in the newspaper reports, and that General Meade always declared that he never directed any such order to be made out; and all the world knows that no such order was executed, nor any attempt made to execute it.

Our army commanders during the Civil War are, of course, now that the war is over, proper subjects for fair criticism, though theories and speculations regarding what might have happened, had the circumstances been different, are, as a general thing, idle. Of course, had Hooker remained in command, the Army of the Potomac might have defeated Lee quite as well as, possibly better than, it did under Meade; but the feeling in the army was generally one of apprehension that a commander who had, not two months before, been badly outgeneraled with nearly three times the force that Lee had at his disposal, might, in the open country of Pennsylvania be outgeneraled again.

In this the army might have been proved mistaken, but a lack of confidence in the ability of its leader is a very heavy handicapping on the eve of a great battle, and in this respect Meade, although comparatively unknown, had a great advantage—an advantage increased very considerably by the results of the battle of Gettysburg.

It is not unusual in war to criticize army commanders for not taking full advantage of their successes in great battles, and in the Civil War it was a very common mode of criticism on both sides. At the very start General Joseph E. Johnston was blamed in some quarters for not pursuing our army of fugitives from the field of Bull Run, and taking possession of the capital, with an army of green volunteers, never in battle before, and scarcely able to move itself, to say nothing of its supplies.

The following year there were not lacking critics who commented on the fact that Lee failed to adopt Stonewall Jackson's suggestion to attack Burnside's army at Fredericksburg, after its repulse, and drive it into the river. Loud complaints were made against McClellan for not driving Lee's army into the Potomac after the battle of Antietam; and so on.

So it appears to be expecting too much of human nature that the critics should abstain from complaints that Meade failed to follow up his victory by capturing Lee's army, either by hurling against it, after the repulse of Pickett's charge, the whole of the Twelfth Corps from the extreme right of our line, supported in "the pursuit" by a division of the Sixth Corps, or afterwards by attacking Lee's army in its entrenched position at Falling Waters, even against the earnest advice of most of his prominent generals.

I am decidedly of the opinion that, if Meade had had at his disposal a division of cavalry to hurl against Lee's centre on the repulse of Pickett's charge, or, more properly speaking, the void left in that centre when the charge was repulsed, Lee's army might have been irretrievably cut in two; but Meade's cavalry divisions had their hands full on the rear and flanks of our army in protecting those from "the force sent to our rear," or rather supposed to be sent to our rear, for it never got there, not so much because Sickles' position on the second day had prevented Longstreet's junction with the force as from the fact that the gallant fight of our cavalry prevented it, and it took Longstreet so long a time to force the Third Corps and its supports back into the position originally intended for it that the question of his making a junction with the force originally intended to go to our rear was no longer one for consideration then, and hence, as General Butterfield says, it is needless to speculate about it now.

The attempt to show that the main battle of Gettysburg took place on the 2d of July, and that the affair of the 3d was a mere episode, will, I think, prove a failure, for the simple reason that the facts do not justify this idea.

The rough sketch herewith will serve to give the general reader a fair idea of the situation.

There can be no question, I think, that General Meade intended originally the Third Corps to occupy the position marked A, in the line of battle (defined in my sketch by double lines). General Sickles, I believe, declares he never received any orders to that effect. Neither did he receive orders to go where he did go.

In cases of this kind there is and can be but one rule in armies. If a soldier is ordered to go to a certain point on a field of battle, he goes there,

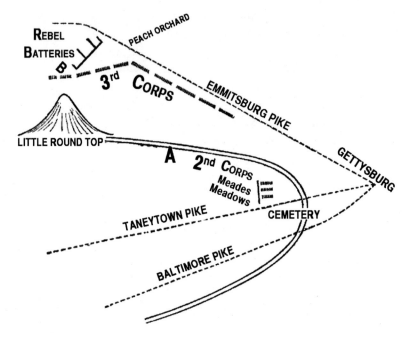

if he can. If he does not get orders to go there, he does not go, with the one single exception that over-whelming necessity requires him to make the move, and this when he is so situated that he cannot solicit or receive the orders of his commanding officer. One of the principal reasons for selecting corps commanders is to obtain generals possessed of the qualifications and judgment requisite for the exercise of such discretion. General Sickles himself exemplifies the rule in disregarding an order he had from the commanding general in his pocket, and marching from Emmetsburg to Gettysburg. He marched: "towards the enemy," and the results justified his judgment.

In the other case, in moving forward on the battlefield to the Emmetsburg Pike, he had no orders, was almost under the very eye of the commanding general, and the very fact of his not receiving orders ought to have been, with him, a reason for still further delay in a forward movement on which the fate of the Army of the Potomac did not turn (nor that of his position). It is true the position at A had some disadvantages. Some portions of it were lower than some portions of the Emmetsburg Pike, but the position along that pike, all the way up to the Peach Orchard, was well commanded by the batteries of the Second Corps, which, however, could not be used without hurting the men of Humphrey's division, Third

Corps, as it fell back in great confusion completely enfiladed by the enemies batteries at B. The case here was an entirely different one from the
first case cited. In that General Sickles had a preparatory order from his
distant commander to make a certain move on a certain contingency (the
enemy assuming the offensive), but even that move was to take place only
after the enemy was held in check long enough to get the trains, etc., out
of the way. Earnest appeals for help came from Gettysburg, where the two
corps (First and Eleventh) were fighting hard to "hold the enemy in check";
and General Sickles decided, and decided properly, to go to their assistance, and marched "to the sound of the guns."

In the other case General Sickles claims to have received no orders,
although almost in sight of the army commander, and on his own responsibility he placed his corps in a faulty position, in which, to avoid his left
being "in the air," he was obliged to form a "broken line," and bend his
left back towards Little Round Top, thus increasing the weakness of his
line and compelling him to call for help almost immediately after the
enemy commenced the attack upon him. This enforced action of the Third
Corps involved a heavy struggle, which included, besides that corps, one
division of the Second and most of the Fifth, seriously endangered a rup-
ture of our main line, and resulted in the advanced line being hammered
into the position which we held to the last, and which General Meade
intended originally should be held from the first.

John Gibbon

*General John Gibbon was not able to attend the gathering of past Get-
tysburg commanders, but he certainly made a significant contribution to the
event by means of the article he wrote. Gibbon exercises little restraint in
responding to the articles written by the other commanders, and targets Sickles for specific rebuke, detailing the various inconsistencies contained in that
officer's recounting of the events that transpired during the fateful battle. He
clearly affixes blame to Sickles for endangering the army by his ill-advised
movement of his corps, and refutes that general's claims that this movement
was in any way responsible for gaining the overall victory on that field. General Butterfield also receives a pointed rebuke from Gibbon concerning the latter's uncomplimentary remarks about General Meade.*

In Gibbon's article, Meade is given just credit as being the architect of the victory at Gettysburg. He shows caustic wit in denouncing Butterfield's contention that Joe Hooker had anything to do with the victory whatsoever, and his arguments in support of Meade ring with a truth and logic that is hard to debate. His statements concerning Meade's orders to the II Corps to march to the field of Gettysburg on the night of July 2 also question Butterfield's claim that he, and not Meade, was responsible for a swift concentration of the army there. But Gibbon saves his most virulent attacks for Dan Sickles. His questions concerning the actions of that officer, combined with his explanations of the tactical situation at the time, portray Sickles' movement of the III Corps line in the most negative way possible. Gibbon stops just short of publicly calling Sickles a liar in denouncing the latter's statements regarding his actions on the field and the council of war held on the night of July 2, which Gibbon is quick to point out Sickles did not even attend. In Gibbon's article, one can clearly see the stance taken by the supporters of General Meade in the Meade/Sickles controversy. With the passing of General Meade, Gibbon became one of the staunchest defenders of the commander's accomplishments, and one of the greatest enemies of the Sickles camp. The historical record favors Gibbon in this controversy, and his version of the events that transpired seems to be the most accurate.

The exception he takes to the premise that the most severe fighting took place on the second day, and that the action of July 3 was merely a sideshow, is both accurate and understandable. To begin with, Pickett's Charge was Robert E. Lee's supreme effort to decide the issue on the field, and maximum force was committed by the Confederates to attempt to break the Union line. If by no other standard, the casualties inflicted on both sides during that day attest to the savagery of the fighting and the importance of the outcome. Gibbon also had a personal reason for taking affront to any attempt to diminish the importance of the third day's fighting. The II Corps played a major role in the fighting that took place on that day, and to relegate Pickett's charge to a role of being anti-climactic would have been tantamount to slighting the sacrifices of the men in the corps in which he was a commanding officer, and to which he ascended to command upon the wounding of General Hancock, until he himself was wounded. Gibbon fought with conspicuous gallantry at Gettysburg, and distinguished himself in command of the 2nd Division of the II Corps. His division earned eternal glory on that day, as the brigades led by Alexander Webb, William Harrow, and Norman Hall, in a line passing through the copse of trees used by Lee as a focal point for the attack, withstood the shelling from Confederate artillery that was heard 150 miles away, in Pittsburgh, Pennsylvania, and then blunted the designs of the infantry in Pickett's Charge.[2]

Following recovery from the wound he received at Gettysburg, Gibbon was assigned to duty with the Cleveland and Philadelphia draft depots. During General Grant's Overland Campaign of 1864, he resumed command of the 2nd Division of the II Corps, participating in all of the engagements of that corps from the Wilderness to the investment of Petersburg. Gibbon was promoted to the rank of major general on June 7, 1864. In January of 1865, he was given command of the newly created XXIV Corps, in the Army of the James. Gibbon participated in the Appomattox Campaign, and was chosen to be one of the Union commissioners to receive the surrender of the Confederate army.

Gibbon remained in the army after the conclusion of the Civil War, serving as colonel of the 36th United States Infantry until 1869, when he assumed command of the 7th U.S. Infantry. The majority of his service was in the West, fighting against the Indians. His infantry arrived on the field of Little Big Horn following the massacre to rescue the survivors and bury the dead. In 1877, he conducted a successful campaign against the Nez Perces. In 1885, Gibbon was promoted to the rank of brigadier general in the regular army, serving until his retirement in 1891. Gibbon retired to Baltimore, Maryland, where he devoted time to Civil War pursuits. He wrote "Personal Recollections of the Civil War" in 1885, and served as commander in chief of the Military Order of the Loyal Legion of the United States. John Gibbon died on February 6, 1896, and was buried at Arlington National Cemetery.[3]

Lieutenant General
James Longstreet, CSA

James Peter Longstreet was born in the Edgefield District of South Carolina on January 8, 1821. He attended West Point, graduating from the academy in the Class of 1842. Longstreet saw service in several campaigns against the Indians, and distinguished himself in the Mexican-American War, where he received two brevet promotions for gallantry. In the years immediately prior to the war, Longstreet had attained the rank of major, and was serving as a paymaster. He resigned his commission in the Federal army, and was appointed a brigadier general in the Confederate service on June 17, 1861, and commanded a brigade at the battle of 1st Manassas. On October 7, 1861, Longstreet was promoted to major general. He led with distinction during the Peninsula Campaign, at 2nd Manassas, and Antietam, and was promoted to the rank of lieutenant general on October 9, 1862.[1] Along with Thomas J. "Stonewall" Jackson, Longstreet provided Robert E. Lee's one-two punch in command of the Army of Northern Virginia's two corps. At Fredericksburg, Major General Ambrose Burnside dashed his army against Longstreet's strong defenses, and at Chancellorsville, Jackson's flank attack sent a superior Federal army reeling from the field. Though the Confederate victory at Chancellorsville was one of the most glorious accomplishments of Southern arms during the war, the mortal wounding of Stonewall Jackson caused a severe dearth in leadership, and necessitated a restructuring of the command structure of the Army of Northern Virginia. General Lee opted to divide his army into three corps, promoting Generals Richard Ewell and Ambrose P. Hill to corps command, along with Longstreet. When Lee started his divisions northward in June of 1863, he did so with two-thirds of his army under the command of untried and untested corps commanders. The Gettysburg Campaign would be a baptism of fire for Ewell and Hill in their new positions, and would leave Longstreet as the only veteran and seasoned corps commander with the army. All three corps commanders were guilty of committing errors on the battlefield during those three days of combat in Pennsyl-

vania, but Longstreet was the only one that was still alive in 1878 to tell his side of the story.

It has been my purpose for some years to give the public a detailed history of the campaign of Gettysburg, from its inception to its disastrous close. The execution of this task has been delayed by reason of a press of personal business, and by reason of a genuine reluctance that I have felt against anything that might, even by implication, impugn the wisdom of my late comrades in arms. My sincere feeling upon this subject is best expressed in the following letter, which was written shortly after the battle of Gettysburg, when there was a sly under-current of misrepresentation of my course, and in response to an appeal from a respected relative that I would make some reply to my accusers:

> Camp, Culpeper Courthouse
> July 24, 1863
>
> My Dear Uncle: Your letters of the 13th and 14th were received on yesterday. As to our late battle, I cannot say much. I have no right to say anything, in fact, but will venture a little for you alone. If it goes to aunt and cousins, it must be under promise that it will go no further. The battle was not made as I would have made it. My idea was to throw ourselves between the enemy and Washington, select a strong position, and force the enemy to attack us. So far as is given to man the ability to judge, we may say with confidence that we should have destroyed the Federal army, marched into Washington, and dictated our terms, or, at least, held Washington and marched over as much of Pennsylvania as we cared to, had we drawn the enemy into attack upon our carefully chosen position in his rear. General Lee chose the plans adopted; and he is the person appointed to choose and to order. I consider it a part of my duty to express my views to the Commanding-General. If he approves and adopts them, it is well; if he does not, it is my duty to adopt his views, and to execute his orders as faithfully as if they were my own. I cannot help but think that great results would have been obtained had my views been thought better of; yet I am much inclined to accept the present condition as for the best. I hope and trust that it is so. Your Programme would all be well enough, had it been practicable; and was duly thought of, too. I fancy that no good ideas upon that campaign will be mentioned at any time that did not receive their share of consideration by General Lee. The few things that he might have overlooked himself were, I believe, suggested by myself. As we failed, I would prefer that all the

blame should rest upon me. As General Lee is our commander, he should have the support and influence we can give him. If the blame (if there is any) can be shifted from him to me, I shall help him and our cause by taking it. I desire, therefore, that all the responsibility that can be put upon me shall go there and shall remain there. The truth will be known in time, and I leave that to show how much of the responsibility of Gettysburg rests on my shoulders.

> Most affectionately yours,
> J. Longstreet.
> To A.B. Longstreet, LL.D., Columbus, Ga.

I sincerely regret that I cannot rest upon that letter. But I have been so repeatedly and so rancorously assailed by those whose intimacy with the Commanding-general in that battle gave an apparent importance to their assaults, that I feel impelled by a sense of duty to give to the public a full and comprehensive narration of the campaign from its beginning to its end; especially when I reflect that the publication of the truth cannot now, as it might have done then, injure the cause for which we fought the battle. The request that I furnish this history to the *Times* comes opportunely, for the appeal just made through the press by a distinguished foreigner for all information that will develop the causes of the failure of that campaign has provoked anew its partisan and desultory discussion, and renders a plain and logical recital of the facts both timely and important.

After the defeat of Burnside at Fredericksburg in December, it was believed that active operations were over for the winter, and I was sent with two divisions of my corps to the eastern shore of Virginia, where I could find food for my men during the winter, and send supplies to the Army of Northern Virginia. I spent several months in this department, keeping the enemy close within his fortifications, and foraging with little trouble and great success. On May 1st I received orders to report to General Lee, at Fredericksburg. General Hooker had begun to throw his army across the Rappahannock, and the active campaign was opening. I left Suffolk as soon as possible, and hurried my troops forward. Passing through Richmond, I called to pay my respects to Mr. Seddon, the Secretary of War. Mr. Seddon was at the time of my visit deeply considering the critical condition of Pemberton's army at Vicksburg, around which Gen. Grant was then decisively drawing his lines. He informed me that he had in contemplation a plan for concentrating a succoring army at Jackson, Miss., under the command of General Johnston, with a view of driving Grant from before Vicksburg by a direct issue at arms. He suggested that possibly my corps might be needed to make the army strong enough to handle Grant, and asked my views. I replied that there was a better plan, in my judgement, for relieving Vicksburg than by a direct assault upon Grant. I proposed that the army then concentrating at Jackson, Miss., be moved swiftly to Tullahoma, where General Bragg was then located with a fine army, confronting an army of about equal strength, under General Rosecranz, and that at the same time the two divisions of my corps be hurried forward to the same point. The simultaneous arrival of these reinforcements would give us a grand army at Tullahoma. With this army General Johnston might speedily crush Rosecranz, and that he should then turn his force toward the north, and with his splendid army march through Tennessee and Kentucky, and threaten the invasion of Ohio. My idea was, that in the march through those States the army would meet no organized obstruction; would be supplied with provisions, and even reinforcements, by those friendly to our cause, and would inevitably result in drawing Grant's army from Vicksburg to look after and protect his own territory. Mr. Seddon adhered to his original views; not so much, I think, from his great confidence in them as rom the difficulty of withdrawing the force suggested from General Lee's army. I was very thoroughly impressed with the practicability of the plan, however, and when I reached General Lee I laid it before him with the freedom justified by our close personal and official relations. The idea seemed to be a new one to him, but he was evidently seriously impressed with it. We discussed it over and over, and I discovered that his main objection to it was that it would, if adopted, force him to divide his army. He left no room to doubt, however, that he believed the idea of an offensive campaign was not only important but necessary.

At length, while we were discussing the idea of a western forward movement, he asked me if I did not think an invasion of Maryland and Pennsylvania by his own army would accomplish the same result, and I replied that I did not see that it would, because this movement would be too hazardous, and the campaign in thoroughly Union States would require more time and greater preparation than one through Tennessee and Kentucky. I soon discovered that he had determined that he would make some forward movement, and I finally assented that the Pennsylvania campaign might be brought to a successful issue if he could make it offensive in strategy, but defensive in tactics. This point was urged with persistency. I suggested that, after piercing Pennsylvania and menacing Washington, we should choose a strong position and force the Federals to attack us, observing that the popular clamor throughout the North would speedily force the Federal General to attempt to drive us out. I recalled to him the battle of Fredericksburg as an instance of a defensive battle, when, with a few thousand men, we hurled the whole Federal army back, crippling and demoralizing it, with trifling loss to our own troops; and Chancellorsville as an instance of an offensive battle, where we dislodged the Federals, it is true, but at such a terrible sacrifice that half a dozen such victories would have ruined us. It will be remembered that Stonewall Jackson once said that "we sometimes fail to drive the enemy from a position; they always fail to drive us." I reminded him, too, of Napoleon's advice to Marmont, to whom he said, when putting him at the head of an invading army, "Select your ground and make your enemy attack you." I recall these points simply because I desire to have it distinctly understood that, while I first suggested to General Lee the idea of an offensive campaign, I was never persuaded to yield my argument against the Gettysburg campaign, except with the understanding that we were not to deliver an offensive battle, but to so manoeuvre that the enemy should be forced to attack us—or, to repeat, that our campaign should be one of offensive strategy, but defensive tactics. Upon this understanding my assent was given, and General Lee, who had been kind enough to discuss the matter with me patiently, gave the order of march.

The movement was begun on the 3rd of June. McLaws' division of my corps moved out of Fredericksburg for Culpeper Courthouse, followed by Ewell's corps on the 4th and 5th of June. Hood's division and Stuart's cavalry moved at the same time. On the 8th we found two full corps (for Pickett's division had joined me then) and Stuart's cavalry concentrated at Culpeper Courthouse. In the meantime a large force of the Federals, cavalry and infantry, had been thrown across the Rappahannock and sent to attack General Stuart. They were encountered at Brandy Station on the morning of the 9th, and repulsed. General Lee says of this engagement: "On the 9th a large force of Federal cavalry, strongly supported by infantry, crossed the Rappahannock at Beverly's Ford and attacked General Stuart. A severe engagement ensued, continuing from early in the morning until late in the afternoon, when the enemy was forced to recross the river with heavy loss, leaving four hundred prisoners, three pieces of artillery, and several colors inour hands." The failure of General Lee to follow up his advantage, by pouring the heavy force concentrated at Culpeper Courthouse upon this detachment of the Federals, confirmed my convictions that he had determined to make a defensive battle, and would not allow any casual advantage to precipitate a general engagement. If he had any idea of abandoning the original plan of a tactical defensive, then, in my judgement, was the time to have done so. While at Culpeper, I sent a trusty scout (who had been sent to me by Secretary Seddon while I was at Suffolk) with instructions to go into the Federal lines, discover his policy, and bring me all the information he could possibly pick up. When this scout asked me, very significantly, where he should report, I replied: "Find me, wherever I am, when you have the desired information." I did this because I feared to trust him with a knowledge of our future movements. I supplied him with all the gold he needed, and instructed him to spare neither pains nor money to obtain full and accurate information. The information gathered by this scout led to the most tremendous results, as will soon be seen.

General A.P. Hill, having left Fredericksburg as soon as the enemy had retired from his front, was sent to follow Ewell, who had marched up the Valley and cleared it of the Federals. My corps left Culpeper on the 15th, and, with a view of covering the march of Hill and Ewell through the Valley, moved along the east side of the Blue Ridge. General Stuart was in my front and on my flank, reconnoitering the movements of the Federals. When it was found that Hooker did not intend to attack, I withdrew to the west side and marched to the Potomac. As I was leaving the Blue Ridge, I instructed General Stuart to follow me, and to cross the Potomac at Shepherdstown, while I crossed at Williamsport, ten miles above. In reply to these instructions, Gen. Stuart informed me that he had discretionary powers; whereupon I withdrew. General Stuart held the gap for awhile, and then hurried around beyond Hooker's army, and we saw nothing more of him until the evening of the 2nd of July, when he came down from York and joined us, having made a complete circuit of the Federal army. The absence of Stuart's cavalry from the main body of the army during the march is claimed to have been a fatal error, as General Lee says: "No report had been received (on the 27th) that the enemy had crossed the Potomac, and the absence of the cavalry rendered it impossible to obtain accurate information." The army, therefore, moved forward as a man might walk over strange ground with his eyes shut. General Lee says of his orders to Stuart: "General Stuart was left to guard the passes of the mountains and to observe the movements of the enemy, whom he was instructed to harass and impede as much as possible, should he attempt to cross the Potomac. In that event, General Stuart was directed to move into Maryland, crossing the Potomac on the east or west of the Blue Ridge, as in his judgement should be best, and take position on the right of our column as it advanced."

My corps crossed the Potomac at Williamsport, and General A.P. Hill crossed at Shepherdstown. Our columns were joined together at Hagerstown on the evening of the 27th. At this point, on the night of the 29th, information was received by which the whole plan of campaign was changed. We had not heard from the enemy for several days, and Gen. Lee was in doubt as to where he was; indeed, we did not know that he had left Virginia. At about 10 o'clock that night Colonel Sorrell, my chief-of-staff, was waked by an orderly, who reported that a suspicious person had just been arrested by the provost-marshal. Upon investigation, Sorrell discovered that the suspicious person was the scout Harrison, that I had sent out at Culpeper. He was dirt-stained, travel-worn, and very much broken down. After questioning him sufficiently to find that he brought very important information, Colonel Sorrell brought him to my headquarters and awoke me. He gave the information that the enemy had crossed the Potomac, marched northwest, and that the head of his column was at Frederick City, on our right. I felt that this information was exceedingly important, and might involve a change in the direction of our march. General Lee had already issued orders that we were to advance toward Harrisburg. The next morning I at once sent the scout to General Lee's headquarters, and followed him myself early in the morning. I found General Lee up, and asked him if the information brought by the scout might not involve a change of direction of the head of our column to the right. He immediately acquiesced to the suggestion, possibly saying that he had already given orders to that effect. The movement toward the enemy was begun at once. Hill marched toward Gettysburg, and my corps followed, with the exception of Pickett's division, which was left at Chambersburg by General Lee's orders. Ewell was recalled from above—he having advanced as far as Carlisle. I was with General Lee most of that day (30th). At about noon the road in front of my corps was blocked by Hill's corps and Ewell's wagon train, which had cut into the road from above. The orders were to allow these trains to precede us, and that we should go into camp at Greenwood, about ten miles from Chambersburg. My infantry was forced to remain in Greenwood until late in the afternoon of the 1st. My artillery did not get the road until 2 o'clock on the morning of the 2nd.

General Lee spent the night with us, establishing his headquarters, as he frequently did, a short distance from mine. General Lee says of the movements of this day: "Preparation had been made to advance upon Harrisburg; but on the night of the 29th information was received from a scout that the enemy had crossed the Potomac, was advancing northward, and that the head of his column had already reached South Mountain. As our communications with the Potomac were thus menaced, it was resolved to prevent his further progress in that direction by concentrating our army on the east side of the mountains." On the morning of the 1st General Lee and myself left his headquarters together, and had ridden three or four miles when we heard heavy firing along Hill's front. The firing became so heavy that General Lee left me and hurried forward to see what it meant. After attending to some details of my march, I followed. The firing proceeded from the engagement between our advance and Reynolds' corps, in which the Federals were repulsed. This recontre was totally unexpected on both sides. As an evidence of the doubt in which General Lee was enveloped, I quote from General R. H. Anderson the report of a conversation had with him during the engagement. General Anderson was resting with his division at Cashtown, awaiting orders. About 10 o'clock in the morning he received a message notifying him that General Lee desired to see him. He found Gen. Lee intently listening to the fire of the guns, and very much disturbed and depressed. At length he said, more to himself than to General Anderson: "I cannot think what has become of Stuart; I ought to have heard from him long before now. He may have met with disaster, but I hope not. In the absence of reports from him, I am in ignorance as to what we have in front of us here. It may be the whole Federal army, or it may be only a detachment. If it is the whole Federal force we must fight a battle here; if we do not gain a victory those defiles and gorges through which we have passed this morning will shelter us from disaster."

When I overtook General Lee at 5 o'clock that afternoon, he said, to my surprise, that he thought of attacking General Meade upon the heights the next day. I suggested that this course seemed to be at variance with the plan of the campaign that had been agreed upon before leaving Fredericksburg. He said: If the enemy is there tomorrow we must attack him." I replied: "If he is there, it will be because he is anxious that we should attack him—a good reason in my judgement for not doing so." I urged that we should move around by our right to the left of Meade and put our army between him and Washington, threatening his left and rear, and thus force him to attack us in such a position as we might select. I said that it seemed to me that if, during our council at Fredericksburg, we had described the position in which we desired to get the two armies, we could not have expected to get the enemy in a better position for us than that he then occupied. I said, further, that his weak point seemed to be his left; hence I thought that we should move around to his left, that we might threaten it if we intended to manouevre, or attack it if we were determined upon a battle.—I called his attention to the fact that the country was admirably adapted for a defensive battle, and that we should surely repulse Meade with crushing loss if we would take position so as to force him to attack us, and suggested that even if we carried the heights in front of us, and drove Meade out, we should be so badly crippled that we could not reap the fruits of victory; and that the heights of Gettysburg were in themselves of no more importance to us than the ground we then occupied, and that the mere possession of the ground was not worth a hundred men to us. That Meade's army, not its position, was our objective. General Lee was impressed by the idea that by attacking the Federals he could whip them in detail. I reminded him that if the Federals were there in the morning it would be proof that they had their forces well in hand, and that with Pickett in Chambersburg and Stuart out of reach, we should be somewhat in detail. He, however, did not seem to abandon the idea of attack on the next day. He seemed under a subdued excitement which occasionally took possession of him when "the hunt was up," and threatened his superb equipoise. The sharp battle fought by Hill and Ewell on that day had given him a taste of victory. Upon this point I quote General Fitzhugh Lee, who says, speaking of the attack on the 3rd: "He told the father of the writer (his brother) that he was controlled too far by the great confidence he felt in the fighting qualities of his people, who begged simply to be 'turned loose,' and by the assuarances of most of his higher officers." I left General Lee quite late on the night of the 1st. Speaking of the battle on the 2nd, General Lee says in his official report: "It had not been intended to fight a general battle at such a distance from our base unless attacked by the enemy; but finding ourselves unexpectedly confronted by the Federal army, it became a matter of difficulty to withdraw through the mountains with our large trains."

When I left General Lee on the night of the 1st, I believed he had made up his mind to attack, but was confident that he had not yet determined as to when the attack should be made. The assertion first made by General Pendleton, and echoed by his confederates, that I was ordered to open the attack at sunrise, is totally false. Documentary testimony upon this point will be presented in the course of this article. Suffice it to say at present that General Lee never in his life gave me orders to open an attack at a specific hour. He was perfectly satisfied that when I had my troops in position and was ordered to attack, no time was ever lost. On the night of the 1st I left him without any orders at all. On the morning of the 2nd I went to General Lee's headquarters at daylight and renewed my views against making an attack. He seemed resolved, however, and we discussed the probable results. He observed the position of the Federals and got a general idea of the nature of the ground. About sunrise General Lee sent Colonel Venable, of his staff, to General Ewell's headquarters, ordering him to make a reconnaissance of the ground in his front, with a view of making the main attack on his left. A short time afterwards he followed Colonel Venable in person. He returned at about 9 o'clock and informed me that it would not do to have Ewell to open the attack. He finally determined that I should make the main attack on the extreme right. It was fully 11 o'clock when General Lee arrived at this conclusion and ordered the movement. In the meantime, by General Lee's authority, Law's brigade, which had been put upon picket duty, was ordered to rejoin my command, and upon my suggestion that it would be better to await its arrival, General Lee assented. We awaited about forty minutes for these troops and then moved forward. A delay of several hours occurred in the march of the troops. The cause of this delay was that we had been ordered by General Lee to proceed cautiously upon the forward movement so as to avoid being seen by the enemy. General Lee ordered Colonel Johnson, of his engineer corps, to lead and conduct the head of the column. My troops, therefore, moved forward under guidance of a special officer of General Lee, and with instructions to follow his directions. I Left General Lee only after the line was stretched out on the march, and rode along with Hood's division, which was in the rear. The march was necessarily slow, the conductor frequently encountering points that exposed the troops to the view of the signal station on Round Top. At length the column halted. After waiting some time, supposing that it would soon move forward, I sent to the front to inquire the occasion of the delay. It was reported that the column was awaiting the movements of Colonel Johnston(sic), who was trying to lead it by some route by which it could pursue its march without falling under view of the Federal signal station. Looking up toward Round Top I saw that the signal station was in full view, and, as we could plainly see this station, it was apparent that our heavy column was seen from their position, and that further efforts to conceal ourselves would be a waste of time.

I became very impatient at this delay, and determined to take upon myself the responsibility of hurrying the troops forward. I did not order

General McLaws forward because, as the head of the column, he had direct orders from General Lee to follow the conduct of Colonel Johnson.

Therefore I sent orders to Hood, who was in the rear and not encumbered by these instructions, to push his division forward by the most direct route so as to take position on my right. He did so, and thus broke up the delay. The troops were rapidly thrown into position and preparations were made for the attack. It may be proper just here to consider the relative strength and position of the two armies. Our army was 52,000 infantry, Meade was 95,000; these are our highest figures and the enemy's lowest. We had learned on the night of the 1st, from some prisoners captured near Seminary Ridge, that the First, Eleventh, and Third corps had arrived by the Emmitsburg road and had taken position on the heights in front of us, and that reinforcements had been seen coming by the Baltimore road just after the fight of the 1st. From an intercepted dispatch we learned that another corps was in camp about four miles from the field. We had every reason, therefore, to believe that the Federals were prepared to renew the battle. Our army was stretched in an elliptical curve, reaching from the point of Round Top around Seminary Ridge, and enveloping Cemetery Heights on the left; thus covering a space of four or five miles. The enemy occupied the high ground in front of us, being massed within a curve of about two miles, nearly concentric with the curve described by our forces. His line was about 1,400 yards from ours. Any one will see that the proposition for this inferior force to assault and drive out the masses of troops upon the heights was a very problematical one. My orders from General Lee were "to envelop the enemy's left and begin the attack there, following up as near as possible the direction of the Emmitsburg road."

My corps occupied our right, with Hood on our extreme right and McLaws next. Hill's corps was next to mine, in front of the Federal centre, and Ewell was on our extreme left. My corps, with Pickett's division absent, numbered hardly 13,000 men. I realized that the fight was to be a fearful one; but being assured that my flank would be protected by the brigades of Wilcox, Perry, Wright, Posey, and Mahone moving en echelon, and that Ewell was to co-operate by a direct attack on the enemy's right, and Hill to threaten his centre and attack if opportunity offered and thus prevent reinforcements from being launched either against myself or Ewell, it seemed that we might possibly dislodge the great army in front of us. At half-past 3 o'clock the order was given General Hood to advance upon the enemy, and, hurrying to the head of McLaw's division, I moved with his line. Then was fairly commenced what I do not hesitate to pro-

nounce the best three hours' fighting ever done by any troops on any battle-field. Directly in front of us, occupying the peach orchard, on a piece
of elevated ground that General Lee desired me to take and hold for his
artillery, was the Third corps of the Federals, commanded by General Sickles. My men charged with great spirit and dislodged the Federals from the
peach orchard with but little delay, though they fought stubbornly. We
were then on the crest of Seminary Ridge. The artillery was brought forward and put into position at the peach orchard. The infantry swept down
the slope and soon reached the marshy ground that lay between Seminary
and Cemetery Ridges, fighting their way over every foot of ground and
against overwhelming odds; at every step we found that reinforcements
were pouring into the Federals from every side. Nothing could stop my
men, however, and they commenced their heroic charge up the side of
Cemetery Ridge. Our attack was to progress in the general direction of
the Emmitsburg road, but the Federal troops, as they were forced from
point to point, availing themselves of the stone fences and boulders near
the mountain as rallying points, so annoyed our right flank that General
Hood's division was obliged to make a partial change of front so as to
relieve itself of this galling flank fire. This drew General McLaws a little
further to the right than General Lee had anticipated, so that the defensive advantages of the ground enabled the Federals to delay our purposes
until they could occupy Little Round Top, which they just then discovered was the key to their position. The force thrown upon this point was
so strong as to seize our right, as it were, in a vise.

Still the battle on our main line continued to progress. The situation
was a critical one. My corps had been fighting over an hour, having
encountered and driven back line after line of the enemy. In front of them
was a high and rugged ridge, on its crest the bulk of the Army of the
Potomac, numbering six to one, and securely resting behind strong positions. My brave fellows never hesitated, however. Their duty was in front
of them and they met it. They charged up the hill in splendid style, sweeping everything before them, dislodging the enemy in the face of a with-
ering fire. When they had fairly started up the second ridge, I discovered
that they were suffering terribly from a fire that swept over their right and
left flanks. I also found that my left flank was not protected by the brigades
that were to move en echelon with it. McLaws' line was consequently
spread out to the left to protect its flank, and Hood's line was extended
to the right to protect its flank from the sweeping fire of the large bodies
of troops that were posted on Round Top. These two movements of exten-

sion so drew my forces out that I found myself attacking Cemetery Hill with a single line of battle against not less than 50,000 troops.

My two divisions at that time were cut down to eight or nine thousand men, four thousand having been killed or wounded. We felt at every step the heavy stroke of fresh troops—the sturdy regular blow that tells a soldier instantly that he has encountered reserves or reinforcements. We received no support at all, and there was no evidence of co-operation on any side. To urge my men forward under these circumstances would have been madness, and I withdrew them in good order to the peach orchard that we had taken from the Federals early in the afternoon. It may be mentioned here as illustrative of the dauntless spirit of these men, that when General Humphreys (of Mississippi) was ordered to withdraw his troops from the charge, he thought there was some mistake, and retired to a captured battery near the swale between the two ridges, where he halted, and when ordered to retire to the new line a second time, he did so under protest. Our men had no thought of retreat. They broke every line they encountered. When the order to withdraw was given a courier was sent to General Lee informing him of the result of the day's work.

Before pursuing this narrative further, I shall say a word or two concerning this assault. I am satisfied that my force, numbering hardly 13,000 men, encountered during that three and a holf hours of bloody work not less than 65,000 of the Federals, and yet their charge was not checked nor their line broken until we ordered them to withdraw. Mr. Whitelaw Reid, writing a most excellent account of this charge to the Cincinnati *Gazette*, says: "It was believed from the terrific attack that the whole rebel army, Ewell's corps included, was massed on our centre and left, and so a single brigade was left to hold the rifle-pits on the right and the rest hurried across the little neck of land to strengthen our weakening lines." He describes, too, the haste with which corps after corps was hurried forward to the left to check the advance of my two-thirds of one corps. General Meade himself testifies (see his official report) that the Third, the Second, the Fifth, the Sixth, and the Eleventh corps, all of the Twelfth except one brigade and part of the First corps, engaged my handful of heroes during that glorious but disastrous afternoon. I found that night that 4,529 of my men, more than one-third of their total number, had been left on the field. History records no parallel to the fight made by these two divisions on the 2d of July at Gettysburg. I cannot refrain from inserting just here an account of the battle of the 2d taken from a graphic account in the New York *World*. It will be seen that the correspondent treats the charge of my 13,000 men as if it were the charge of the whole army. The account is as follows:

"He then began a heavy fire on Cemetery Hill. It must not be thought that this wrathful fire was unanswered. Our artillery began to play within a few moments, and hurled back defiance and like destruction upon the rebel lines. Until 6 o'clock the roar of cannon, the rush of missles and the bursting of bombs filled the air. The clangor alone of this awful combat might well have confused and awed a less cool and watchful commander than General Meade. It did not confuse him. With the calculation of a tactician and the eye of an experienced judge, he watched from his head-quarters on the hill whatever movement under the murky cloud which enveloped the rebel lines might first disclose the intention which it was evident this artillery firing covered. About 6 o'clock P.M., silence, deep, awfully impressive but momentary, was permitted, as if by magic, to dwell upon the field. Only the groans—unheard before—of the wounded and dying, only a murmur, a warning memory of the breeze through the foliage; only a low rattle of preparation of what was to come embroidered this blank stillness. Then, as the smoke beyond the village was lightly borne to the eastward, the woods on the left were seen filled with dark masses of infantry, three columns deep, who advanced at a quick step. Magnificent! Such a charge by such a force—full forty-five thousand men, under Hill and Longstreet—even though it threatened to pierce and anni-hilate the Third corps, against which it was directed, drew forth cries of admiration from all who beheld it. General Sickles and his splendid com-mand withstood the shock with a determination that checked but could not fully restrain it. Back, inch by inch, fighting, falling, dying, cheering, the men retired. The rebels came on more furiously, halting at intervals, pouring volleys that struck our troops down in scores. General Sickles, fighting desperately, was struck in the leg and fell. The Second corps came to the aid of his decimated column. The battle grew fearful. Standing firmly up against the storm, our troops, though still outnumbered, gave back shot for shot, volley for volley, almost death for death. Still the enemy was not restrained. Down he came upon our left with a momentum that nothing could check. The rifled guns that lay before our infantry on a knoll were in danger of capture. General Hancock was wounded in the thigh, General Gibbon in the shoulder. The Fifth corps, as the First and Second waivered anew, went into the breach with such shouts and such volleys as made the rebel column tremble at last. Up from the valley behind another battery came rolling to the heights, and flung its contents in an instant down in the midst of the enemy's ranks. Crash! Crash! With discharges deafening, terrible, the musketry firing went on. The enemy, reforming after each discharge with wondrous celerity and firmness, still pressed up the declivity. What hideous carnage filled the minutes between the appearance of the Fifth corps and the advance to the support of the rebel columns of still another column from the right, I cannot bear to tell. Men fell, as the leaves fall in autumn, before those horrible discharges. Faltering for an instant the rebel columns seemed about to recede before the tempest. But their officers, who could be seen through the smoke of the conflict galloping and swinging their swords along the lines, rallied them anew, and the next instant the whole line sprang forward, as if to break through our own by mere weight of numbers. A division from the Twelfth corps, on the extreme right, reached the scene at this instant, and at the same time Sedgwick came up with the Sixth corps, having finished a march of nearly thirty-six consecutive hours. To what rescue they came their officers saw and told them. Weary as they were, barefooted, hungry, fit to drop for slumber, as they were, the wish for victory was so blended with the thought of exhaustion that they cast themselves, in turn, en masse into line of battle, and went down on the enemy with death in their weapons and cheers on their lips. The rebel's camel's back was broken by this "feather." His line staggered, reeled and drifted slowly back, while the shouts of our soldiers, lifted up amid the roar of musketry over the bodies of the dead and wounded, proclaimed the completeness of their victory."

It may be imagined that I was astonished at the fact that we received no support after we had driven the Federals from the peach orchard and one thousand yards beyond. If General Ewell had engaged the army in his front at that time (say 4 o'clock) he would have prevented their massing their whole army in my front, and while he and I kept their two wings engaged Hill would have found their centre weak, and should have threatened it while I broke through their left and dislodged them. Having failed to move at 4 o'clock, while the enemy was in his front, it was still more surprising that he did not advance at 5 o'clock with vigor and promptness, when the trenches in front of him were vacated or rather held by one single brigade (as General Meade's testimony before the Committee on the Conduct of the War states). Had he taken these trenches and scattered the brigade that held them, he would have found himself in the Federal's flank and rear. His attack in the rear must have dislodged the Federals, as it would have been totally unexpected—it being believed that he was in front with me. Hill charging upon the centre at the same time would have increased their disorder and we should have won the field. But Ewell did not advance until I had withdrawn my troops, and the First corps, after winning position after position, was forced to withdraw from the field with two corps of their comrades within sight and resting upon their arms. Ewell did not move until about dusk (according to his own report). The real cause of Ewell's non-compliance with General Lee's orders was that he had broken his line of battle by sending two brigades off on some duty up the York road. General Early says that my failure to attack at sunrise was the cause of Ewell's line being broken at the time I did attack. This is not only absurd but impossible. After sunrise that morning Colonel Venable and General Lee were at Ewell's headquarters discussing the policy of opening the attack with Ewell's corps. They left Ewell with this definite order: that he was to hold himself in readiness to support my attack when it was made. It is silly to say that he was ready at sunrise, when he was not ready at 4 o'clock, when the attack was really made. His orders were to hold himself in readiness to co-operate with my attack when it was made. In breaking his line of battle he rendered himself unable to support me when he would have been potential. Touching the failure of the supporting brigades of Anderson's division to cover McLaws' flank by enchelon movements, as directed, there is little to be said. Those brigades acted gallantly, but went astray early in the fight. General Anderson in his report says: "A strong fire was poured upon our right flank, which had become detached from McLaws' left." General Lee, alluding to the action of these two brigades, says: "But having become separated from McLaws', Wilcox's and Wright's brigades advanced with great gallantry, breaking successive lines of the enemy's infantry and compelling him to abandon much of his artillery. Wilcox reached the foot and Wright gained the crest of the ridge itself, driving the enemy down the opposite side; but having become too separated from McLaws, and gone beyond the other two brigades of the division they were to attack in front and on both flanks, and compelled to retire, being unable to bring off any of the captured artillery, McLaws' left also fell back, and it being now nearly dark General Longstreet determined to await the arrival of Pickett." So much for the action of the first day.

I did not see General Lee that night. On the next morning he came to see me, and fearing that he was still in his disposition to attack, I tried to anticipate him by saying: "General, I have had my scouts out all night, and I find that you still have an excellent opportunity to move around to the right of Meade's army and manoeuvre him into attacking us." He replied, pointing with his fist at Cemetery Hill: "The enemy is there, and I am going to strike him." I felt then that it was my duty to express my convictions; I said: "General, I have been a soldier all my life. I have been with soldiers engaged in fights by couples, by squads, companies, regiments, divisions and armies, and I should know as well as any one what soldiers can do. It is my opinion that no 15,000 men ever arrayed for battle can take that position," pointing to Cemetery Hill. General Lee in reply to this ordered me to prepare Pickett's division for the attack. I should not have been so urgent had I not foreseen the hopelessness of the proposed assault. I felt that I must say a word against the sacrifice of my men; and then I felt that my record was such that General Lee would or could not misconstrue my motives. I said no more, however, but turned away. The most of the morning was consumed in waiting for Pickett's men and getting into position. The plan of assault was as follows: Our artillery was to be massed in a wood from which Pickett was to charge, and it was to pour a continuous fire upon the cemetery. Under cover of this fire, and supported by it, Pickett was to charge.

Our artillery was in charge of General E.P. Alexander, a brave and gifted officer. Colonel Walton was my chief of artillery, but Alexander being at the head of the column, and being first in position, and being besides an officer of unusual promptness, sagacity and intelligence, was given charge of the artillery. The arrangements were completed about one o'clock. General Alexander had arranged that a battery of seven 10-pound howitzers, with fresh horses and full caissons, were to charge with Pickett, at the head of his line, but General Pendleton, from whom the guns had been borrowed, recalled them just before the charge was made, and thus deranged this wise plan. Never was I so depressed as upon that day. I felt that my men were to be sacrificed, and that I should have to order them to make a hopeless charge. I had instructed General Alexander, being unwilling to trust myself with the entire responsibility, to carefully observe the effect of the fire upon the enemy, and when it began to tell to notify Pickett to begin the assault. I was so much impressed with the hopelessness of the charge that I wrote the following note to General Alexander: "If the artillery fire does not have the effect to drive off the enemy or greatly demoralize him, so as to make our efforts pretty certain, I would prefer that you should not advise General Pickett to make the charge. I shall rely a great deal on your judgement to determine the matter, and shall expect you to let Pickett know when the moment offers."

To my note the General replied as follows: "I will only be able to judge the effect of our fire upon the enemy by his return fire, for his infantry is but little exposed to view, and the smoke will obscure the whole field. If, as I infer from your note, there is an alternative to this attack, it should be carefully considered before opening our fire, for it will take all of the artillery ammunition was have left to test this one thoroughly, and if the result is unfavorable, we will have none left for another effort, and even if this is entirely successful it can only be so at a very bloody cost." I still desired to save my men and felt that if the artillery did not produce the desired effect I would be justified in holding Pickett off. I wrote this note to Colonel Walton at exactly 1:30 P.M.: "Let the batteries open. Order great precision in firing. If the batteries at the peach orchard cannot be used against the point we intend attacking, let them open on the enemy at Rocky Hill." The cannonading which opened along both lines was grand. In a few moments a courier brought a note to General Pickett (who was standing near me) from Alexander, which, after reading, he handed to me. It was as follows: "If you are coming at all you must come at once, or I cannot give you proper support; but the enemy's fire has not slackened at all; at least eighteen guns are still firing from the Cemetery itself." After I had read the note Pickett said to me: "General, Shall I advance?" My feelings had so overcome me that I could not speak for fear of betraying my want of confidence to him. I bowed affirmation and turned to mount my horse. Pickett immediately said: "I shall lead my division forward, sir." I spurred my horse to the wood where Alexander was stationed with artillery. When I reached him he told me of the disappearance of the seven guns which were to have led the charge with Pickett, and that his ammunition was so low that he could not properly support the charge. He informed me that he had no ammunition with which to replenish. I then saw that there was no help for it, and that Pickett must advance under his orders. He swept past our artillery in splendid style, and the men marched steadily and compactly down the slope. As they started up the ridge over one hundred cannon from the breastworks of the Federals hurled a rain of cannister, grape and shells down upon them; still they pressed on until half way up the slope, when the crest on the hill was lit with a solid sheet of flame as the masses of infantry rose and fired. When the smoke cleared away Pickett's division was gone. Nearly two-thirds of his men lay dead on the field, and the survivors were sullenly retreating down the hill. Mortal man could not have stood that fire. In half an hour the contested field was cleared and the battle of Gettysburg was over.

When this charge had failed I expected that of course the enemy would throw himself against our shattered ranks and try to crush us. I sent my staff officers to the rear to assist in rallying the troops, and hurried to our line of batteries as the only support that I could give them, knowing that my presence would impress upon every one of them the necessity of holding the ground to the last extremity. I knew if the army was to be saved those batteries must check the enemy. As I rode along the line of artillery I observed my old friend Captain Miller, Washington Artillery, of Sharpsburg record, walking between his guns and smoking his pipe as quietly and contentedly as he could at his campfire. The enemy's skirmishers were then advancing and threatening assault. For unaccountable reasons the enemy did not pursue his advantage. Our army was soon in compact shape, and its face turned once more toward Virginia. I may mention here that it has been absurdly said that General Lee ordered me to put Hood's and McLaws' divisions in support of Pickett's assault. General Lee never ordered any such thing. After our troops were all arranged for assault General Lee rode with me twice over the lines to see that everything was arranged according to his wishes. He was told that we had been more particular in giving the orders than ever before; that the commanders had been sent for and the point of attack had been carefully designated, and that the commanders had been directed to communicate to their subordinates, and through them to every soldier in the command, the work that was before them, so that they should nerve themselves for the attack and fully understand it. After leaving me he again rode over the field once, if not twice, so that there was really no room for misconstruction or misunderstanding of his wishes. He could not have thought of giving any such an order. Hood and McLaws were confronted by a largely superior force of the enemy on the right of Pickett's attack. To have moved them to Pickett's support would have disengaged treble their number of Federals, who would have swooped down from their rocky fastnesses against the flank of our attacking column and swept our army from the field. A reference to any of the maps of Gettysburg will show from the position of the troops that this would have been the inevitable result. General Lee and myself never had any deliberate conversation about Gettysburg. The subject was never broached by either of us to the other. On one occasion it came up casually and he said to me (alluding to the charge of Pickett on the 3d), "General, why didn't you stop all that thing that day." I replied that I could not under the circumstances assume such a responsibility, as no discretion had been left me.

Before discussing the weak points of the campaign of Gettysburg, it is proper that I should say that I do so with the greatest affection for General Lee and the greatest reverence for his memory. The relations existing between us were affectionate, confidential, and even tender, from the first to last. There was never a harsh word between us. It is then with a reluctant spirit that I write a calm and critical review of the Gettysburg campaign, because that review will show that our Commanding General was unfortunate at several points. There is no doubt that General Lee, during the crisis of that campaign, lost the matchless equipoise that usually characterized him, and that whatever mistakes were made were not so much matters of deliberate judgement as the impulses of a great mind disturbed by unparalleled conditions. General Lee was thrown from his balance (as is shown by the statement of General Fitzhugh Lee) by too great confidence in the prowess of his troops and (as is shown by General Anderson's statement) by the deplorable absence of General Stuart and the perplexity occasioned thereby. With this preface I proceed to say that the Gettysburg campaign was weak in these points—adhering, however, to my opinion that a combined movement against Rosecranz in Tennessee and a march toward Cincinnati would have given better results than could possibly have been secured by the invasion of Pennsylvania: First, the offensive strategically but defensive tactical plan of the campaign as agreed upon should never have been abandoned after we entered the enemy's country. Second, if there ever was a time when the abandonment of that plan could have promised decisive results, it was at Brandy Station, where, after Stuart had repulsed the force thrown across the river, we might have fallen on that force and crushed it, and then put ourselves in position, threatening the enemy's right and rear, which would have dislodged him from his position at Fredericksburg and given us the opportunity for an effective blow. Third, General Stuart should not have been permitted to leave the general line of march, thus forcing us to march blindfolded into the enemy's country; to this may be attributed, in my opinion, the change of policy of the campaign. Fourth, the success obtained by the accidental rencontre on the 1st should have been vigorously prosecuted and the enemy should have been given no time to fortify or concentrate. Fifth, on the night of the 1st the army should have been carried around to Meade's right and rear, and posted between him and his capitol, and we could have maneuvered him into an attack. Sixth, when the attack was made on the enemy's left on the 2d by my corps, Ewell should have been required to co-operate by a vigorous movement against his right and Hill should have moved against his centre. Had this been done his army would have been dislodged beyond question. Seventh, on the morning of the 3d it was not yet too late to move to the right and maneuver the Federal into attacking us. Eighth, Pickett's division should not have been ordered to assault Cemetery Ridge on the 3d, as we had already tested the strength of that position sufficiently to admonish us that we could not dislodge him. While the co-operation of Generals Ewell and Hill, on the 2d, by vigorous assault at the moment my battle was in progress, would in all probability have dislodged the Federals from their position, it does not seem that such success would have yielded the fruits anticipated at the inception of the campaign. The battle as it was fought would, in any result, have so crippled us that the Federals would have been able to make good their retreat, and we should soon have been obliged to retire to Virginia with nothing but victory to cover our waning cause.

The morale of the victory might have dispirited the North and aroused the South to new exertions, but it would have been nothing in the game being played by the two armies at Gettysburg. As to the abandonment of the tactical defensive policy that we had agreed upon, there can be no doubt that General Lee deeply deplored it as a mistake. His remark, made just after the battle, "It is all my fault," meant just what it said. It adds to the nobility and magnanimity of that remark when we reflect that it was the utterance of a deep-felt truth rather than a mere sentiment. In a letter written to me by General Lee in January, 1864, he says: "Had I taken your advice at Gettysburg instead of pursuing the course I did, how different all might have been." Captain T.J. Gorie, of Houston, Texas, a gentleman of high position and undoubted integrity, writes to me upon this same point as follows: "Another important circumstance which I distinctly remember was in the winter of 1864, when you sent me from East Tennessee to Orange Courthouse with dispatches for General Lee. Upon my arrival there General Lee asked me in his tent, where he was alone with two or three Northern papers on his table. He remarked that he had just been reading the Northern official report of the Battle of Gettysburg; that he had become satisfied from reading those reports that if he had permitted you to carry out your plans on the third day, instead of making the attack on Cemetery Hill, we would have been successful." I cannot see, as has been claimed, why the absence of General Lee's cavalry should have justified his attack on the enemy. On the contrary, while they may have perplexed him, I hold that it was an additional reason for his not hazarding an attack. At the time the attack was ordered we were fearful that our cavalry had been destroyed. In case of a disaster, and a forced retreat, we should have had nothing to cover our retreat. When so much was at stake as at Gettysburg the absence of the cavalry should have prevented the taking of any chances.

As to the failure of Stuart to move with the enemy to the west side of the Blue Ridge, I can only call attention to the fact that General Lee gave him discretionary orders. He doubtless did as he thought best. Had no discretion been given him he would have known and fallen into his natural position—my right flank. But authority thus given a subordinate general implies an opinion on the part of the commander that something better than the drudgery of a march along our flank might be open to him, and one of General Stuart's activity and gallantry should not be expected to fail to seek it. As to Ewell's failure to prosecute the advantage won on the 1st, there is little to be said, as the Commanding-General was on the field. I merely quote from his (General Ewell's) official report. He says: "The enemy had fallen back to a commanding position that was known to us as Cemetery Hill, south of Gettysburg, and quickly showed a formidable front there. On entering the town, I received a message from the Commanding-General to attack the hill, if I could do so to advantage. I could not bring artillery to bear on it; all the troops with me were jaded by twelve hours' marching and fighting, and I was notified that General Johnson was close to the town with his division, the only one of my corps that had not been engaged, Anderson's division of the Third corps, having been halted to let them pass. Cemetery Hill was not assailable from the town, and I determined with Johnson's division to take possession of a wooded hill to my left, on a line with and commanding Cemetery Hill. Before Johnson got up the Federals were reported moving to our left flank—our extreme left—and I could see what seemed to be his skirmishers in that direction. Before this report could be investigated by Lieutenant T.T. Turner, of my staff, and Lieutenant Robert Early, sent to investigate it, and Johnson placed in position, the night was far advanced." General Lee explains his failure to send positive orders to Ewell to follow up the flying enemy as follows: "The attack was not pressed that afternoon, the enemy's force being unknown and it being considered advisable to await the arrival of the rest of our troops. Orders were sent back to hasten their march, and in the meantime every effort was made to ascertain the numbers ond positions of the enemy and find the most favorable point to attack."

Pursuit "pell-mell" is sometimes justified in a mere retreat. It is the accepted principle of action in a rout. General Early, in his report of this day's work, says: "the enemy had been routed." He should therefore, have been followed by everything that could have been thrown upon his heels, not so much to gain the heights, which were recognized as the rallying point, but to prevent his rallying at all in time to form lines for another battle. If the enemy had been routed this could and should have been done. In the "Military Annals of Louisiana," (Napier Bartlett, Esq.,) in the account of this rout, he says: "Hays had received orders through Early from General Ewell (though Lee's general instructions were subsequently the reverse) to halt at Gettysburg and advance no further in case he should succeed in capturing that place. But Hays now saw that the enemy were coming around by what is known as the Baltimore road, and were making for the heights—the Cenetery Ridge. This ridge meant life or death, and for the possession of it the battles of the 2d and 3d were fought. Owing to the long detour the enemy was compelled to make, it was obvious that he could not get his artillery in position on the heights for one or two hours. The immediate occupation of the heights by the Confederates, who were in position to get them at the time referred to, was a matter of vital importance. Hays recognized it as such and presently sent for Early. The latter thought as Hays, but declined to disobey orders. At the urgent request of General Hays, however, he sent for General Ewell. When the latter arrived many precious moments had been lost. But the enemy, who did not see its value until the arrival of Hancock, had not yet appeared in force." General Hays told me ten years after the battle that he "Could have seized the heights without the loss of ten men." Here we see General Early adhering to orders when his own convictions told him he should not do so, and refusing to allow General Hays to seize a point at a moment when he admitted and knew that disregard of the order would have made more secure the point at issue when the order was given.

Before closing this article I desire to settle finally and fully one point concerning which there has been much discussion, viz: the alleged delay in the attack upon the 2d. I am moved to this task not so much by an ambition to disolve the cloud of personal misrrepresentation that has been settled about my head, and by a sense of duty which leads me to determine a point that will be of value to the historian. It was asserted by General Pendleton, with whom the carefulness of statement or deliberateness of judgement has never been characteristic, but who has been distinguished for the unreliabity of his memory, that General Lee ordered me to attack the enemy at sunrise on the 2d. General J.A. Early has, in positive terms, indorsed this charge, which I now proceed to disprove. I have said that I left General Lee late in the night of the 1st, and that he had not yet determined when the attack should be made; that I went to his headquarters early the next morning and was with him for some time; that he left me early the next morning and went to Ewell's headquarters with the express view of seeing whether or not the main attack should be made then, and that he returned at about 9 o'clock; and that after discussing the ground for some time he determined that I should make the main attack, and at 11 o'clock gave me the order to prepare for it. I now present documents that sustain these assertions.

The first letter that I offer is from Colonel W.H. Taylor, of General Lee's staff. It is as follows:

Norfolk, Va., April 28, 1875.

Dear General: I have received your letter of the 20th instant. I have not read the article of which you speak, nor have I ever seen any copy of General Pendleton's address; indeed, I have read little or nothing of what has been written since the war. In the first place, because I could not spare the time; and in the second, of those whose writings I have heard I deem but very few entitled to any attention whatever. I can only say that I never before heard of "the sunrise attack" you were to have made as charged by General Pendleton. If such an order was given you I never knew of it, or it has strangely escaped my memory. I think it more than probable that if General Lee had had your troops available the evening of the previous day of which you speak, he would have ordered an early attack, but this does not touch the point at issue. I regard it as a great mistake on the part of those who, perhaps because of political differences, now undertake to criticise and attack your war record. Such conduct is most ungenerous, and I am sure meets the disapprobation of all good Confederates with whom I have had the pleasure of associating in the daily walks of life.

Yours very respectfully,
W.H. Taylor

The next letter is from Colonel Charles Marshall, of General Lee's staff, who was in charge of all the papers left by General Lee. It is as follows:

Baltimore, Md., May 7, 1875

Dear General: Your lett of the 20th ult. Was received and should have had an earlier reply but for my engagements preventing me from looking at my papers to find what I could on the subject. I have no personal recollections of the order to which you refer. It certainly was not conveyed by me, nor is there anything in General Lee's official report to show the attack on the 2d was expected by him to begin earlier, except that he notices that there was not proper concert of action on that day.

Respectfully,
Charles Marshall

The a letter from A.L. Long, who was General Lee's military secretary:

Big Island, Bedfore, Va., May 31. 1875

Dear General: Your letter of the 20th, ult., refering to an assertion of General Pendleton's, made in a lecture delivered several years ago, which was recently published in the *Southern Historical Society Magazine* substantially as follows: "That General Lee ordered General Longstreet to attack General Meade at sunrise on the morning of the 2d of July." has been received. I do not recollect of hearing of an order to attack at sunrise, or at any other designated hour, pending the operations at Gettysburg during the first three days of July, 1863.

Yours truly,
A.L. Long"

I add the letter of Colonel Venable, of General Lee's staff, which should of itself be conclusive. I merely premise it with the statement that it was fully 9 o'clock before General Lee returned from his reconnaissance of Ewell's lines:

University of Virginia, May 11, 1875

General James Longstreet:
Dear General: Your letter of the 25th ultimo. With regard to Gen. Lee's battle order on the 1st and 2d of July at Gettysburg, was duly received. I did not know of any order for attack on the enemy at sunrise on the 2d, nor can I believe any such order was issued by Gen. Lee to General Ewell to ask him what he thought of the advantages of an attack on the enemy from his position. (Colonel Marshall had been sent with a similar order on the night of the 1st). General Ewell made me ride with him from point to point of his lines, so as to see with him the exact position of things. Before he got through the examination of the enemy's position General Lee came himself to General Ewell's lines. In sending the message to General Ewell, General Lee was explicit in saying that the question was whether he should move all the troops around on the right and attack on that side. I do not think that the errand on which I was sent by the Comanding General is consistent with the idea of an attack at sunrise by any portion of the army.

Yours, very truly,
Chas. S. Venable

I add upon this point the letter of Dr. Cullen, medical director of the First corps:

Richmond, Va., May 18, 1875

General James Longstreet:
Dear General—Yours of the 16th ult. Should have received my immediate attention, but before answering it I was desirous of refreshing my memory of the scenes and incidents of the Gettysburg campaign by conversation with others who were with us and who served in different corps of the command. It was an astounding announcement to the survivors of the First army corps that the disaster and failure at Gettysburg was alone and solely due to its commander. And that had he obeyed the orders of the commander-in-chief that Meade's army would have been beaten, before its entire force had assembled, and its final discomfiture thereby made certain. It is a little strange that these charges were not made while General Lee was alive to substantiate or disprove them, and that seven years or more were permitted to pass in silence regarding them. You are fortunate in being able to call upon the Adjutant-General and the two confidential officers of General Lee's staff for their testimony in the case, and I do not think that you will have any reason to fear their evidence. They knew every order that was issued for that battle, when and where the attacks were to be made, who were slow in attacking, and who did not make attacks that were expected to be made. I hope, for the sake of history and for your brave military record, that a quietus will at once be put on this subject. I distinctly remember the appearance in our headquarter camp of the scout who brought from Frederick the first account that General Lee had of the definite whereabouts of the enemy; of the excitement at General Lee's headquarters among couriers, quartermasters, commissaries, etc., all betoking some early movement of the commands dependent upon the news brought by the scout. That afternoon General Lee was walking with some of us in the road in front of his headquarters and said: "To-morrow, gentlemen, we will not move to Harrisburg as we expected, but will go over to Gettysburg and see what General Meade is after." Orders had then been issued to the corps to move at sunrise on the morning of the next day, and promptly at that time the corps was put on the road. The troops moved slowly a short distance when they were stopped by Ewell's wagon trains and Johnson's division turning into the road in front of them, making their way from some point north to Cashtown or Gettysburg. How many hours we were detained I am unable to say, but it must have been many for I remember eating a lunch or dinner before moving again. Being anxious to see you I rode rapidly by the troops (who, as soon as they could get into the road, pushed hurriedly by us also), and overtook you about dark at the hill this side of Gettysburg, about half a mile from the town. You had been at the front with General Lee and were returning to your camp, a mile or two back. I spoke very exultingly of the victory we were thought to have obtained that day, but

was surprised to find that you did not take the same cheerful view of it that I did, and presently you remarked that it would have been better had we not fought than to have left undone what we did. You said that the enemy were left occupying a position that it would take the whole army to drive them from and then at a great sacrifice. We soon reached the camp, three miles, perhaps, from Gettysburg, and found the column near by. Orders were issued to be ready to march at "daybreak," or some earlier hour, next morning. About 3 o'clock in the morning, while the stars were shining, you left your headquarters and rode to General Lee's, where I found you sitting with him after sunrise looking at the enemy on Cemetery Hill. I rode then into Gettysburg and was gone some two hours, and when I returned found you still with General Lee. At 2 or 3 o'clock in the day I rode with you toward the right, when you were about to attack, and was with you in front of the peach orchard when Hood began to move towards Round Top. General Hood was soon wounded and I removed him from the field to a house near by.

> I am yours, very truly,
> J.S.D. Cullen

I submit next an extract from the official report of General R.H. Anderson:

Upon approaching Gettysburg I was directed to occupy the position in line of battle which had first been vacated by Pender's division, and to place one brigade and battery of artillery a mile or more on the right. Wilcox's brigade and Captain Ross' battery, of Lane's battalion, were posted in the detached position, while the other brigades occupied the ground from which Pender's division had first been moved. We continued in position until the morning of the 2d, when I received orders to take up a new line of battle on the right of Pender's division, about a mile and a half further forward. In taking the new position the Tenth Alabama regiment, Wilcox's brigade, had a sharp skirmish with the body of the enemy who had occupied a wooded hill on the extreme right of my line.... Shortly after the line had been formed I received notice that Lieutenant-General Longstreet would occupy the ground on my right, and that he would be in a direction nearly at right angles with mine, and that he would assault the extreme left of the enemy and drive him toward Gettysburg.

From a narrative of General McLaws, published in 1873, I copy the following:

On the 30th of June, I had been directed to have my division in readiness to follow General Ewell's corps. Marching toward Gettysburg, which it was intimated we would have passed by 10 o'clock the next day (the first of July), my division was accordingly marched from its camp and lined along the road in the order of march by 8 o'clock the 1st of

July. When the troops of Ewell's corps—it was Johnson's division in charge of Ewell's wagon trains, which were coming from Carlisle by the road west of the mountains—had passed the head of my column, I asked General Longstreet's staff officer, Major Fairfax, if my division should follow. He went off to enquire, and returned with orders for me to wait until Ewell's wagon train had passed, which did not happen until after 4 o'clock P.M. The train was calculated to be fourteen miles long, when I took up the line of march and continued marching until I arrived within three miles of Gettysburg, where my command camped along a creek. This was far into the night. My division was leading Longstreet's corps, and of course the other divisions came up later. I saw Hood's division the next morning, and understood that Pickett had been detached to guard the rear. While on the march, at about 10 o'clock at night, I met General Longstreet and some of his staff coming from the direction of Gettysburg, and had a few moments conversation with him. He said nothing of having received an order to attack at daylight the next morning. Here I will state that until General Pendleton mentioned it about two years ago when he was on a lecturing tour, after the death of General Lee, I never heard it intimated even that any such order had ever been given.

I close the testimony on this point by an extract from a letter from General Hood. He writes:

I arrived with my staff in front of the heights of Gettysburg shortly after daybreak, as I have already stated, on the morning of the 2d of July. My division soon commenced filing into an open field near me, when the troops were allowed to stack arms and rest until further orders. A short distance in advance of this point, and during the early part of the same morning, we were both engaged in company with Generals A.P. Hill and Lee in observing the position of the Federals. General Lee, with coat buttoned to the throat, sabre belt around his waist and field glasses pending at his side, walked up and down in the shade of large trees near us, halting now and then to observe the enemy. He seemed full of hope, yet at times buried in deep thought. Colonel Freemantle, of England, was ensconced in the forks of a tree not far off with glasses in constant use examining the lofty position of the Federal army. General Lee was seemingly anxious that you should attack that morning. He remarked to me: "The enemy is here, and if we do not whip him he will whip us." You thought it better to await the arrival of Pickett's division, at that time still in the rear, in order to make the attack, and you said to me subsequently, while we were seated together near the trunk of a tree: "General Lee is a little nervous this morning. He wishes me to attack. I do not wish to do it without Pickett. I never like going into a battle with one boot off.

Having thus disproved the assertions of Messrs. Pendleton and Early in regard to this rumored order for a sunrise attack, it appears that they are worthy of no further recognition; but it is difficult to pass beyond them without noting the manner in which, by their ignorance, they marred the plans of their chief on the field of battle. Mr. Pendleton robbed Pickett's division of its most important adjunct, fresh field artillery, at the moment of its severest trial, and thus frustrated the wise and brilliant programme of assault planned by General Alexander, and without the knowledge of that officer. (See narrative of General Alexander in the *Southern Historical Papers* for September 1877.) General Early broke up General Lee's line of battle on the 2d of July by detaching part of his division on some uncalled-for service, in violation of General Lee's orders, and thus prevented the co-operative attack of Ewell ordered by General Lee.

It is proper to discuss briefly, at this point, the movements of the third day. The charge of that day as made by General Pickett was emphatically a forlorn hope. The point designated by General Lee as the point of attack seemed to be about one mile from where he and I stood when he gave his orders. I asked him if the distance we had to overcome under a terrific fire was not more than a mile. He replied: "No; it is not more than fourteen hundred yards." So that our troops, when they arose above the crest, had to advance this distance under the fire of about half the Federal army, before they could fire a shot. Anything less than thirty thousand fresh veterans would have been vainly sacrificed in this attempt. The force given me for this work was Pickett's division (or rather part of it), about 5,500 men, fresh and ready to undertake anything. My supporting force of probably 8,000 men had bloody noses and bruised heads from the fight of the previous day, and were not in physical condition to undertake such desperate work. When fresh they were the equals of any troops on earth; but every soldier knows that there is a great difference between fresh soldiers and those who have just come out of a heavy battle. It has been charged that the delay of the attack on the third day was the cause of the failure of Ewell to co-operate with Pickett's attack. Colonel Taylor says that Ewell was ordered to attack at the same time with me, mine being the main attack. He says:

> General Longstreet's dispositions were not completed as soon as was expected ... General Ewell, who had orders to co-operate with General Longstreet, and who was, of course, not aware of any impediment to the main attack, having reinforced General Johnson during the night of the 2d, ordered his forward early the next morning. In obedience to these instructions, General Johnson became hotly engaged before General Ewell could be informed of the halt that had been called upon our right.

Let us look at the facts of this. Instead of "Making this attack at daylight," General Ewell says: "Just before the time fixed for General Johnson's advance the enemy attacked him to regain the works captured by Stuart the evening before." General Meade in his official report, says: "On the morning of the 3d, General Geary, having returned during the night, attacked at early dawn the enemy, and succeeded in driving him back and reoccupying his former position. A spirited contest was maintained along this portion of the line all the morning, and General Geary, reinforced by Wharton's brigade of the Sixth corps, maintained his position and inflicted very severe loss upon the enemy." Now to return to my end of the line. At about sunrise General Lee came to me and informed that General Pickett would soon report to me, and then ordered that his troops were to be used as a column of assault, designating the point of assault, and that portions of the Third corps were to be used in support. About 7 o'clock General Pickett rode forward and stated that his troops would soon be upon the field and asked to be assigned his position. Colonel W.W. Wood, of Pickett's division, in his account of the day, says: "If I remember correctly, Pickett's division and the artillery were all in position by 11 A.M." Hence we see that General Geary attacked General Ewell at least one hour before I had received my orders for the day; that at the very moment of my receiving these instructions General Ewell was engaged in a "spirited contest"; that this contest had continued several hours before General Pickett's troops came upon the field, and that the contest was virtually over before General Pickett and the artillery were prepared for the battle. When these arrangements were completed and the batteries ordered to open, General Ewell had been driven from his positions and not a footstep was made from any other part of the army in my support. That there may have been confusion of orders on the field during the second and third days I am not prepared to deny, but there was nothing of the kind about the headquarters of the First corps.

General Wilcox steps forward as a willing witness in all concerning the battle of Gettysburg, and seems to know everything of General Lee's wishes and the movements of the First corps, and in fact everything else except his own orders. His brigade was the directing brigade for the echelon movement that was to protect McLaws' flank. He went astray at the opening of the fight, either through ignorance of his orders or a misapprehension or violation of them. Had he but attended to his own brigade instead of looking to the management of the general battle, the splendid exhibition of soldiery given by his men would have given better results.

I have not seen criticism of the Comte de Paris upon the campaign, but I gather from quotations that he adduced as one of the objections to the invasion of Pennsylvania that the Federals would do superior fighting upon their own soil. The Confederates, whom I have read after, deny that this is true. Although not technically correct the Count is right in the material point. The actual fighting on the field of Gettysburg by the army of the Potomac was not marked by any unusual gallantry, but the positions that it occupied were held with much more than usual tenacity of purpose.

There is little to say of the retreat of General Lee's army to the Potomac. When we reached South Mountain, on our retreat, we learned that the Federal cavalry was in strong force threatening the destruction of our trains then collecting at Williamsport, and that it was also intercepting our trains on the road and burning some of our wagons. Upon the receipt of this intelligence, General Lee ordered me to march as rapidly as possible to the relief of our trains. By a forced march we succeeded in clearing the road and reached Williamsport in time to save our supply trains. We then took position covering the crossing there and at Falling Water, a short distance below. As the other corps arrived they were assigned positions and we went to work, as rapidly as possible to strengthen our line with field-works. On the 13th General Lee informed me that the river had fallen sufficiently at Williamsport to allow us to ford, and that the bridge at Falling Water had been repaired, and that he would that night recross the river with his entire army. I suggested as a matter of convenience and to avoid confusion, that it might be better to pass the trains over that night, with everything not essential to battle, and let his troops remain in position until the night of the 14th; that if the rest of his line was as strong as mine we could easily repulse any attack that might be made, and thus recover some of the prestige lost by the discomfiture at Gettysburg. After we crossed the Potomac we soon found that the Federals were pushing along the west side of the Blue Ridge with the purpose of cutting off our retreat to Richmond. General Lee again sent my corps forward to prevent this effort on the part of General Meade, and we succeeded in clearing the way, and holding it open for the Third corps that followed us. General Ewell, however, was cut off, and was obliged to pass the mountains further south. The First corps reached Culpeper Courthouse on the 24th.

In the month of August, 1863, while lying along the Rapidan, I called General Lee's attention to the condition of our affairs in the West, and the progress that was being made by the army under General Rosecranz, in cutting a new line through the State of Georgia, and suggesting that a successful march, such as he had started on would again bisect the Southern country, and that when that was done the war would be virtually over. I suggested that he should adhere to his defensive tactics upon the Rapidan, and reinforce from his army the army lying in front of Rosecranz—so that it could crush that army and then push on to the West. He seemed struck with these views, but was as much opposed to dividing his army as he was in the spring when I first suggested it. He went down to Richmond to arrange for another offensive campaign during the fall. While there several letters passed between us, only two of which I have preserved in connected form. The result of this correspondence was, however, that I was sent with two divisions—Hood's and McLaw's—to reinforce our army then in Georgia. The result of this movement was the defeat of Rosecranz at Chickamauga, when the last hope of the Confederacy expired with the failure of our army to prosecute the advantage gained by this defeat. The letters are appended herewith:

Richmond, August 31, 1863.

Lieutenant General J. Longstreet,
Headquarters Army of Northern Virginia
General: I have wished for several days past to return to the army, but have been detained by the President. He will not listen to my proposition to leave to morrow.

I hope you will use every exertion to prepare the army for offensive operations, and improve the condition of men and animals. I can see nothing better to be done than to endeavor to bring General Meade out and use our efforts to crush his army while in the present condition.

The Quartermaster's Department promise to send up 3,000 bushels of corn per day, provided the cars can be unloaded and returned without delay. I hope you will be able to arrange it so that the cars will not be detained. With this supply of corn if it can be maintained, the condition of our animals should improve.

Very respectfully and truly yours,
R.E. Lee.

Headquarters, September 2, 1863.

General: Your letter of the 31st is received. I have expressed to Generals Ewell and Hill your wishes, and am doing all that can be done to be well-prepared with my own command. Our greatest difficulty will be in preparing our animals.

I don't know that we can reasonably hope to accomplish much here by offensive operations, unless we are strong enough to cross the Potomac. If we advance to meet the enemy on this side he will in all probability go into one of his many fortified positions. These we cannot afford to attack.

I know but little of the condition of our affairs in the West, but am inclined to the opinion that our best opportunity for great results is in Tennessee. If we could hold the defensive here with two corps and send the other to operate in Tennessee with that army, I think that we could accomplish more than by an advance from here.

The enemy seems to have settled down upon the plan of holding certain points by fortifying and defending, while he concentrates upon others. It seems to me that this must succeed unless we concentrate ourselves and at the same time make occasional show of active operations at all points.

I know of no other means of acting upon that principle at present, except to depend upon our fortifications in Virginia, and concentrate with one corps of this army and such as may be drawn from others in Tennessee and destroy Rosecranz's army.

I feel assured that this is practicable, and that greater advantages will be gained than by any operations from here.

I remain, General, very respectfully,
Your obedient servant,
James Longstreet, Lieut-General.

It will be noticed by those who have watched the desultory controversy maintained upon the subject, that after I had proved the fallacy of General Pendleton's and General Early's idea of a sunrise attack, they fall back upon the charge that I delayed in bringing my troops into action, waiving all question of an order from General Lee. I have shown that I did not receive orders from General Lee to attack until about 11 o'clock on the 2d, that I immediately began my dispositions for attack; that I waited about forty minutes for Laws' brigade, by General Lee's assenting authority; that by especial orders from General Lee my corps marched into position by a circuitous route, under the direction and conduct of Col. Johnson of his staff of engineers; that Colonel Johnson's orders were to keep the march of the troops concealed, and that I hurried Hood's division forward in the face of these orders, throwing them into line by a direct march, and breaking up the delay occasioned by the orders of Gen. Lee. I need only add that every movement or halt of the troops on that day was made in the immediate presence of General Lee, or in his sight—certainly within reach of his easy and prompt correction. I quote in this connection the order that I issued to the heads of departments in my corps on the 1st. I present the order issued to Colonel Walton of the artillery, similar orders having been issued to the division commanders:

> Headquarters, First Army Corps,
>
> Colonel: The Commanding General desires you to come on to night as fast as you can without distressing your men or animals. Hill and Ewell have sharply engaged the enemy and you will be needed for to-morrow's battle. Let us know where you will stop to-night
>
> Respectfully,
> G.M. Sorrell, A.A. General.

I offer also a report made by General Hood touching on this march. He says:

> While lying in camp near Chambersburg information was received that Hill and Ewell were about to come into contact with the enemy near Gettysburg. My troops, together with McLaws' division, were at once put in motion upon the most direct road to that point, which we reached after a hard march at or before sunrise on July the 2d. So imperative had been our orders to hasten forward with all possible speed that on the march my troops were allowed to halt and rest only about two hours during the night from the 1st to the 2d of July.

It appears to me that the gentlemen who made the above-mentioned charges against me have chosen the wrong point of attack. With their motives I have nothing to do; but I cannot help suggesting that if they had charged me with having precipitated the battle instead of having delayed it, the records might have sustained them in that my attack was made about four hours before General Ewell's. I am reminded in this connection of what a Federal officer, who was engaged in that battle, said to me when we were talking over the battle and the comments it had provoked. He said: "I cannot imagine how they can charge you with being late in your attack, as you were the only one that got in at all. I do not think their charge can be credited."

In conclusion I may say that it is unfortunate that the discussion of all mooted points concerning the battle was not opened before the death of General Lee. A word or two from him would have settled all points at issue. As it is, I have written an impartial narrative of the facts as they are, with such comments as the nature of the case seemed to demand.

Controversy concerning the battle of Gettysburg began to rear its ugly head almost as soon as the smoke cleared from the Pennsylvania hills and fields. A scathing letter from Brigadier General Ambrose Ransom Wright appeared in a Georgia newspaper some three weeks following the battle, and caused a furor that led to Wright being brought up on charges for court martial. Though he was later acquitted of any wrongdoing, Wright had fired one of the opening shots in a public debate that lasts to this day.

General Longstreet, in his submission to the Philadelphia newspaper, states that he has come to the decision to speak out about the "mistakes" made at Gettysburg because of the incessant recent attacks that were being made upon him by many officers having a close personal tie to Robert E. Lee. This is somewhat misleading. The fact is that the controversy had been festering since 1866, when William Swinton published his Campaigns of the Army of the Potomac. This book was the first authoritative Union account of the war to be released.[2] Swinton ascribed to General Longstreet's version of the battle, and placed blame for the Confederate defeat on the shoulders of Generals Lee, Ewell, and Early. Though a number of Lee's supporters quickly rallied to his defense, Lee himself declined to enter into a public debate. It is difficult to say whether doing so would have squashed or intensified the controversy. As Lee assumed full responsibility for the failure to defeat the Union army immediately following Pickett's charge, it would be reasonable to assume that a similar statement, issued after the end of hostilities, would have had the effect of laying the matter to rest. It would also have prevented a lifelong rift that developed between men that had formerly been his subordinate officers and comrades. The fact that Lee refused to make such a statement may be significant. He was silent in assuming blame for the failure at Gettysburg, even though it was in his character to do so, if he felt that such blame was warranted and deserved. Was this because he felt he was not solely responsible, because his plans had not been fully carried out by subordinates? Was Lee's silence on the matter indicative of a belief that he had been failed at Gettysburg, that his plan of battle could have succeeded if it had been carried out with celerity and enthusiasm? It was not in Lee's character to sacrifice a brother officer for the sake of maintaining his own reputation, and if he did indeed feel that there was responsibility enough to go around, he was not the type to point fingers or make accusations. By not stepping forward and answering the charges being made against him, he might have been following the strict code of honor that had so defined his life, but in doing so, he only added to the speculation and controversy that continues to this day.

General Longstreet begins his narrative with a statement that seems to *be in conflict with his contemporary writing. He states that he had an interview with Secretary of War James Seddon, in Richmond, while he and his army were marching from Suffolk to join Lee at Fredericksburg. Longstreet discloses that the subject of this meeting was a need to relieve the pressure on Vicksburg, and states that the discussion centered around plans to send him and his corps to the Western Theater in an attempt to blunt the designs of the Federals in that sector. He continues to say that the objective of such a move would be the invasion of Kentucky, and possibly Ohio. These statements set the tone for Longstreet's arguments that the invasion of Pennsylvania was a mistake, and that critical errors were made in not allocating the resources of the Confederacy to other theaters of the war, at that time.*

This meeting took place on May 6, following the conclusion of the battle of Chancellorsville. Longstreet had missed that battle, his corps not reaching Lee in time to lend the weight of his numbers to the effort to protect Richmond and turn back Hooker's massive Army of the Potomac. With the immediate threat in Virginia removed, the time seemed right to examine Confederate options in other theaters of operation. General Ulysses S. Grant's army was threatening the capture of Vicksburg, Mississippi, and the severing of the last remaining portion of the Mississippi River open to Confederate travel. How to best support the Confederate armies under Braxton Bragg, John C. Pemberton, and Joseph E. Johnston became the overriding topic of conversation. Lee had come to be thought of as being invincible by the administration. His most recent victory at Chancellorsville seemed to prove that he could prevail regardless of the odds. Had he not defeated a vastly superior Federal army without the assistance of Longstreet's corps? The politicians in Richmond speculated that Lee would easily be able to assume the offensive while one or two of Longstreet's divisions was sent west to bolster the situations confronting either Bragg or Pemberton. In his post-war writings, General Longstreet appears to have been completely in favor of this plan, and he offers it as an alternative to the Pennsylvania Campaign that was finally adopted. But Longstreet was, at the time, fully aware of the critical situation Lee's army was in, and he doubted the results to be obtained by a transfer of his divisions to the west.

To be sure, Lee had won a glorious victory at Chancellorsville, but in doing so he had seriously impaired the efficiency of his own army. Casualties in the Confederate ranks were approximately 21 percent, or about 13,000 men. The defeated Army of the Potomac had suffered 15 percent casualties, something over 17,000 men. The problem was that Hooker's army had outnumbered Lee's by more than two-to-one at the inception of the campaign, and even though the Confederates had suffered 4,000 less casualties than had the

Federals, the disparity in numbers between to contending forces was alarm-
ing. The Federal army had been forced to retreat, and Lee had won the field,
but the threat was quite ominous. Hooker was positioned just across the Rap-
pahannock River, free to move his divisions in any direction, at any time. Lee
badly needed the reinforcement of Longstreet's corps to face this challenge, as
his own army had been reduced to just under 50,000 men. If Longstreet's divi-
sions were sent west, Lee would be compelled to assume the defensive, and he
would most likely have to surrender Northern Virginia to the invaders and
retire to the trenches around Richmond. This would place the Federal army
on the doorstep of the Confederate capital and would prevent Lee from being
able to adequately sustain his army. Longstreet was well aware of these con-
tingencies at the time, and his later assertions that he fully supported a move-
ment of his divisions to the west are not consistent with his contemporary
expressions. In a letter to his friend and confidant, Senator Louis Wigfall,
dated May 13, 1863, Longstreet stated that "There is a fair prospect of a for-
ward movement. That being the case we can spare nothing from this army to
reinforce in the West. On the contrary we should have use of our own and the
balance of our Armies if we could get them." He went on to state that if they
could get a sufficient force across the Potomac they "could demand Lincoln to
declare his purpose. If it is a Christian purpose enough of blood has been shed
to satisfy any principles. If he intends extermination we should know it at once
and play a little at that game whilst we can." Longstreet says that it seems to
him that Pemberton is not a fighting man, and "the fewer troops he had the
better." He ends his letter by telling Wigfall that he has come to the conclu-
sion that the army in Virginia could not be of assistance to Pemberton and his
situation at Vicksburg.[3] *Clearly, his post-war recollection of the policy he*
favored clashes with the sentiments he expressed at the time. He also fails to
mention anything about a defensive campaign. Instead, he makes the state-
ment that once across the Potomac, the Confederates would be able to "demand
Lincoln to declare his purpose." This is hardly consistent with his later claims
that he consented to the campaign only under the condition that it be con-
ducted as a defensive operation.

After a brief recounting of the battle of Brandy Station, and the subse-
quent movements of the Army of Northern Virginia, Longstreet's narrative
enters into a discussion of the fatal errors committed during the Pennsylvania
Campaign. First of these is the absence of General J.E.B. Stuart's cavalry, and
the consequent blinding of Lee's army. The historic record shows that more
than half of the Confederate cavalry remained with the main army, and that
the portion that accompanied Stuart was in the minority. Some have argued

that Stuart's absence did not materially injure the campaign, stating that Lee still had sufficient resources at hand to attend to the intelligence needs usually provided by the cavalry. This might have been so if Lee was conducting a defensive campaign, and his only intelligence concerns were guarding against an unexpected thrust by the enemy. Such was not the case in Pennsylvania. The Confederate horse was detailed to guard important passes, and protect lines of supply and communication along the march. It was also asked to serve as the guide for three independently moving corps as they tramped through Pennsylvania, providing information as to lines of march and enemy garrison positions. In addition, it was called on to screen the army from Hooker's force, and provide information concerning the movements of that army. While the cavalry remaining with Lee's army would probably have been more than sufficient to cope with the demands of a defensive campaign, it proved inadequate to the increased responsibilities of such a large-scale offensive movement. To be sure, Stuart's forces were sorely missed by the army and its commander, and the presence of Stuart himself was missed almost as much as the force he commanded.

Debate has gone back and forth as to the extent of the injury caused to the Army of Northern Virginia by the lack of cavalry prior to the battle being fought. However, the responsibility for Stuart's absence not having been much debated, it is generally attributed to Lee's discretionary orders, which it is assumed that Stuart exceeded. Upon Lee's shoulders is placed the blame for Stuart's failure to provide the necessary intelligence that might have prevented the chance encounter that led to the battle of Gettysburg. But is that really the case? Was Lee ultimately responsible for Stuart's absence? Longstreet states that he was. But Longstreet fails to mention the role he played in Stuart's ride around the Federal army, one that leaves him more accountable for the situation than his superior. When the army started its northward trek from Culpeper Courthouse, Stuart was with Longstreet, and under his orders. Longstreet acknowledges this himself in his narrative that appeared in the Century Magazine, by stating "I ordered General Stuart, whom I considered under my command, to occupy the gaps with a part of his cavalry...." He continues, however, to state that Stuart informed him that Lee had authorized him to follow the Federal army with a portion of his command.[4] Once again, Longstreet infers that Lee's interference caused a blunder in the strategically superior operations he was then conducting. What he fails to mention is that he was directly responsible for Stuart's cavalry being cut off from the main body of Lee's army, that he had in fact ordered the movement that created the situation. Colonel John S. Mosby wrote "I have recently discovered documents *in the archives of the War Department that set at rest the question of Stuart's alleged disobedience of orders, and show that General Longstreet then approved a plan which he now condemns as 'a wild ride around the Federal army.' He directed Stuart to pass around the rear of the enemy in preference to crossing west of the ridge, in order to prevent disclosing our designs."*

The order in question is the following:

Headquarters, Millwood, June 22d, 1863, 7 P.M.
Major-General J.E.B. Stuart, Commanding Cavalry.

General: General Lee has enclosed to me this letter for you to be forwarded to you provided you can be spared from my front, and provided you think you can move across the Potomac without disclosing our plans. He speaks of your leaving via Hopewell Gap and passing by the rear of the enemy. If you can get through by that route, I think that you will be less likely to indicate what our plans are than if you cross by passing to our rear. I forward the letter of instructions with these suggestions. Please advise me of the condition of affairs before you leave, and order General Hampton—whom I suppose you will leave here in command—to report to me at Millwood either by letter or in person, as may be most agreeable to him. Most respectfully, J. Longstreet, Lieutenant-General. N.B. I think that your passage of the Potomac by our rear at the present moment will in a measure disclose our plans. You had better not leave us, therefore, unless you can take the proposed route in rear of the enemy. J. Longstreet, Lieutenant-General.[5]

This order shows that General Longstreet had full authority to stop Stuart's movement had he so desired, as Lee gave him the discretion to retain Stuart if he thought it best to do so. It also shows that Longstreet not only approved the movement, he directed that it not be made unless the route taken was around the rear of the Federal army, placing the Hooker's force between the Confederate horse and the main body. General Longstreet fixes the blame for the first of his list of errors committed squarely on the shoulders of Stuart and Lee, and assumes no responsibility whatsoever for any involvement on his own part, but it is evident that he was not only a participant in the incident, he was a prime motivator. Though he denounces the absence of the cavalry during the campaign, he had the authority to prevent it, and furthermore had established the only permissible line of march that it could take place as being one that would separate it from the army. He states that "General Stuart should not have been allowed to leave the general line of march, thus forcing us to march blindfolded into the enemy's country." If General Longstreet had entertained any apprehensions about the wisdom of the move, he had full authority to prevent it from taking place. Given the tone of his narrative, and the fact that he states he constantly advised caution to General Lee, argued against movements he felt to be risky, and attempted to sway Lee from an offensive mind-set to a defensive one, it is reasonable to assume that he would have availed himself of the opportunity to keep Stuart well in hand, when it was within his power to do so. Instead, he not only abdicated his authority to prevent the move, he granted it his full blessing and determined the line of march. When the movement proved to be a mistake, he then disavowed any personal responsibility and placed the blame squarely on the shoulders of Lee and Stuart.

General Longstreet next turns his attention to the failure on the part of the Confederates to secure and fortify Cemetery Hill on the evening of July 1. Blame for this failure is primarily ascribed to Lieutenant General Richard Ewell, but Lee is also held to account by virtue of his not taking personal control of the situation and pushing the attack forward. Longstreet cites numerous firsthand accounts of the situation existing on the ridge during the closing hours of the fist day's battle, and all of them support his supposition that a determined thrust by Confederate forces would have pushed the Federals off the ridge and gained the high ground for Southern arms. Union testimony substantiates Longstreet's charge, and shows that a golden opportunity was lost when Ewell declined to order an advance on the position that was so thinly held. Historians have long considered what might have been the outcome at Gettysburg if Stonewall Jackson had not been killed at Chancellorsville, and had still been in command of his old corps on the hills of Pennsylvania. Surely, Jackson would have pressed his advantage, and, flushed with victory, would have pursued the fleeing Federals as long as daylight permitted him to do so, driving the few defenders from the crest, and altering the course of the battle, and maybe the war. But Jackson was dead, and his successor, General Ewell, was a newly promoted corps commander, still coming to grips with his increased responsibilities and authority. Unsure of himself, and unwilling to commit a costly error in his first engagement as a corps commander, Ewell hesitated and balked when it came to throwing his corps against an unknown enemy on a commanding position. Caution got the better of him, and instead of following his instincts in pressing a routed foe, he worried about the potential possibilities for disaster that awaited him on Cemetery Ridge. His failure to occupy the high ground on the battlefield that evening was certainly a turning point of the battle, and Longstreet is correct in listing it as an error in the campaign. But what is the level of Lee's involvement in the mistake that was made? Clearly, Lee intended that Cemetery Ridge be taken, and had issued orders to Ewell directing him to undertake the fulfillment of that desire. The point of contention in those orders were the words "if practicable," which allowed Ewell *a degree of discretionary authority in making the charge. There is no doubt that Lee wanted the heights taken, and felt that it was an obtainable objective. As was his custom, he couched his orders in words that allowed his subordinate to exercise a certain degree of autonomous authority in carrying them out, however. Ewell chose to invoke this autonomy, and declined to attack.*

Lee trusted the judgment of his subordinate on the scene. Should he have intervened personally and taken direct control of the situation in front of Cemetery Hill? Possibly. The historical record shows that it would have been the intelligent thing to do, but that is evaluating the situation with the benefit of hindsight. At that time, on the field, Lee was accepting the evaluation of a commander he both knew and trusted. True, Ewell was new to corps command, but he was a veteran division commander who had seen combat on many hard-fought fields, and who had distinguished himself upon every one of them. Lee had no reason to question his judgment or suspect his lack of movement. His only fault was in accepting the judgment of a subordinate who, to that time, had proven himself fully worthy of his confidence. General Longstreet is quite correct in pointing out the missed opportunity on the evening of July 1, and General Ewell is certainly found lacking in his reluctance to order the attack, but involving Lee in the assessment of blame is done as a result of knowing all the facts, after the event had transpired, and is not relevant to the decisions Lee made at the time, with the knowledge he then possessed.

General Longstreet next lists Lee's failure to move around the Federal right on the night of July 1st, to interpose the Confederate army between the Union army and Washington, and thus force Meade to come off of his high ground and attack Lee at a point of his own choosing. Longstreet cites the statistics from the victory at Fredericksburg, and strengthens his argument by quoting "Stonewall" Jackson and saying that the Confederates sometimes failed to move the Federals, but the Federals "always" failed to move the Confederates. But would Longstreet's proposed movement had produced the desired result he claimed? Meade's Army of the Potomac was not the only Federal force in the area, and if Lee's army threatened Washington, it would not be the only force arrayed against the Confederate thrust.

Major General William French was stationed at Harper's Ferry, with a force of some 9,000. General Hooker had attempted to add this force to his army as it marched north to meet Lee, but the request had been denied. In the light of a drive against Washington, it most certainly would have been released to operate with the Army of the Potomac. Major General Darius Couch commanded two divisions of newly raised troops in the vicinity of Harrisburg, Pennsylvania. These were a portion of the 50,000 new soldiers that had joined the army as a result of President Lincoln's urgent call for volunteers on June 15, in response to Lee's invasion of the North.[6] While it is true that green, untested troops are usually no match for seasoned veterans, the North had not hesitated to commit dozens of such regiments to battle at Antietam, only six months before, and would surely have ordered their use in defending Washington from capture. Major General Robert Milroy was in the vicinity of Everrett, Pennsylvania with almost 3,000 men from his command that had been forced to evacuate Winchester, Virginia. In addition, there were close to 1,500 additional militia within easy supporting distance of Milroy, posted in the several mountain gaps leading to Altoona, Pennsylvania.[7] These were but a portion of the aggregate force the Union had available to concentrate in front of Lee's army. The addition of the available forces in the region could have swelled Meade's ranks to numbers that approximated the armies recently commanded by Generals Burnside and Hooker, roughly 120,000 to 130,000 in size. While it is true that Lee had bested both of those commanders, despite the disparity of numbers being two-to-one between his army and the enemy, he had done so on home turf, on ground that was not only of his choosing, but was familiar to him. Now, Lee was deep in enemy territory, far removed from his base of supply and communication. He was on unfamiliar ground, and in the enemy's backyard. The Federal's ability to concentrate forces against him was greatly enhanced, while his ability to replace losses or augment his existing force was almost non-existent. Lee knew that to stand and entice an attack from Meade was to invite the possibility of a crushing defeat from which the South could not recover. Any delay of action favored the Federals, allowing them the opportunity of concentrating superior forces at the point of attack. Celerity of movement, combined with a defeat of the Union army, in detail, was what Lee had envisioned.

The chance encounter at Gettysburg had not been in his plans, but the strength and position of the opposing armies presented to Lee what he felt to be his best chance to attain the objectives of his offensive. Two Federal corps, the First and the Eleventh, had already been crippled in the first day's fighting. If Lee could effect a like result on a couple more of Meade's corps, he would level the playing field somewhat, and might possibly have enabled himself to adopt the defensive strategy Longstreet urged. As it was, he was faced to his front by a mighty host, and surrounded by that which could speedily be sent to confront him. If he was to stay in Pennsylvania, and if the campaign was to have any chance for success, he must fight, he must attempt to injure the Federal army to the extent that he would gain an advantage in future operations. To have withdrawn from the field, marched his army around the right of the Fed-

erals, and assumed a position between that army and Washington, inviting an attack, would have placed him in the position of waiting to be overwhelmed by vastly superior forces, and at the same time would have seriously effected the morale of his own army. If a concentration of Union forces threatened the safety of his army, it is certainly possible that he could have withdrawn back into Virginia, without fighting a battle, but that would have had the effect of providing the enemy with a bloodless victory that emboldened their cause at the same time it disheartened the resolve of the Southerners. The fact is that Lee did not have many good options open to him on the night of July 1, 1863. The course he chose was the one that offered the best opportunity to accomplish his mission and achieve his goals, if all the pieces fell into place. At Gettysburg, however, the pieces did not fall the way Lee envisioned them, and the end result was far from that which was contemplated.

Throughout his narrative, General Longstreet paints the picture that General Lee had strayed from the campaign plan he had adopted, in agreement with Longstreet, of conducting a defensive operation. Longstreet had first made these statements while Lee was still alive, and Lee disavowed that the conversation had taken place, and flatly denied that he had ever given a promise to conduct the campaign in the manner Longstreet described. He stated that he never would have thought of confining himself to such a rigid plan of operations, thus limiting his possibilities for success.[8] General Longstreet had just recently returned from independent command, in the Suffolk area, where he had become accustomed to calling the shots. Longstreet had always been free with his advice and suggestions, but now, with the death of Jackson, he viewed his own prominence as being almost the equal of Lee. It is probable that he made his suggestions on how he felt the campaign should unfold and that Lee listened to this advice courteously, as was his manner, without adding his approval to it. Though Longstreet was well-acquainted with Lee's conduct and manner, it is possible that he misconstrued courtesy for assent.

Union General Henry Hunt made a rational assessment of Lee's situation at Gettysburg. He states that though Longstreet urged his commander to force Meade's army from its stronghold "by interposing between him and Washington and threatening his communications, to force him to attack the Confederate army in position; but General Lee probably saw that Meade would be under no such necessity; would have no great difficulty in obtaining supplies, and—disregarding the clamor from Washington—could play a waiting game, which it would be impossible for Lee to maintain in the open country. He could not advance on Baltimore or Washington with Meade in his rear nor could his army subsist itself in a hostile region which would soon swarm with additional enemies. His communications could be cut off, for his recommendation to assemble even a small army at Culpeper to cover them and aid him had not been complied with. A battle was a necessity to Lee, and a defeat would be more disastrous to Meade, and less so to himself, at Gettysburg than at any point east of it.... It is more probable that General Lee was influenced by cool calculation of this nature than by hot blood, or that the opening success of a chance battle had thrown him off his balance."[9]

Longstreet's next alleged error in judgment was the ordering of his corps to attack on the Confederate right without being properly supported by the forces of Ewell and Hill. A sub-plot to this allegation brings the question of whether or not the attack was intended by Lee to take place on the morning of July 2 to the forefront. Longstreet charges that his corps was left unsupported to fight the entire Union army. The historic record shows Longstreet's statement to be utterly false. In fact, it is a slight to the courageous efforts put forth by thousands of Confederate troops that battled on the field that day.

Lieutenant General Ambrose P. Hill, holding the center of the Confederate line, had been ordered to support Longstreet's advance on the right, and to move his brigades forward as soon as Longstreet's men were fairly engaged. A letter from Brigadier General Ambrose R. Wright, written to his wife on July 9, 1863, sheds some light on the subject and calls to task a major point of Longstreet's defense. Wright relates that "On Thursday morning, July 2d, our whole army having been placed in position, except General Pickett's Division, of Longstreet's corps ... which had not come up, we prepared to attack the enemy ... strongly posted on a mountain range."[10] The reader will note that General Wright states that his brigade, as well as the rest of the army, so far as he knew by the units surrounding him (the brigades of Generals Carnet Posey and William Mahone on his left, and William Perry and Cadmus Wilcox on his right), were ready for action on the morning of July 2, in preparation for supporting the attack that was to be launched by Longstreet on the Confederate right. He states that the lines were formed and ready that morning, anticipating the movement on the right. If Lee had not intended an early attack, as Longstreet claims, then why were Hill's lines formed and ready to step out seven hours or more before the engagement was finally initiated? Their movement was contingent upon Longstreet's advance, being in a supporting role, and it was not necessary for them to be in place before the anticipated advance of the right. A.P. Hill did not survive the war to give testimony, but all indications lead one to believe that he formed his lines of battle at the time he did because he anticipated the attack to be made much earlier than it was. While it is improbable that Lee intended the attack to be made at sunrise, as *some of his partisans later avowed, it seems consistent with the actions of Hill's corps that the assault was expected to be made earlier, rather than later. A sunrise assault would have necessitated the positioning of the army during the preceding night. The movements of Lee's army do not lend credence to this assertion, but they most certainly support the allegations that the attack on the right was tardy in its execution.*

No commander wants to hold his troops in an attack formation for several hours, waiting for the order to advance to be given. A junior lieutenant understands that this is detrimental to the morale of those troops making the attack, and should be avoided whenever possible. Why then would Hill form his lines and compel them to be in readiness for the majority of the morning and afternoon unless he was awaiting a movement that he understood was to take place at an earlier hour? Once Hill's lines were formed, his men became the captives of Longstreet. Not knowing at what moment the attack on the right would finally be made, Hill's men were compelled to remain in formation and await the unfolding of events on their right.

When Longstreet's infantry surged forward on the right, Hill's troops were given the attack order at 5 P.M. Major General Richard Anderson's division, to which the aforementioned brigades belonged, moved forward toward the Emmitsburg Road, aiming for the Union line, posted roughly in the vicinity of what would become the "High Water Mark" on the following day. The Federals were aligned on a ridge between the Emmitsburg Road and the Taneytown Road. From their left to right they had the II Corps divisions of Andrew A. Humphreys, John Gibbon, and Alexander Hays. Wilcox and Wright surged forward, and effectively spearheaded he Confederate advance on that part of the field. Humphreys and Gibbon were sorely pressed, and the Union line was driven back upon the Taneytown Road. The brigades of Posey and Mahone, on Wright's left, lagged behind, leaving Wright's left flank exposed and unprotected. Wright sent General Anderson word of this development, and a response was received that both Generals had been ordered to advance their brigades. In the meantime, Perry's Brigade, on Wright's right flank, gave way, and streamed for the rear. Wright and Wilcox continued forward, with both of Wright's flanks and Wilcox's left flank hanging in the air. The two remaining Confederate brigades pushed home their attack, driving the Federals from a strong position behind a stone fence, where Wright's men captured some 20 pieces of artillery, after having shot down all of the cannoneers. But without support, the advance could not be sustained. Union reinforcements were pouring into the gap created by Perry's withdrawal, and were threatening to encircle Wright's Brigade and cut them off from the rest of the army. Wright was forced to cut his way out of the encirclement, in an effort to regain his own lines and safety. This he was successful in doing, though by the time he reached the safety of Seminary Ridge there were only 600 men remaining of the 1,600 he had begun the assault with. The situation with Wilcox's brigade was very similar, as that general also reached the crest of the Federal position before being forced to retire by Union forces attacking his flank where Perry's Brigade had been. ll Hill's assault had pinned down the II Corps, and had actually pierced the Union line at the point of attack. The assaults of Posey and Mahone were poorly executed, and Perry's withdrawal at the critical point of the fighting prevented the Confederates from exploiting their breakthrough and possibly severing the Union line on Cemetery Hill, but there is no denying that Longstreet received the support of Hill's corps that he alleges he never got. In fact, it was the near success of the Confederate troops on this part of the field that led General Lee to settle upon his battle strategy for the third and final day. As stated, Hill's assault was poorly orchestrated, and yet the desired results were nearly achieved. If two determined brigades could come so close to cracking the Union line, what might be expected of three divisions arrayed against that same point?

As shown, Longstreet was supported in his attack by A.P. Hill's corps on his left, but what about Ewell's corps on the far left of the Confederate line? Did Ewell undertake offensive operations designed to support Longstreet's movements? Ewell had been ordered to coordinate his attack on the Confederate left with that of Longstreet's on the right. When Longstreet's advance was underway, Ewell's artillery on Benner's Hill opened on the Federal positions on Culp's Hill and East Cemetery Hill. The Union artillery was protected by strong earthworks, and its response was such that the Confederate guns were quickly knocked out of action. With his artillery silenced, and the Union guns raking his line, Ewell declined to order his infantry forward. Several precious hours were allowed to pass before Ewell finally ordered an attack, but by the time his troops formed up to assault Culp's Hill Longstreet's attack on the right was coming to a close. Ewell's hesitation had allowed Meade to shift troops from General Henry W. Slocum's Twelfth Corps to help stem the tide in Longstreet's front, and Ewell thus failed to pin down the enemy on his part of the line to prevent them from shifting reinforcements to aide Sickles' battered Third Corps on the Union left. In the end, Longstreet received support from Hill's corps. Ewell's corps failed to provide the diversionary attack that Lee had intended. Because of this, Longstreet's men were forced to face a larger portion of the Union army than had been expected when Lee ordered the attack, but they did not face the entire Federal army, as Longstreet claims. More than

2,000 casualties in Anderson's division attest to the fact that these troops held down their portion of the battlefield and gave Longstreet the best support they could.[12]

As for General Longstreet's argument that his attack on July 2 was not late, and that there had never been a time assigned to its inception, the historic record seems to invalidate his statements. Longstreet is very specific in relating the time of 11 A.M. as being the moment when he was first acknowledged of the definite intent of his commander to attack the enemy on his portion of the line. In his own narrative, he mentions talking with Lee early in the morning, but he passes off this meeting by saying that he had gone to try to convince Lee to pull his army out of line and swing it around the flank of the Federals. In fact, this meeting was much more than an opportunity for Longstreet to continue his arguments against the management of the campaign. This was a planning meeting, attended by Generals Lee, Hill, Longstreet, Hood, and Heth. The four generals gathered on Seminary Ridge at 5:30 A.M. to observe the enemy position on their left flank, and to plot out what they saw against the map. This was an extension of Lee's mindset from the previous night, when he had informed Longstreet and Hill "Gentlemen, we will attack the enemy in the morning as early as practicable." It was also the reason Hill had his brigades in line of battle early on the morning of the 2nd, awaiting the movements of Longstreet he was ordered to support. It also explains the agitation many officers reported seeing in Lee's conduct as morning gave way to afternoon.[13] While it is probable that General Lee did not specifically order a time for the assault to begin, he intended it to be earlier, rather than later, and General Hill understood, even if Longstreet says he did not.

General Longstreet's assertion is that the next mistake made at Gettysburg was the failure to move around the Federal flank following the fighting of July 2, when such a move could still have produced the desired results of prying the Union army from its stronghold. This argument is thin, at best. There had been no change in the situation at Gettysburg that made the move any more desirable on the night of July 2 than it had been on the night of July 1. In fact, it would be far more dangerous to undertake than it had been twenty-four hours before. The Army of the Potomac was now fully concentrated and at its maximum strength. The Sixth Corps had arrived on the field during the 2nd, as had the other various units and detachments that had been separated from the field on the night of the 1st. Meade now had his army firmly in hand and was prepared to meet any activities the Confederates might undertake. The flanking movement was not a good option on the night of July 1. It was even a worse choice on the night of July 2.

General Longstreet's last point of contention with Lee's management of the battle is the ordering of Pickett's charge. He contends that this was the final great mistake made by Lee upon those Pennsylvania fields, and infers the ludicrous nature of the orders by stating that the attack was to be made against a portion of the Union line that had already been assailed, and found to be impregnable, on July 2. In retrospect, it is easy to condemn an attack that resulted in two-thirds of the attacking force becoming casualties, while the objective of the mission was not attained. But history cannot be viewed through the ideal vision of hindsight. Robert E. Lee had gained his reputation as an army leader by means of his application of the Napoleonic principles of war that he had learned many years before at the Military Academy at West Point. He was an absolute master at gathering together superior force at the point of attack, to place overwhelming force in his offensive assaults. His mastery of this principle was what had enabled him to defeat Union armies that were numerically superior to his own on many fields. At Chancellorsville, Salem Church, 2nd Manassas, and a host of other fields, Lee had been successful in marshalling assault forces that were superior at the point of attack. To be sure, the application of this military axiom had also failed Lee occasionally, most notably at the battle of Malvern Hill. Still, his adherence to this style of fighting was a logical choice. At most times, the Army of Northern Virginia was inferior to the Army of the Potomac, and Lee was forced to maximize his resources by clustering his forces where they were needed most. The tactic had proven itself to be so effective, on so many battlefields, that Lee came to rely on it as a staple of his tactical and strategic planning. Gettysburg was no exception. Outnumbered by more than two-to-one at Chancellorsville, Stonewall Jackson's attack had crushed the Union line and won a most unexpected victory for Confederate arms. Why would the situation at Gettysburg be any different? Especially since the disparity in numbers favored the Confederates much more at Gettysburg than it had at Chancellorsville. On the third day at Gettysburg, Lee planned an offensive strategy that had served him well on so many other fields of battle; it's as simple as that. As for the charge that Lee's selection of the location for the assault was faulty, remember that the troops belonging to Generals Wright and Wilcox had penetrated the Union line at that point on the previous day. They had broken the infantry, captured some twenty pieces of artillery, and effected a lodgment in the center of the Union's defensive position. This had been accomplished despite the fact that the attack on that portion of the line had been poorly coordinated and executed. These two brigades had been fighting virtually alone, and had almost succeeded. What could be accomplished by a well-executed attack, with a massive assault force, along *this same point? Lee envisioned a repeat of the crushing blow at Chancellorsville when he drew up his plans for the battle of July 3. Ewell would attack on the Union right, pinning down the Federal troops positioned there, and keeping Meade from shifting forces from that sector to support his center. Stuart would take his cavalry around the Union flank, and menace the enemy position from the rear, poised to support any break through that might occur. Longstreet's main attack column, three divisions strong, would deliver the knock-out punch in this pincer movement, proving to be the superior force at the point of attack. At least that is the way it was drawn up in Lee's mind. But events began to spiral out of control almost from the start. Ewell's forces were engaged prematurely, and the fighting on that part of the field had already sputtered out before Longstreet's battle lines moved forward. Stuart's cavalry met a Union cavalry that had been infused with confidence from their strong showing at Brandy Station. The Federal horsemen accomplished what they had not yet done in the first two years of war: They defeated and threw back a concerted effort made by the cavalry of the Army of Northern Virginia.*

The concerted effort that Lee had planned was falling apart, and unity of action was becoming a forlorn hope by the time General Pickett ordered his division forward. According to Longstreet's paper, one would conclude that Pickett made this charge alone, that his division was solely responsible for the success or failure of the endeavor. Conspicuous by absence is any mention of the divisions of Generals Pettigrew and Trimble, who also took part in the desperate undertaking. Longstreet focuses his entire narrative on Pickett, almost as if that division was the only responsibility he had in the engagement. Indeed, he had stationed himself with Pickett's men, monitored the progress of the attack from that point only, and had conducted himself in every way as if Pickett was his only consideration in the attack. Pettigrew and Trimble were left pretty much on their own, and their men were subject only to the orders of their own division commanders. Regrettably, most historians have adopted Longstreet's sentiments in focusing only upon the activities of Pickett's division in reporting "Pickett's Charge." Noted historian Colonel Edward Stackpole, in his book They Met at Gettysburg, *is representative of the lack of attention given to the other two divisions involved in the attack. Stackpole devotes twenty-three pages to the chapter on Pickett's charge, but his coverage of Pettigrew is limited to the following lone paragraph: "Pettigrew's division, advancing on the left towards Hancock's right at Ziegler's Grove, was in trouble. A Federal regiment, which had been stationed in extended order west of the Emmitsburg Road, was wheeled at a right angle as the Confederates moved toward the ridge, to be greeted by a deadly flanking fire that badly shook Pet-*

tigrew's brigades. On they came, however, until every weapon of the Federal arsenal on that part of the front opened on them simultaneously. Human flesh and nerves simply couldn't stand such punishment. The Southern lines broke, the men ran for cover, and the dead and wounded covered the field."[14] Trimble's division, on Pickett's right and rear, gets even less notice in the text, barely a mention. Fully eighteen and one half of the nineteen pages in this chapter are devoted solely to Pickett, and this is to be found in most popular histories of the battle.

But what of the movements of Pettigrew and Trimble? The fact is that this was the final breakdown in the concerted effort Lee had envisioned when ordering the assault. The three divisions were not handled as a single assault force, rather, they were allowed to operate independently of one another, with no efforts being made to coordinate their activities. When the Confederate line stepped out of the woods, Pettigrew's division attracted the bulk of the attention coming from the Union line. Pettigrew's men were subjected to a fearful bombardment that cut gaping holes in the advancing gray line. Pickett's men were relatively untouched, during this time, and advanced in parade-perfect ranks. The Union pressure caused Pettigrew's line to stray to the left, forcing Pickett to execute an oblique movement of 45 degrees to maintain contact with Pettigrew's right flank.[15] Pettigrew's men surged forward, made contact with the Union line, and actually pierced the position reminiscent of Wright and Wilcox the previous day, and Armistead yet to come. But Pettigrew's troops could not sustain the impetus of the attack. They were still drawing the bulk of the Federal attention, and the pressure forced them back, retiring from the position they had so dearly won. This left Pickett to advance with no support on his left flank, and it allowed the Federals to now concentrate their full and undivided attention upon his column. Though his brigades advanced in grand style, each step forward saw gaping holes torn in his lines. The 4,500 men that he had begun the assault with were being diminished with each yard of ground they traversed toward their goal. In front of them, at the critical angle to which they were marching, Meade had concentrated 6,000 Federal troops. Thus, Pickett was advancing, over open ground, to make an attack with a force that was only seventy-five percent of the enemy when the assault was commenced. His chances of success were almost nonexistent, and the fact that Armistead was able to pierce the Federal position at all is a marvel and a testament to the fighting spirit of the troops he led.

Where was Trimble's division, on Pickett's right? The division was lagging dangerously behind both Pickett and Pettigrew. The brigades of Generals Wilcox and Lang were not in position to support Pickett's thrust against *the angle until the charge had already disintegrated and the survivors of Armistead's breakthrough were being gobbled up by the Union victors. Despite this fact, these two lone brigades were thrown forward. They had not conformed their march to that of Pickett's, having marched straight forward, instead of making an oblique movement to the left, to maintain contact with Pickett's right flank, and thus they were completely alone, facing the entire might of the Union position. For a while, Wilcox and Lang were unsure as to whether Pickett was retreating, or had merely been temporarily pushed back by a Federal counter-thrust. General George Stannard charged Lang's left flank with the 14th and 16th Vermont, and the 2nd Florida Infantry ceased to exist, with almost all of the survivors surrendering to the Federal attackers. With both flanks in the air, sorely pressed on three sides, and finally realizing that Pickett was quitting the field, Wilcox and Lang ordered a retreat.*

By the disparity in coverage afforded to the attacks made by Pettigrew and Trimble, one would naturally deduce that their losses were much less than those sustained by Pickett. Quite the opposite is true. Casualty figures are listed at fifty percent for both Pettigrew and Trimble, while those given for Pickett are at forty percent. Of the more than 11,500 men that Lee had assembled for the assault, almost 6,000 became casualties. On the Federal side, there had been 6,000 men collected for the defense of the angle. Of these, some 1,500 fell as casualties, or twenty-five percent. The Union defenders had been able to fight the engagement in three separate encounters, each time facing a detail that was numerically inferior to their own, and advancing across open ground to attack a prepared position of great strength. This was the final unraveling of Lee's plans for a concerted assault on the Union line. The massive force that he had collected was allowed to attack the enemy strong point in piecemeal fashion, by individual divisions, and the attack never achieved the concentration of force that had been intended. The Union army had been allowed to fight detachments of approximately 4,000 men each, instead of being compelled to stand fast against a force numbering almost double their own size. Where lies the responsibility for this? To be sure, much of it rests with the Union army, and the ability to alter the march of the attacking columns by forcing Pettigrew's lines to sway to the left. But what part is played by General Longstreet in this final chapter of the battle? Longstreet was in tactical command of the entire attacking force, not just the division belonging to General Pickett. As such, he should have been exerting efforts to coordinate the assault, to maximize the effect of the forces gathered to overpower the Union line. As previously stated, the general attached himself to Pickett's command, and there he remained. Pettigrew and Trimble were left to execute their parts of the movement alone, without any significant amount of supervision from their direct superior. The result was a self-fulfilling prophesy on the part of Longstreet. While it is open to debate whether or not the Confederate attack could have been successful, given the fact that Ewell's and Stuart's part of the scheme had already come to naught, it is true that the Union line was pierced twice by these piecemeal attacks, in which every advantage was given to the Federals. What might have been the result of an assault where superior forces were marshaled at the point of attack? This is left to be a topic for conjecture and speculation. The fact is that it never materialized in the manner intended, and Longstreet must assume at least a portion of the blame. He did not want to make the attack, argued against it as much as he could, and failed to support it with the energy and enthusiasm any subordinate officer owes to his superior. In all endeavors, it is generally accepted that it is honorable to lose, so long as all that can be done to win has been attempted. With Pickett's Charge, the defeat was sustained without the benefit of this type of exertion, and that has laid the groundwork for all of the controversy that has followed. The battle may have ended precisely as it did, a crushing defeat to Confederate arms, but one will never know what might have been the result if maximum effort had been given to this maximum gamble. With so much at stake, this was not the time to be lobbying for an alternate plan of campaign, or brooding over the refusal of a commander to adopt a subordinate's advise or counsel, it was a time to put one's shoulder to the wheel and carry out the mission to the best of one's ability. Regardless of whether the reader agrees with Longstreet or not concerning the conduct of the campaign and the opportunities offered by the advice he forwarded, it is hard to imagine that anyone could state that he did all he could to insure the success of the operations Lee adopted.

After Gettysburg, General Longstreet and his corps was transferred to Georgia, where they participated in the battle of Chickamauga. The Confederates scored a victory on this field, largely due to Longstreet and his men. A brief and unsuccessful stint in independent command, at Knoxville, Tennessee, preceded his return to the Army of Northern Virginia in time to take part in the Battle of the Wilderness, in the spring of 1864. From that time, to the end of the war, Longstreet and his corps participated in every major engagement of the Army of Northern Virginia, including the surrender at Appomattox Courthouse.

Following the war, James Longstreet settled in New Orleans. He became a Republican and renewed his pre-war friendship with General Ulysses S. Grant. This move served to further the alienation he experienced with fellow officers who had arisen to contest his statements made regarding the battle of

Gettysburg. In 1880, Grant appointed him minister to Turkey. In 1896, his book, From Manassas to Appomattox, *was published, in which he recounted many of the charges he had been making for three decades. From 1897 to 1904, he was commissioner of Pacific railroads, under Presidents McKinley and Roosevelt. James Longstreet died on January 2, 1904, at Gainesville, Georgia, where he was buried.*[16] *Longstreet emerges as one of the most controversial figures to wear the gray during the war. He is held as both a hero and a scapegoat by historians and enthusiasts of the period, depending upon individual slant. As one of the top commanders in the Confederate army, he wielded tremendous influence upon the outcome of battles and campaigns, and the final battle he fought, one that consumed over thirty years of his life, was to push any blame for the defeat at Gettysburg away from himself. In doing so, he became a lightening rod for criticism and contempt from those who supported General Lee and his decisions.*

General Fitzhugh Lee, CSA

Fitzhugh Lee was born on November 19, 1835, at "Clermont," Fairfax County, Virginia. He was the nephew of both General Robert E. Lee and General Samuel Cooper. Lee graduated near the bottom of his class from West Point in 1856, before being assigned to duty on the frontier, where he sustained wounds from an engagement with the Indians. The year 1861 found him back at West Point, where he was serving as an assistant instructor of tactics, with the rank of 1st lieutenant. Lee resigned his commission in May of 1861 to serve at the same rank on the staff of General Joseph E. Johnston. After serving at the battle of 1st Manassas, Lee was promoted to the rank of lieutenant colonel, and given command of the 1st Virginia cavalry in August of 1861. He served with distinction during the Peninsular Campaign, and was promoted to the rank of brigadier general on July 24, 1862. Lee took part in all of the campaigns of the Army of Northern Virginia through the Gettysburg Campaign, following which he was promoted to the rank of major general, on August 3, 1863.[1] As both a relative of Robert E. Lee and a subordinate of J.E.B. Stuart, it might seem natural that Fitzhugh Lee would wish to defend the reputations of his commanding officers during the Pennsylvania Campaign, and he was among the first to respond to Longstreet's paper after it appeared in print.

The "great battle of Gettysburg" has always occupied a prominent position in the mind of the Confederate soldier. This surpassing interest is due from the fact that there prevails, through-out the South, a wide-spread impression that had the plans of the Southern chieftan been fully endorsed, entered into, and carried out by his corps commanders, the historic "rebel yell" of triumph would have resounded along Cemetery Ridge upon that celebrated 2d July, 1863, and re-echoing from the heights of Round Top, might have been heard and heeded around the walls of Washington, Baltimore, and Philadelphia. There is a ghastliness about that picture of the struggle at Gettysburg, that the blood of the heroes who perished there serves but to increase; and over that splendid scene of human courage and human sacrifice, there arises like the ghost of Banquo at Macbeth's banquet, a dreadful apparition, which says that the battle was lost to the Southern troops because "someone blundered." Military critics, foreign and native, have differed as to the individual responsibility of what was practically a Confederate defeat. The much abused cavalry is lifted into great prominence and is constrained to feel complimented by the statement of many of these critics that the failure to crush the Federal army in Pennsylvania in 1863 can be expressed "in five words" (General Heth, in a late paper to the Philadelphia *Times*), viz: "the absence of our cavalry"; but such language implies an accusation against General J.E.B. Stuart, its commander, who has been charged with a neglect of duty in not reporting the passage of the Potomac by Hooker's army (afterwards Meade's), and with disobedience of orders, which resulted in placing the Federal army between his command and the force of General Lee, thereby putting out the eyes of his own "giant." There are those who bring our troubles to the door and cast them at the feet of General Ewell, the gallant commander of the Second corps, who is charged with not obeying his chief's orders, by following up his success and occupying Cemetery Heights upon the afternoon of July 1st.

Others confidently agree with Colonel Taylor, General Lee's adjutant, that "General Longstreet was fairly chargeable with tardiness" on the 2nd July, in not making his attack earlier; and again it is stated, that his charging column upon the 3rd, which moved so magnificently to assault the positions of the Federals, was not composed of all the troops General Lee designed should be placed in it.

And last, but by no means least, the Confederate Commander-in-Chief himself is now for the first time charged with everything relating to the disaster of Gettysburg, and the whole accountability for the results of the battle are pointedly placed upon his shoulders by one of his subordinates, in a paper prepared for the Philadelphia *Times*. To whom, therefore, it may be asked, can the loss of the battle of Gettysburg be properly attributed—to Stuart, or Ewell, or Longstreet, or to General Lee? Very many of us who are deeply interested in the subject may honorably differ as to that, but upon the splendid courage displayed by the rank and file of the Confederate army upon those first three days in July, 1863, wherever tested, the world unites in perfect harmony.

We were indeed "within a stone's throw of peace" at Gettysburg—and although in numbers as 62,000 is to 105,000, before any portion of either army had become engaged—yet the advantages were so manifestly on General Lee's side in consequence of the more rapid concentration of his troops upon a common point, that the heart of every Southern soldier beat with the lofty confidence of certain victory.

Any new light, therefore, thrown upon the matter in discussion, should be well-sifted before permitting it to shine for the benefit of the future historian, less it dazzle by false rays the sympathetic minds of generations yet to come.

The Philadelphia *Times* of November 3rd, 1877, in commenting upon some additional points furnished that paper by General Longstreet as an addenda to his article published in that same issue says: "The letter from General Longstreet which accompanies these enclosures dwells particularly upon a point which he wishes to have his readers understand. It is that while General Lee on the battle-field assumed all the responsibility for the result, he afterwards published a report that differs from the report he made at the time while under that generous spirit. General Longstreet and other officers made their official reports upon the battle shortly after its occurrence, and while they were impressed with General Lee's noble assumption of all the blame, but General Lee having since written a detailed and somewhat critical account of the battle, Longstreet feels himself justified in discussing the battle upon its merits."

Whilst claiming the same privilege as a Confederate soldier, I, yet, would not have exercised it, being only a cavalryman, who added to his "jingling spur" not even a "bright sabretache," but only a poor record, were it not my good fortune to have known long and intimately the Commander-in-Chief, and to have conversed with him frequently during and since the war, upon the operations of the Army of Northern Virginia.

First then, let us examine the charge that the battle of Gettysburg was lost by the "absence of our cavalry." The cavalry of General Lee's army in the Gettysburg campaign consisted of the brigades of Hampton, Fitzhugh Lee, W.H.F. Lee's (under Chambliss), Beverly Robertson, Wm. E. Jones, Imboden, and Jenkins, with a battalion under Colonel White. The first three named accompanied Stuart on his circuit around the Federal army, reaching Gettysburg on the 2nd of July—Jones and Robertson were left to hold the gaps of the Blue Ridge, and did not get to the vicinity of Gettysburg until after the battles; so that of all the force I ennumerate, Jenkins' brigade and White's battalion alone crossed the Potomac with the army. (Imboden's command was detached along the Baltimore & Ohio railroad, and was not in the fight at Gettysburg). Stuart after fighting at Brandy Station, on the 9th of June, a large body of Federal cavalry supported by infantry, and forcing them to recross the Rappahannock river with a loss (to them) of "four hundred prisoners, three pieces of artillery, and several colors" (General Lee's report), marched into Loudon county upon the right flank of the army, and was engaged in a series of conflicts, terminating with Pleasonton's cavalry corps and Barnes' division of infantry, upon the 21st June, which caused him to retire to the vicinity of Ashby's Gap in the Blue Ridge, our infantry being upon the western side of the mountains.

Leaving the brigade before mentioned to hold the position, Stuart then, in the exercise of a discretion given him by General Lee and so stated in his report, determined to pass to the rear of the Federal army and cross the Potomac at Seneca Falls, a point between that army and their capital. Thus, it will be seen, including the brigade and battalion of cavalry which composed the vanguard of the army, that over one-half of the cavalry was left in position to be used by General Lee.

Hooker, in his dispatch to the President, June 21st (Report on the Conduct of the War, volume 1, page 279) referring to Stuart's command, says: "This cavalry force has hitherto prevented me from obtaining satisfactory information as to the whereabouts of the enemy; they had masked all their movements." General Hooker had reference to the five brigades holding the country between his army and the marching column of General Lee—Jenkins being in front of the advanced corps (Ewell's) with Colonel White's battalion, in addition to his own command. The cavalry corps, by the return of May 31st, 1863, numbered 9,536. According to a letter from Major McClellan, Stuart's A.A.G., this force was divided about as follows: Hampton, 1,200; Fitz Lee, 2,000; W.H.F. Lee, 1,800; Jones, 3,500; Robertson, 1,000. It is proper to state that the figures above refer to the enlisted men present for duty. The total effective strength (Inclusive of officers) numbered, according to Walter Taylor, at that date, 10,292. (I am satisfied , from a conversation with General Robertson, that McClellan overestimates the number of men in Jones' brigade, and therefore underestimates the number in some of the other brigades.) There is no authenticated return after the above date until August. After the return above cited, the losses at Brandy Station fight, the three days fighting in Loudon, the encounter at Westminster, Maryland, Hanover, Pennsylvania, and other points, occurred, together with the usual reduction of mounted troops from long and rapid marching. It is proper to say that the return quoted did not include the commands of Jenkins, Imboden, or White. General Stuart, in his report (August No., 1876, *Southern Historical Society Papers,* p. 76) estimated Jenkins' brigade, on leaving Virginia, at 3,800 troopers. I think this number is probably a misprint; from the best information I can get, this brigade numbered at that time 1,600. (See Rodes' official report.) Adding this last number to 4,500 (McClellan's estimate of Robertson's and Jones' brigade,) and putting White's battalion at 200, the result is a cavalry force of 6,300 doing duty for the main army, and greater in numerical strength than the three brigades Stuart carried with him, which at Gettysburg numbered less than 4,000. Whilst not endorsing Stuart's march as the best movement under the circumstances, I assert that he had the Commanding-General's permission to make it; (General Lee's report, *Southern Historical Society Papers* for July, 1876, page 43;) that it involved a loss of material and men to the enemy and drew Kilpatrick's and Gregg's divisions of cavalry from their aggressive attitude on Meade's flank and front, leaving only Buford's to watch for the advance of our troops, and hence we find only his two brigades in the Federal front on the first of July; that it kept the Sixth Federal corps, some 15,000 men, from reaching Gettysburg until after 3 P.M. on the 2nd of July; that it caused General Meade to send General French to Frederick, to protect his communications, with from 5,000 to 7,000 men (the latter figure is Walter Taylor's estimate, page 113, "Four Years with General Lee") and prevented that body of troops from being made use of in other ways—which force, Butterfield says, Hooker (before being relieved) contemplated throwing, with Slocum's corps, in General Lee's rear; and finally, that there was inflicted a loss upon the enemy's cavalry of confessedly near 5,000. (Stuart's report, p. 76, August No., 1876, *Southern Historical Society Papers.*) The Federal army crossed the Potomac upon the 26th June. General Lee heard it on the night of the 28th, from a scout, and not from his cavalry commander. Stuart crossed between the Federal army and Washington on the night of the 27th, and necessarily, from his position, could not communicate with General Lee. He sent information about the march of Hancock towards the river, and after that was not in position to do more. The boldness of General Lee's offensive strategy, in throwing his army upon one side of the Potomac whilst leaving his adversary upon the other, made it particularly necessary for him to know the movements of the Federal army. Stuart, with his experience, activity, and known ability for such work, should have kept interposed always between the Federal army and his own, and whilst working close on Meade's lines, have been in direct communication with his own army commander. It is well known that General Lee loitered, after crossing the Potomac, because he was ignorant of the movements and position of his antagonist. For the same reason he groped in the dark at Gettysburg. From the 25th of June to July 2d, General Lee deplored Stuart's absence, and almost hourly wished for him, and yet it was by his permission his daring chief of cavalry was away. General Stuart cannot, therefore, be charged with the responsibility of the failure at Gettysburg. Did such failure arise from Ewell and Hill not pushing their success on the 1st of July? I have always been one of those who regarded it a great misfortune that these two corps commanders did not continue to force the fighting upon that day. Each had two divisions of their corps engaged, thus leaving one division to each corps, viz., Johnson of Ewell's, and Anderson of Hill's, at their service for further work— something over 10,000 men. The four divisions engaged upon the Confederate side in the battle amounted to about 22,000. The loss after the repulse of the enemy, in Early's division, amounted to 586 (Early's review of Gettysburg, December number of *Southern Historical Society Papers,* 1877, page 257) leaving him still about 4,500 fighting men. Heth says (see his paper in Philadelphia *Times,* September 22d, 1877) he went into that fight with 7,000 muskets, and lost 2,700 men killed and wounded. He was still left with 4,300. Estimating those four divisions, at the close of the action, at an average of 4,500 men apiece, we had 18,000 men; add the 10,000 of the two divisions not engaged, and there will be found 28,000 men ready to move on, flushed with victory and confident of success. General Early, in a letter to me, places the effective force in Ewell's and Hill's corps, on the morning of the 2nd, at 26,000 men. Upon the Federal side there had been engaged the First and Eleventh corps (save one brigade, Smith's of Steinwehr's division, left on Cemetery Hill as a reserve) and Buford's two brigades of cavalry. As bearing directly upon this portion of the subject, I give a letter from Major General Hancock, and also one from Colonel Bachelder. (The latter remained on the field of Gettysburg for eighty-four days after the battle, making sketches and collecting data, and has since engaged, forty-seven of them being Generals Commanding. General Hancock writes of him to General Humphrey's: "Mr. Bachelder's long study of the field has given him a fund of accurate information in great detail, which I believe is not possessed by any one else.")

Letter from General Winfield Hancock

New York, January 17th, 1878.

My Dear General:

I am in receipt of yours of the 14th inst., and in reply have to say, that in my opinion, if the Confederates had continued the pursuit of General Howard on the afternoon of the 1st July at Gettysburg, They would have driven him over and beyond Cemetery Hill. After I had arrived upon the field, assumed the command, and made my dispositions for defending that point (say 4 P.M.), I do not think the Confederate force then present could have carried it. I felt certain at least of my ability to hold it until night, and sent word to that effect back to General Meade, who was then at Taneytown. Please notice the following extract from my testimony before the committee on the "Conduct of the War" on that point—Vol. 1, page 405, March 22nd, 1864:

"When I arrived and took the command, I extended the lines. I sent General Wadsworth to the right to take possession of Culp's Hill with his division. I directed General Geary, whose division belonged to the Twelfth corps, (its comander, General Slocum, not having then arrived,) to take possession of the high ground towards Round Top.

"I made such dispositions as I thought wise and proper. The enemy evidently believing that we were reinforced, or that our whole army was there, discontinued their great efforts, and the battle for that day was virtually over. There was firing of artillery and skirmishing all along the front, but that was the end of that day's battle. By verbal instructions, and in the order which I had received from General Meade, I was directed to report, after having arrived on the ground, whether it would be necessary or wise to continue to fight the battle at Gettysburg, or whether it was possible for the fight to be had on the ground Gen. Meade had selected. About 4 o'clock P.M. I sent word by Maj. Mitchell, aide-de-camp, to General Meade, that I would hold the ground until dark, meaning to allow him time to decide the matter for himself.

"As soon as I had gotten matters arranged to my satisfaction, and saw that the troops were being formed again, and I felt secure, I wrote a note to General Meade, and informed him of my views of the ground at Gettysburg. I told him that the only disadvantage which I thought it had was that it could be readily turned by way of Emmetsburg, and that the roads were clear for any movement he might make. I had ordered all the trains back, as I came up, to clear the roads."

When I arrived upon the field, about 3 P.M., or between that and 3:30, I found the fighting about over—the rear of our troops were hurrying through the town pursued by the Confederates. There had been an attempt to reform some of the Eleventh corps as they passed over Cemetery Hill, but it had not been very successful. I presume there may have been 1,000 to 1,200 at most, organized troops of that corps, in position on the hill. Buford's cavalry, in a solid formation, was showing a firm front in the plain just below (in line of battalions in mass, it is my recollection) Cemetery Hill, to the left of the Taneytown road.

I at once sent Wadsworth's division of the First corps, and a battery of artillery, to take post on Culp's Hill, on our right. The remainder of the First corps I placed on the right and left of the Taneytown road, connecting with the left of the Eleventh corps. These were the troops already on the battle-field when I had arrived and had made my dispositions.

About the time the above-described dispositions were made, Williams' division of the Twelfth army corps came upon the field and took position to the right and rear of Wadsworth's division of the First corps, and, subsequently, Geary's division of the Twelfth corps arriving, I caused it to move to our left and occupy the higher ground towards Round Top, to prevent any local turning of my left, (feeling safe as to the front).

You will perceive that up to the time I transferred the command of our forces on the field to my senior, Major-General Slocum, who arrived there between 6 and 7 o'clock P.M., these two divisions of his corps (Williams' and Geary's) were all the fresh troops that had actually marched on the battle-field.

Please see, on this point, the following extract from my official report of that battle:

"At this time the First and Eleventh corps were retiring through the town closely pursued by the enemy. The cavalry of General Buford was occupying a firm position on the plain to the left of Gettysburg, covering the rear of the retreating corps. The Third corps had not yet arrived from Emmettsburg.

"Orders were at once given to establish a line of battle on Cemetery Hill, with skirmishers occupying that part of the town immediately in our front. The position, just on the southern edge of Gettysburg, overlooking the town and commanding the Emmetsburg and Taneytown roads, and the Baltimore turnpike, was already partially occupied, on my arrival, by direction of Major-General Howard.

"Some difficulty was experienced in forming the troops of the Eleventh corps, but by vigorous efforts a sufficiently formidable line was established to deter the enemy from any serious assault on the position. They pushed forward a line of battle for a short distance east of the Baltimore turnpike, but it was easily checked by the fire of our artillery.

"In forming the line I received material assistance from Major-General Howard, Brigadier-General Warren, Brigadier-General Buford, and officers of General Howard's command.

"As soon as the line of battle mentioned above was shown by the enemy, Wadsworth's division, First corps, and a battery, (thought to be the Fifth Maine,) were placed on the eminence just across the turnpike, and commanding completely this approach. This important position was held by the division during the remainder of the operations near Gettysburg.

"The rest of the First corps, under Major-General Doubleday, was on the right and left of the Taneytown road, and connected with the left of the Eleventh corps, which occupied that part of Cemetery Hill immediately to the right and left of the Baltimore turnpike.

"A division of the Twelfth corps, under Brigadier-General Williams, arrived as these arrangements were being completed, and was established, by order of Major-General Slocum, some distance to the right and rear of Wadsworth's division.

"Brigadier-General Geary's division of the Twelfth corps arriving on the ground subsequently and not being able to communicate with Major-General Slocum, I ordered the division to the high ground to the right of and near Round Top mountain, commanding the Gettysburg and Emmettsburg road, as well as the Gettysburg and Taneytown road to our rear."

The third corps, however, was in close proximity, coming up on the Emmettsburg road, and a portion of it arrived upon the field before night. The Second corps did not reach the field that evening, only because I halted it about three miles in rear of Gettysburg, where an important road came in from the direction of Emmettsburg, to prevent any turning of the left of our army, in case General Lee should make any movement of that nature on the evening of the 1st, or early on the morning of the 2d. I consider that, had a prolonged struggle taken place that evening (after the dispositions which I have already described as having been made by me), portions at least, of both the Second and Third corps, might have been brought forward in time to have taken part in it. For a sudden assault or a brief contest, they would not, however, have been available before dark. In reference to the numbers of the First corps, after it had fallen back from in front of the town, and reformed on Cemetery Hill, I have seen a statement in Bates' "Battle of Gettysburg," page 82, fixing them at 2,450 men; but as to the correctness of this estimate, I cannot speak with any certainty.

As to the Eleventh corps, I have already stated that I did not think there were more than 1,000 to 1,200 organized men of that corps in position on Cemetery Hill at the time I arrived there, and these were a portion of Steinwher's division, which, with the artillery of the corps, was left there by Howard when he marched up in the morning.

In reference to the numbers of the Second, Third, and Twelfth corps, our returns of June 30th give their strength, "present for duty," as follows:

Second corps,—12,088 men.

Third corps,—11,799 men.

Twelfth corps,—8,056 men.

The Fifth corps came up during the night of the 1st, and morning of 2d, from Hanover—see following extract from testimony of General S.W. Crawford, who comanded a division in that corps, on that point:

"I was in the rear division of the corps (Fifth), and on the evening of the 1st July I marched through Hanover and along the road through

McSherrytown, marching until between two and three o'clock in the morning, and bivouacked at a town called Brushtown; and before dawn on Thursday, the 1nd of July, a staff-officer of General Sykes, then commanding the corps, rode to my headquarters and directed me to march my men, without giving them any coffee, at once to the field. I placed the column in motion and arrived before noon in the rear of the other divisions of the corps."

The Sixth corps was at Manchester on the evening of the 1st, and marched all of that night and until two o'clock P.M. on the 2nd, before it reached the field.

It has been stated "that Steinwher's division of Howard's corps, on the first day, threw up lunettes around each gun, on Cemetery Hill—solid works of such height and thickness to defy the most powerful bolts which the enemy could throw against them—with smooth and perfectly level platforms on which the guns could be worked."

This is a great error; there were no works of the kind above described on that field when I arrived there, and all that I saw in the way of "works" were some holes (not deep) dug to sink the wheels and trains of the pieces.

I am, very truly yours,
Winf'd Hancock.

Letter from John E. Bachelder, Esq.

You ask; "How many troops would have opposed Hill and Ewell had the attack been continued on the first day?" For reasons already explained, I am not prepared to give historically, the exact numbers, but I will say that there was but one brigade that had not been engaged: Smith's of Steinwher's division, which, with one battery remained in reserve on Cemetery Hill; Costar's brigade of the same division was sent out to cover the retreat of the Eleventh corps, but was met soon after it emerged from the town by Hoke's and the left of Hay's brigades and repulsed.

There is no question but what a combined attack on Cemetery Hill, made within an hour, would have been successful. At the end of an hour the troops had been rallied, occupied strong positions, were covered by stone walls, and under the command and magnetic influence of General Hancock—who in the meantime had reached the field—would, in my opinion, have held the position against any attack from the troops then up.

But at 6 o'clock everything was changed; both armies were reinforced at that hour, and had the battle been renewed after that it would have been by fresh troops on either side, with all the chances of a new battle. At 6 o'clock, Johnson's division entered the town; and Anderson's division might have reached there at the same time if it had been ordered to do so. The head of the Twelfth corps also reached the battle field at 6

P.M., but not being required at Cemetery Hill, Geary's division was moved to the left to occupy the high land near Round Top, and Williams' division was turned to its right as it moved up the Baltimore pike, crossed Wolf Hill, with orders to seize the high land on the Confederate left, where Johnson's division subsequently spent the night.

If, therefore, Hill and Ewell had renewed the attack at 6 P.M., with their full commands, the two divisions of the Twelfth corps would have been in position to meet it. This, as before remarked, would have been a new phase of the battle, fought by fresh troops, and therefore subject to all the uncertainties of battle; but with strong probabilities in favor of Confederate success. The First corps had been engaged in a long and severe contest, in which it was everywhere beaten and had suffered heavily. The Eleventh corps had also suffered as much, and portions of it were badly demoralized. On the contrary, the Confederate forces would have continued the engagement with the prestige of victory. Several brigades had been badly cut up, but others had fired scarcely a shot, and the presence of General Lee, who had now arrived, would have given a new impulse to the battle. It is probable strong efforts would have been made to hold the position until the troops of the Third and Second corps could be brought up. Although General Sickles reached the field at an earlier hour, only two brigades of his command arrived that night—these reaching the field at sunset. Two brigades were left at Emmettsburg to hold the pass towards Fairfield, and General Humphreys, with two brigades of his division, reached the field at 1 o'clock the next morning. The Second corps was ordered to move up to Gettysburg, but General Hancock met it on the road on his return to Taneytown, where he went to report to General Meade, and not considering its presence necessary, ordered it to go into bivouac. In case of an engagement, however, these troops could hardly have reached the field before nightfall.

By this brief explanation you will see that the best chance for a successful attack was within the first hour, and unquestionably the great mistake of the battle was the failure to follow the Union forces through the town, and attack them before they could reform on Cemetery Hill. Lane's and Thomas' brigades, of Pender's division, and Smith's of Early's division, were at hand for such a purpose, and had fired scarcely a shot. Dole's, Hoke's, and Hays' brigades were in good fighting condition, and several others would have done good service. The artillery was up, and in an admirable position to have covered an assault, which could have been pushed, under cover of the houses, to within a few rods of the Union position.

I have a nominal list of casualties in the First and Eleventh corps, but not at my command at present. If you desire anything additional I shall be pleased to furnish it, if at my disposal.

I am sir, yours with respect,
Jno. B. Bachelder.

These letters unquestionably show that had we known it at the time, the position on the heights fought for on the 2nd could have been gained on the afternoon on the 1st by continuing without delay the pursuit of the Federals. It will be observed that they also affirm that the success of an attack made by us after an hour's delay would have been involved in doubt. General Hancock says that an attempt had been made "to reform some of the Eleventh corps as they passed over Cemetery Hill, but it had not been successful; and that when he arrived there, about 3 P.M., there were only some 1,000 or 1,200 troops on the hill, with Buford's cavalry in front; and that up to 6 P.M. the troops that had been collected from the First and Eleventh corps had only been reinforced by Williams' and Geary's divisions of the Twelfth corps, under Slocum—numbering together by return of June 30th, 8,056.

The number collected in the First Corps amounted to 2,450—(Bates, page 82, and also Doubleday's, its commander's testimony). Of the Eleventh, (see Hancock,) 1,200. Estimating Buford's cavalry at about 2,500, we would have a Federal force, up to 6 P.M., of 13,206, opposed to our 26,000. Birney's division of the Third corps (Sickles) were the next troops to arrive; they came up about sunset, less one brigade left at Emmettsburg, and numbered, at that hour, 4,500.

Humphrey's division of that corps did not reach the field until towards midnight—(General Humphreys, in a letter to me). It will be noticed, however, that General Hancock says that portions of the Second and Third corps, had our assault been sudden or the contest brief, would not have been available until dark. If these figures are correct, I am authorized in reaffirming that "a little more marching, perhaps a little more fighting," would have gained for us the possession of the heights on the evening of the 1st of July.

On the other hand, General Early, in a masterly review of those operations in the December number *Southern Historical Society Papers*, 1877, gives some strong reasons, which at the time prevented a further advance, made more convincing by the fact of its being well known that he desired to move on after the retreating Federals. I can well imagine that, with the existing doubt as to what portion of the Federal army was then within supporting distance of the First and Eleventh corps, the arrival at a most inopportune moment of what proved to be a false report, that the enemy were advancing on the York road, which would have brought them in the rear of the Confederate troops; the time consumed in investigating the report; the apparent strength of the enemy's position; would all combine to make a subordinate commander hesitate to take the responsibility of beginning another battle; more especially as his chief was close at hand. I know, too, how easy it is, in the light of subsequent events, to criticise an officer's action. "Young man, why did you not tell me that before the battle?" General Lee is reported to have said to an officer who was commenting upon some of the movements at Gettysburg, "Even as stupid a man as I am can see it all now," illustrates the point.

Being at the commencement of the war Ewell's chief-of-staff, knowing his soldierly qualities, and loving his memory, God forbid that I should utter one word to detract from the splendid record he has left behind him. His corps being more advanced than Hill's after the action was over, and he being the senior officer present, has caused his conduct on the first, in not pursuing the enemy, to be criticized; of course, after the arrival of his chief, all responsibility was taken from Ewell in not ordering the troops forward—it was assumed by and is to be placed upon General Lee.

While the capture of Cemetery Hill on the 1st would have probably thrown Meade back on the already selected line of Pipe Clay creek, in gaining it we would have shattered the Twelfth corps—possibly portions of two others—and the Federal army offering battle with three or more of its corps beaten, would have been a less formidable antagonist than we found it on the 2d, from Culp's Hill to Round Top. The Confederates, too, would have suffered an additional loss; but the victor, in most instances, loses less in proportion to the vanquished, except in an attack on fortified places. General Hancock, the opposing commander, does not ennumerate this as one of those.

To the operations of the 2d of July I now direct attention, not with the view of going over the whole ground, because it has been fully covered by official reports of the higher officers operating there and by recent papers, some of them bearing exhaustingly upon the subject, but for the purpose of examining some of the statements contained in General Longstreet's article, written and published by the Philadelphia *Times* in its issue of November the 3rd, 1877. It is charged by persons, particularly from the North, that Longstreet's political apostasy, since the war, has made his comrades forget his services during that period. Upon that point, whilst I believe, as General Lee once said to me in Lexington, (referring to a letter he had received from General Longstreet, asking an endorsation of his political views,) that "General Longstreet has made a great mistake," I concede the conscientious adoption of such opinions by General Longstreet. The fact that he differs widely, and has not acted politically with the great majority of his old comrades since the war, has nothing to do with his undoubted ability as a soldier during the contest. I saw him for the first time on the 18th of July, 1861, at Blackburn's Ford, on the Bull Run, and was impressed with his insensibility to danger. I recollect well my thinking, there is a man that cannot be stampeded. For the last time I saw him the night before the surrender at Appomattox Courthouse, and there was still the bull-dog tenacity, the old genuine sang froid about him which made all feel he could be depended upon to hold fast to his position as long as there was ground to stand upon. These solid characteristics were always displayed by him during the four years of war, and gained for him the sobriquet of "General Lee's old war-horse." But when General Longstreet writes for the public prints a paper which has generally been construed as an attack upon the reputation of General Lee, it will be criticized by a great many; by me, because I find it difficult to reconcile many of his statements with facts in my possession. While there are very few who will deny that General Longstreet was a hard fighter when once engaged, I have never found any one who claimed that he was a brilliant strategist; indeed, upon the only occasions when he exercised an independent command, Suffolk and Knoxville, the results in the public mind were not satisfactory. It is, therefore, with some surprise we learn from his paper that when in Richmond, en route from Sufflok to join General Lee at Fredericksburg, he paused to tell Mr. Seddon (then Secretary of War), how to relieve Pemberton at Vicksburg. Our astonishment is increased when we read further, that before entering upon the campaign of 1863, he exacted a promise from General Lee that the "campaign should be one of offensive strategy, but defensive tactics, and upon this understanding my (his) assent was given," and that therefore General Lee "gave the order of march." Our wonder culminates when finally we are told that he had a plan to fight the battle different from General Lee's, and that General Lee had since said it would have been successful if adopted.

The invasion of Maryland and Pennsylvania was undoubtedly undertaken with a view of manoeuvering the Federal army, then in front of Fredericksburg, to a safer distance from the Confederate capital; to relieve Virginia of the presence of both armies; to subsist our troops upon new ground, that the old might recuperate, and with the idea a decisive battle fought elsewhere might be more productive of substantial results. These premises admitted, not only is gross injustice done to the memory of General Lee, in believing he crossed the Potomac bound fast by a promise to a subordinate to make the movement "strategically offensive, tactically defensive," as charged by General Longstreet, but such reported promise contains a positive reflection upon General Lee's military sagacity. As well might the Czar of Russia, acting as commander-in-chief of his army, have so committed himself to the Grand Duke Nicholas, or under like circumstances, the Sublime Porte have tied himself up to Osman Pasha, the hero of Plevna. The truth is, General Lee and his army were full of fight, their "objective point" was the Federal army of the Potomac, and "those people" the Confederate chief had resolved to strike whenever and wherever the best opportunity occurred, "strategically offensive and tactically defensive," to the contrary notwithstanding. An army of invasion is naturally an offensive one in strategy and tactics, and history rarely points to an instance where it has been concentrated on a given point to patiently await an attack. The distance from its base making supplies a difficult matter to procure, in itself regulates the whole question.

An army so situated must move or fight. The absurdity of Longstreet's statement is shown in admitting the presumption, General Lee knew all this; nor can we reconcile with the facts of the case General Longstreet's expression, wherein he says that his paper in the *Times* is called out by the fact that he has "been so repeatedly and rancorously assailed by those whose intimacy with the Commanding-General, in that battle, gives an importance to their assaults."

His communications just after the war to Mr. Swinton, the historian, were in substance the same attack upon General Lee which he has repeated in this paper. It was, therefore, in him, and came out before any of the utterances now complained of were made. The official reports of General Ewell, Early, and Pendleton, written soon after the battle, clearly stated it was well understood and expected that General Longstreet would make the main attack early in the morning of the 2nd of July.

If these reports furnished the "sly under-current of misrepresentation" of his course, why did he not ask his chief to correct their statements, and set him right upon the record? His revelations, if accepted now, would greatly injure the military reputations of General Lee, Ewell, and Hill. Alas! Not one of whom live, for history's sake, to defend their stainless fame.

I propose to show, first, it was General Lee's intention to attack at sunrise or as soon as possible thereafter; second, the probable result of such an attack promptly made at an early hour, and, third, to examine the statement that General Longstreet had a plan to fight the battle different from General Lee's, which plan General Lee has since said would have been successful if adopted.

On the night of July 1st two corps of General Lee's army lay in close proximity to the enemy, ready, willing, and expecting to fight as early as possible on the next morning; and two divisions, McLaws' and Hood's, of the three in the remaining corps the same night bivouacked some four miles to the rear.

The natural inference to be deduced from their positions would be that the Federal troops hastening up would concentrate and fortify in front of the two corps already in position, while the force in rear would be used to attack at the most vulnerable and available point. That such was General Lee's intention I think can be as clearly established as that General Longstreet did not, upon the 2nd of July, 1863, use due dillegence in carrying out the wishes of his chief.

General Early, a division-commander in Ewell's corps, in a recent paper on Gettysburg, gives a detailed narrative of a conference which General Lee held on the evening of the 1st with Ewell, Rodes, and himself, in which General Lee seemed very anxious for an attack to be made as early as possible next morning, and after being persuaded that it would not be best to make the main attack in Ewell's front said, "Well, if I attack from my right, Longstreet will have to make the attack—Longstreet is a very good fighter when he gets in position and gets everything ready, but he is so slow." General Early further states that General Lee left the conference with the distinct understanding that he would order Longstreet up to make the attack early the next morning.

The official reports of General Ewell, Early, and Pendleton, all confirm this testimony. General A.P. Hill, in his official report of the battle of Gettysburg, says, speaking of the operations of the morning of the 2nd, "General Longstreet was to attack the left flank of the enemy and sweep down his line, and I was directed to co-operate with him." General Long, one of the witnesses introduced by General Longstreet, who was at that time General Lee's military secretary, says, (in the portion of his letter which General Longstreet found it convenient to leave out, but which Gen. Early was fortunately able to supply,) "that it was General Lee's intention to attack the enemy on the 2nd of July as early as practicable, and it is my opinion that he issued orders to that effect." In letters published in the *Southern Historical Society Papers* for August and September, 1877, General Long gives various details which demonstrate that General Lee expected Longstreet to attack early in the morning of the 2nd; that, at 10 o'clock, "General Lee's impatience became so urgent that he proceeded in person to hasten the movements of Longstreet; that he was met by the welcome tidings that Longstreet's troops were in motion; and that, after further annoying delays, at 1 o'clock P.M. General Lee's impatience again urged him to go in quest of Longstreet." Col. Walter H. Taylor, of General Lee's staff, whose letter General Longstreet gives to show that he did not hear the order for an early attack, says, in his article published in the *Southern Historical Society Papers* for September, 1877, "it is generally conceded that General Longstreet on this occasion was fairly chargeable with tardiness"; that he had been urged the day before by General Lee "to hasten his march"; and, that, on the morning of the 2nd, "General Lee was chafed by the non-appearance of the troops, until he finally became restless and rode back to meet General Longstreet and urge his forward."

General Lindsay Walker, chief-of-artillery of Hill's corps, in a letter to me, says:

Letter from General R. Lindsay Walker

Richmond, Va., January 17th, 1878

General Fitz. Lee:

My dear Sir: I cheerfully comply with a request to give you the following brief statement:

I was, at Gettysburg, as I continued to be to the surrender at Appomattox Courthouse, chief of artillery of the Third corps, (Lieutenant-General A.P. Hill, commanding,) and it was, therefore, necessary for me to know on the evening of the 1st of July what dispositions of my artillery to make for the next day. I have a strong impression that I heard General Lee say that evening that he wished the battle opened at the earliest possible moment the next morning by a simultaneous attack on both flanks, and that this conversation took place with Generals Lee, Longstreet, Hill, and perhaps Ewell.

But I am positive that in receiving my instructions from General Hill, on the night of the 1st of July, he told me that the orders were for the attack on the heights to be made at daybreak the next morning on both flanks—that the Third corps was to co-operate as circumstances might determine—and that the artillery should be held in readiness to support either flank, or to advance in front as should be decided.

We were ready at daybreak the next morning, and waited impatiently for the signal. Between 9 and 10 o'clock, I was lying under the shade of a tree near Colonel W.F. Pougue, who commanded that day the reserve artillery of my corps, when General Lee rode up to him and, mistaking him for one of General Longstreet's officers, administered to him a sharp rebuke for being there instead of hurrying into position on the right. Colonel Pougue explained that he was in Hill's, not Longstreet's command, and General Lee at once apologized and eagerly asked, "Do you know where General Longstreet is?" Colonel Pougue referred him to me, and I immediately came forward from my position (where I had heard distinctly the conversation), and offered to ride with General Lee to where I thought he could find General Longstreet. As we rode together General Lee manifested more impatience than I ever saw him show upon any other occasion; seemed very much disappointed and worried that the attack had not opened earlier, and very anxious for Longstreet to attack at the very earliest possible moment. He even, for a little while, placed himself at the head of one of the brigades to hurry the column forward.

I was fully satisfied then, as I am now, that General Lee had decided to attack early on the morning of the 2d; that he was bitterly disappointed at the protracted delay, and that this delay enabled Meade to concentrate his forces and to occupy key positions, which we could have seized in the morning, and thus lost us a great victory.

> I have the honor to be sir,
> Very respectfully, your obd't serv't,
> R.L. Walker.

At daylight on the morning of the 2d General Longstreet was at General Lee's headquarters renewing his protest against making an attack, but General Lee "seemed resolved to attack," so says General Longstreet. As General Lee afterwards became so worried at the non-appearance of General Longstreet's troops, is it not a fair presumption that General Longstreet had already received his instructions? General Hood, writing to Longstreet, says, "General Lee was seemingly anxious you should attack that morning, and you said to me, the General is a little nervous this morning; he wishes me to attack; I do not wish to do so without Pickett."

In General Longstreet's official report we find that "Laws' brigade was ordered forward to its division during the day and joined about noon on the 2d. Previous to his joining I received instructions from the Commanding-General to move with the portion of my command that was up, to gain the Emmettsburg road on the enemy's left," ... and that "fearing that my force was too weak to venture to make an attack, I delayed until General Laws' brigade joined its division." And yet in face of this, his official report, he charges the responsibility of the delay of his attack to General Lee in his recent paper to the *Times*, by writing that after receiving from General Lee the order to attack at 11 o'clock, he waited for Laws' brigade to come up, and that "General Lee assented." The two statements, it will be readily preceived, are at variance.

General Hood says he arrived, with his staff, in front of the heights of Gettysburg shortly after daybreak on the morning of the 2d, and that his troops soon filed into an open field near by. Colonel Walton, chief of artillery, Longstreet corps, states that his reserve artillery arrived on the field about the same hour and reported themselves ready to go into battle. The Commanding-General was impatient—why the delay then until 4 P.M. in what General Lee intended to be his main attack?

General Longstreet, in his narrative, contends that the delay of several hours in the march of his column to the right was General Lee's fault, since the column was moved under the special directions of Colonel Johnston, an engineer officer of the Comanding-General, and having for the time the authority of General Lee himself, which he, Longstreet, could not set aside. Although he finally "became very impatient at this delay and determined to take the responsibility of hurrying the troops forward," which he did by what he seems to regard an ingenious flanking of General Lee's orders, viz., marching Hood, who was in McLaws' rear and not governed by Lee's dilatory orders, "by the most direct route" to the position assigned him. If the military principle here established by General Longstreet is correct, why would not it have been that much better to have simply left a platoon at the head of this command to go through the form of following General Lee's engineer, and hasten on with the remainder of his command?

But in his official report (which he should have consulted) Longstreet says: "Engineers sent out by the Commanding General and myself guided us by a road which would have completely disclosed the move—some delay ensued in seeking a more convenient route." It contains no hint that he lost "several hours by the blundering" of General Lee's engineer, Colonel S. P. Johnston, the gallant engineer officer mentioned by General Longstreet, tells me that he read the paper in the *Times* "with some surprise, particularly that portion where reference is made to the part I took in the operations of the 2d July," and says that he "had no idea that I (he) had the confidence of the great Lee to such an extent that he would entrust me with the conduct of an army corps moving within two miles of the enemy's line, while the lieutenant-general was riding at the rear of the column." Colonel Johnston, and I state it on his authority, was ordered by General Lee to make a reconnaissance on the enemy's left early on the morning of the 2d. On that errand he left army headquarters about 4 A.M. Upon returning he was required to sketch upon a map General Lee was holding the route he had taken, and was soon ordered to ride with General Longstreet. NO OTHER ORDERS HE RECEIVED. In obedience to such instructions he joined the head of Longstreet's corps about 9 A.M., and then it was about three miles from Round Top, by the route selected for its march. "After no little delay (I quote from Colonel Johnston's words) the column got in motion and marched under cover of the ridge and woods until the head of the column got to about one and a half miles of the position finally taken by General Hood's division. Here the road turned to the right and led over a high hill to where it intersected a road leading back in the direction of the Round Top. When we reached the bend of the road, I called General Longstreet's attention to the hill over which he would have to pass, in full view of the enemy, and also to a route across the field, shorter than the road and completely hidden from the enemy's observation. General Longstreet preferred the road, and followed it until the head of his column reached the top of the hill. He then halted McLaws and ordered Hood forward. At the time our movement was discovered we were not more than a mile and a half from the position finally reached by Hood. Had General McLaws pushed on by the route across the field he would have been in position in less than an hour; yet General Longstreet says 'several hours' were lost by his taking the wrong road. The delay of 'several hours' cannot be attributed to General Longstreet's taking the wrong road (whether he or I is to blame for that), but in the delay in starting, the slowness of the march, the time unnecessarily lost by halting McLaws, and the time lost in getting into action after the line was formed. The fact that General Lee ordered me to make a reconnaissance and return as soon as possible, led me to believe, if he intended to attack at all, such an attack was to be made at an early hour."

Colonel Johnston did not even know where General Longstreet was going. He supposed he had been ordered to ride with him simply to give him the benefit of his reconnaissance. He must be surprised then, as he states, to find himself considered by Gen. Longstreet in charge of McLaws' division, First corps, Army of Northern Virginia. I dwell on this point because it is a most important one. Gettysburg was lost by just this delay of "several hours."

Facts, however, do not warrant us in believing that General Longstreet was always so particular in following officers sent by General Lee to guide his column, because many of us recall that in the opening of the spring campaign of 1864, General Lee sent an engineer officer to General Longstreet, then encamped near Gordonsville, to guide him to the point they wanted him in the wilderness, but this officer was pushed aside by General Longstreet's saying he knew the route and had no use for his services. As a consequence, he lost his way and reached the wilderness twenty-four hours behind time, just as A.P. Hill was about to sustain a terrible disaster which Lee gallantly averted. This incident comes direct from General Lee himself, who cited it as an instance of Longstreet's habitual slowness.

From known facts then, it seems clearly established that to General Longstreet and not to General Lee, as the former claims, must be attributed the delay in the attack of the 2nd.

Let us now enquire what would have been the probable results of an earlier attack. From very accurate data in my possession I am enabled to give the following as the position of the Federal forces on the 2nd of July.

I begin on their right: At 6 A.M. Culp's Hill was only occupied by Wadsworth's division, First corps, and Steven's Fifth Maine battery, Wadsworth's command being much shattered by the fight of the 1st. On our extreme left opposed to Wadsworth, were three brigades of Johnson's division, Ewell's corps. One of his brigades, Walker's, was in position faced to the left to guard the flank of our army. In front of Walker lay William's division of the Twelfth corps, and two regiments of Lockwood's independent brigade, and the Fifth corps, except Crawford's division, which arrived on the field about twelve o'clock. (Crawford's testimony before Committee on Conduct of the War).

The Eleventh corps occupied Cemetery Hill with the artillery attached to the First and Eleventh corps., except Stevens' battery, before mentioned. Doubleday's division of the First corps was massed in rear of Cemetery Hill, while Robertson's division of the same corps extended to the left along Cemetery Ridge, embracing that portion of it assaulted by Longstreet on the 3rd.

From the left of Robertson the line was occupied for about three quarters of a mile beyond which point two brigades of Humphreys' division of the Third corps were massed, and on their left two brigades of Birney's division of same corps, and constituting all of that corps then up—Birney and Humphreys having each left a brigade at Emmettsburg. General Humphreys, in a private letter to me, says "Birney reached Gettysburg about sunset the first day, leaving one brigade at Emmettsburg—with Birney there were probably 4,500, and at Emmettsburg 1,500. My division (Second division, Third corps) reached the ground towards midnight of July 1st, leaving one brigade at Emmettsburg—with me there were about 4,000, and at Emettsburg about 1,200.

"The return of the Third corps for the 30th of June, 1863, gives officers and enlisted men, infantry, present for duty 11,942; but there were less than 11,000 present at the battle. My impression is that the corps did not exceed 10,000 present on the ground.."

These four brigades of the Third corps lay a little west of the crest of the ridge. The crest proper was held by Geary's division of the Twelfth corps from the night before, but about this time they began to move over to Culp's Hill, where they formed on a prolongation of Wadsworth's line, already mentioned. In front of the Third corps was Buford's two brigades of cavalry; and these troops at the time mentioned, 6 A.M., except some batteries of artillery, constituted all the troops then up. Mark the point— the Second corps, Hancock's, 12,088, by the return of June 30th, was in bivouac three miles in rear on the night of the 1st, (nearly as far from the Federal as Longstreet was from the Confederate lines). It broke camp at an early hour, and a little after 6 A.M. had reached that portion of the Taneytown road, running along the slope of Little Round Top. Between the hours of 6 and 9 A.M. some important changes were made. Let us commence on the Federal right again. Williams had assumed command of the Twelfth corps, and Ruger had taken his division, and with Lockwood's regiments, had moved over to Culp's Hill and formed on a prolongation of Geary's line. Notice how Meade was increasing the forces opposed to our left—the Fifth corps numbering, on the 10th of June, 1863, 10,136 for duty, to which was added a portion of the Pennsylvania reserves, some 4,000 or 5,000, (Butterfield, then chief of Meade's staff, testimony before Committee on Conduct of the War, pg. 428,) moved across Rock Creek, was massed and held in reserve, where it lay until called upon to support Sickles in the afternoon, when its place was taken by the Sixth corps, which arrived at 3 P.M., having marched 32 miles since 9 P.M. on the first— (Meade's testimony before the Committee on the Conduct of the War, page 438). This was the largest of the seven corps Meade had at Gettysburg, and on the 10th of June, 1863, numbered for duty, 15,408. (Butterfield, page 428). It will be perceived that when two-thirds of Longstreet's corps went into camp four miles in rear of the field of Gettysburg, on the evening of the first of July, Sedgewick, with over 15,000 men, was 32 miles away. Upon his arrival, about the hour above named, he was ordered to relieve the Fifth corps. The latter corps was then ordered to move to the rear of Round Top; it reached there and was massed half a mile in rear between 4 and 5 P.M. Caldwell's division of the Second corps occupied Round Top just before the Fifth corps got up. (Meade.) Wadsworth's division and the Eleventh corps continued to occupy its first position until the close of the battle. Doubleday remained in the position before named until night, but Robertson's division was relieved by the Second corps, which had arrived at 7 A.M., and gone into position on Cemetery Ridge. The two remaining brigades of the Third corps left at Emettsburg got up about 9 A.M., relieving Buford's cavalry, which was ordered back to Westminster to protect the depot of supplies. About the same time General Tyler came up with eight batteries of artillery. At half-past 10 A.M. Major McGilverey reached the field with the artillery reserve and ammunition train. At this hour the Federal army was all up, except one regiment of Lockwood's brigade, Sixth corps, whose movements have been previously given. At about 11 A.M. General Sickles ordered a reconnaissance, and at 12, advanced his command and occupied the intermediate ridge, extending his line to the foot of Round Top. Round Top was occupied as a signal station; the Fifth, it will be recollected, was, after 4 P.M., massed in its rear.

I ask a careful perusal of the positions, strength, and time of arrival upon the battlefield of the Federal troops on the 2d of July, as here given. I think it will show that an attack at daybreak or sunrise, or at an hour preceding 9 A.M., nay, even 12 M., would have combined many elements of success. General Lee knew it, and to use Longstreet's own words, "was impressed with the idea that by attacking the Federals he could whip them in detail." General Lee, it seems, as was habitual with him, had a correct idea of the situation. His army, except a portion of the cavalry and one division of infantry, was practically concentrated on the night of July 1st, and could have attacked, if necessary, at daylight on the 2d. General Meade arrived, in person, at 1 A.M. on the 2d, and was engaged in getting his army up until after 2 P.M. on that day. He commanded at Gettysburg seven corps of infantry, viz., First, Second, Third, Fifth, Sixth, Eleventh, and Twelfth, and three divisions of cavalry, viz., Buford's, Kilpatrick's, and Gregg's—the last two reaching the field after Buford left. The First corps went into battle on the 2d with 2,450 men (Bates' History of Gettysburg, page 52, and Doubleday's testimony—who commanded it after Reynolds' death—page 309, Committee on the Conduct of the War); the Second Corps being put at 12,088 (return of June 30th); the Third, including the two brigades not then up, 10,000 (General Humphreys' letter to me); the Fifth at 10,136; the Eleventh at 3,200 (this corps numbered 10,177 on the 10th of June. General Hancock said he could not find but 1,200 organized on the afternoon of the 1st of July, after their little difficulty with Ewell and Hill. Wadsworth's division, of that corps, went into the fight on the 1st with 4,000 men, and on the morning of 2d but 1,600 answered to their names—Wadsworth's testimony, page 413). The Twelfth corps, by the return of the 30th of June, numbered 8,056. These six corps numbered, then, on the 2d of July, before the Sixth corps reached the field, 45,930. The cavalry and 4,000 Pennsylvania reserves are not included in this statement of the Federal force. Ewell and Hill's corps numbered together about 28,000 men on the morning of the 2d, and Longstreet says he had, without Pickett, some 13,000 men, making our strength (leaving out the cavalry, too,) some 41,000. General Lee could have had his 41,000 men in hand at daybreak, whereas General Meade could not count upon all of his 45,930 until after 12 M., Crawford's division, Fifth corps, not getting up, until then. General Longstreet, by an early attack, would have undoubtedly seized Round Top, for even as late as the attack was made, General Warren, Meade's chief of engineers, (Warren's testimony before the Committee on the Conduct of the War, page 377), says he went by General Meade's directions to Round Top, and from that point, "I could see the enemy's line of battle. I sent word to General Meade that he would at once have to occupy that place very strongly. He sent as quickly as possible a division of General Sykes' corps, (Fifth,) but before they arrived the enemy's line of battle, I should think a mile and a half long, began to advance and the battle became very heavy at once. The troops under General Sykes arrived barely in time to save Round Top, and they had a very desperate fight to hold it." An attack at that point even before 12 o'clock would have been successful, because Sykes was then in reserve behind Meade's right and could not have gotten up. And Meade testifies (page 332) that Sykes, by hurrying up his column, fortunately was able to drive the enemy back and secure a foothold upon that important position, viz., Round Top, "the key point of my whole position," General Meade says. And again, that, "if they had succeeded in occupying that, it would have prevented me from holding any of the ground I subsequently held until the last." Behold the sagacity of General Lee! He wanted to attack early so as to "whip the Federals in detail," and selected the very point admitted by his able opponent to be his "key point." It seems he would have gained the position if he could have imparted more velocity to the commander on his right. General Lee's plan seems, in a military sense, almost faultless. An English writer has said of General Lee, that with a character as near perfect has been hitherto vouchsafed to mortals, there was yet in it, for a military man, a slight imperfection, viz., "a disposition too epicene." To the tender and loving heart of the woman he united the strong courage and will of the man, but a reluctance to oppose the wishes or desires of others, or to order them to do things disagreeable to them which they would not fully consent to or enter into. Perhaps herein lies the secret of his troubles on the 2d of July. He was fully alive, on his part, to the necessity of an early attack, and he saw with an unerring eye the "key point," but in view of the unwillingness of the commander of the troops he had determined to begin the battle with, and who was at his headquarters at daylight arguing against, instead of making the attack, he may not have put his orders in that positive shape from which there could be no evasion, no appeal. General Hood, in a letter to me, says "I did not hear General Lee give the direct order to do so, but merely as he (General Lee) often did, suggested the attack." If Hood is correct, the suggestion had the strength of an order in General Lee's own mind at least, because upon no other theory can we explain his personal actions and impatience on that morning or his own words to others. The attempt of General Longstreet to hold General Lee to the full responsibility of the failure at Gettysburg, because, in a spirit of magnanimity which has excited the highest admiration both in this country and in Europe, he said on the field of Gettysburg, "It is all my fault," as he had said in like spirit to Stonewall Jackson at Chancellorsville, "The victory is yours, not mine," will excite only surprise and not carry conviction to the minds of the old soldiers of General Lee, who knew the General's habit of self-deprecation. The effort must therefore fail in its purpose.

Now let us scrutinize the statement of General Longstreet that he had a plan to fight the battle of Gettysburg, which was submitted to General Lee and refused by him at the time, but which he afterwards regretted not having adopted, as it would have been successful. General Dick Taylor, in recent paper, says: "That any subject involving the possession or exercise of intellect should be clear to Longstreet and concealed from Lee, is a startling proposition to those possessing knowledge of the two men."

Readers of the history of the four years of "War between the States" will doubtless agree with General Taylor. General Lee's plan of battle at Gettysburg, in the light of subsequent facts, could not have been more admirably arranged if he had have possessed, in lieu of his own grand genius, the McCormick telescope, and the centre and both flanks of the Federal army had been within its focus. Why should he then have regretted that he had not adopted the plan of another? About one month after the battle of Gettysburg General Lee wrote a letter to the President of the Confederacy, in which, after undervaluing his own ability, he says, "Everything, therefore, points to the advantages to be derived from a new commander, and I the more anxiously urge the matter upon your Excellency, from my belief that a younger and abler man than myself can readily be obtained. I know that he will have as gallant and brave an army as ever existed to second his efforts, and it would be the happiest day of my life to see at its head a worthy leader—one who could accomplish more than I could perform, and all that I have wished. I hope your Excellency will attribute my request to the true reason, the desire to serve my country." To this the Honorable Jefferson Davis, in the course of his reply, responds, "But suppose, my dear friend, that I were to admit, with all their implications, the points which you present, where am I to find that new commander who is to possess the greater ability which you believe to be required? I do not doubt the readiness with which you would give way to one who could accomplish all that you have wished; and you will do me the justice to believe that if Providence should kindly offer such a person, I would not hesitate to avail myself of his services. To ask me to substitute you by some one, in my judgement, more fit to command or who would possess more of the confidence of the army or of the reflecting men of the country, is to demand an impossibility."

I give extracts from these two letters because, some two years ago, General Lee's whole letter to Mr. Davis was reproduced in some of the public prints. It was followed by General Longstreet's letter to his uncle, (again republished in his paper to the *Times*,) and which first gave to the world the information that another plan to fight this great battle had been considered by the Commander of the Confederate army. This news was in turn succeeded by an extract from a letter from General Lee to General Longstreet wherein he says, "Had I taken your advise at Gettysburg, instead of pursuing the course I did how different all might have been." Following this came an extract from a letter of Captain Gorie to General Longstreet. The captain had been sent as a bearer of dispatches from General Longstreet, then in Tennessee, to General Lee at Orange Courthouse. In this extract Captain Gorie tells us that, "upon my arrival there General Lee asked me in his tent, where he was alone, with two or three Northern papers on his table. He remarked that he had just been reading the Northern official reports of the battle of Gettysburg, and that he had become satisfied that, if he had permitted you to carry out your plans on the 3rd day, instead of making the attack on Cemetery Hill, we would have been successful."

These little extracts which General Longstreet used again in his narrative, seem to appear as a desirable connection, and to ring out a public notice, that the younger and abler man referred to by General Lee was the commander of his First army corps, and as there are witnesses still living to testify that General Longstreet once said in the house of the late John Alexander, at Campbell Courthouse, just after the surrender at Appomattox, that in case of another war he would never fight under General Lee again, it is fair to presume that he, too, was conscious of his own superiority, if all this be true.

Very many of us were not able to reconcile these reported utterances of General Lee with facts within our own knowledge, and General Longstreet was asked more than once to publish the whole letter that he claimed to have received from General Lee, that we might see the connection before and after the short sentence he permitted only to be known. His reply in this was concluded in hasty language foreign to the enquiry, and he failed to produce anything more. In the narrative in the *Times*, once again appears the same sentence, "only that and nothing more." It is possible that after General Lee's plans had been frustrated and his opportunity lost, he would naturally regret that he had not taken the advice of the one who urged him not to attack.

In the Rev. Wm. Jones' "Personal Reminiscences, Anecdotes, and Letters of Lee," page 156, we find that General Lee, in speaking (to Professor White, of Washington and Lee University,) of the irreparable loss the South had sustained in the death of Jackson, said with emphasis: "If I had had Stonewall Jackson at Gettysburg, we should have won a great victory." How, by General Lee's or General Longstreet's plan? Tell me, you who knew Jackson best, if he had been in command of troops, say four miles in rear of the battle-field on the night of the 1st of July, 1863, and General Lee had SUGGESTED to him to attack from his right on the morning of the 2d, what hour would he have attacked Meade's "key-point" on Round Top? Would the hour have approached nearer to 4 A.M. or 4 P.M.? For General Lee has said, "I had such implicit confidence in Jackson's skill and energy that I never troubled myself to give him detailed instructions— the most general instructions were all that he needed." But as bearing upon this point stronger, if possible, than Lee's wish for Jackson at Gettysburg, is the following language in a letter to me from a gentleman extensively known and universally noted for the purity of his life and the conscientiousness of his character, and who now worthily fills the responsible position of Governor of his State. This letter was written some two years ago in response to a note of mine sending him the published controversy between General Longstreet and Early in reference to the operations at Gettysburg. The high character of the writer gives to his statements great weight, but the letter being a private one, would have been kept from the public had not General Longstreet paraded what he terms "the weak points of the campaing of Gettysburg," in attempting to show the "eight" mistakes committed by General Lee.

The name of the author is not now given, because I do not wish to draw him into the discussion, but it is at the disposal of any one who questions the facts. His letter bears the date April 15th, 1876:

> Major-General Fitzhugh Lee:
> My Dear Sir: I am in receipt to-day of your letter of the 14th inst., with its interesting inclosures in reference to the battle of Gettysburg. I have not had the leisure to follow closely the controversy to which the article refers, but I remember perfectly my conversation with General Lee on this subject. He said plainly to me "that the battle would have been gained if General Longstreet had obeyed the orders given him and had made the attack early instead of late." He said further, "General Longstreet, when once in a fight, was a most brilliant soldier; but he was the hardest man to move I had in my army."

Does this testimony prove that General Lee regretted that he had not adopted another's plan to fight the battle of Gettysburg, or is it not cumulative to all the other well-known facts? Gen. Pleasonton, Meade's cavalry commander, writes a paper for the Philadelphia *Times*, January 19th, 1878, in which he tells us what he said to Meade after our repulse on the 3rd, and this is it: "I rode up to him, and after congratulating him on the splendid conduct of his army I said, 'General, I will give you half an hour to show yourself a great general. Order the army to advance while I take the cavalry; get in Lee's rear and we will finish the campaign in a week.'" A Sandwich Islander, knowing nothing about the war except what he might read in these papers of Generals Longstreet and Pleasonton, but of a humane and benevolent disposition, would inwardly rejoice that they did not command their respective armies lest the historic feat of the "Kilkenny Cats" should have been eclipsed by not even leaving to the public their two tales.

In conclusion, let our fancy picture the grim veterans of the Army of Northern Virginia paraded in their camp grounds in that month of August, 1863, to hear the announcement that Mr. Davis had accepted the resignation of their chief, would there not have resounded from front to rear, from flank to flank, "Le Roi est mort"? but when the "younger and abler man," whoever he might be, assumed command, the mummies of the Pyramids on the skeleton bones beneath the ruins of Pompeii could not be more silent than the refusal of these heroes to sing to Lee's successor, "Vive Le Roi."

Aye, as certain as that the day will roll around, when "the secrets of all hearts shall be disclosed," so sure would the Angel of Peace have donned her white and shining robes in that hour that General Lee bid farewell to the Army of Northern Virginia and mounted "Traveller" to ride away from his people. The termination of the war would indeed have simplified the duties of "the younger and abler man!"

General Fitz Lee lists the main reasons given for the defeat at Gettysburg, and then proceeds to state the strengths of the opposing armies at Gettysburg as being 62,000 for the Confederates and 105,000 for the Federals. This estimate is given some fifteen years after the battle, when statistical information for both sides was readily available. The best available compilations for both armies place the Union army at approximately 78,000 and the Confederate army at about 70,000. Though the Army of Northern Virginia was still inferior to its Union counterpart, the disparity was far less than Fitz Lee states, and far better than it had been on any recent meeting between the two armies. Lee certainly had access to these statistics, and it is curious why he would provide numbers that were so erroneous. The heroic deeds performed by the soldiers of the Confederate army upon the hills and fields of Pennsylvania won eternal fame and glory for the supporters of the Southern cause, and were not in need of enhancement through increasing the odds they faced.

Lee then goes into a detailed explanation of the reasons for Stuart's ride around the Federal army, the authority he had to do so, the numbers involved, and the numbers remaining with Robert E. Lee's main body. His information shows that more than one half of the Southern cavalry remained with the army, and he seeks to exonerate both Stuart and Lee from any blame by stating that Stuart had permission to make the ride, while the army retained sufficient numbers of mounted troops to perform the scouting and screening duties needed to safeguard its movements and provide intelligence. In clearing Stuart, his immediate superior, Lee is quite correct that Robert E. Lee granted permission for the raid, but he stops short in describing the chain of command that led to this movement. He fails to cite General Longstreet's part played in the whole affair, and the fact that Longstreet had final approval over the raid, and in fact ordered the precise route by which it must be begun. Stuart was

definitely not at fault for his absence from the army. He was exercising latti-
tude granted to him by his superiors, and was in full compliance with the orders
he had been given. The fact that he became separated and cut off from the
main body, due to the movements of the Federal army, was just one of the
uncertainties of war. It was an unfortunate and unforeseen circumstance that
is blameless, yet it has been the subject of blame for more than a century. In
retrospect, it is easy to see that Stuart should not have been permitted to make
this raid. At the time it was allowed, neither Robert E. Lee, nor J.E.B. Stu-
art, envisioned that the cavalry assigned to it would be lost to the main body.
Both officers were confident that the column would be able to perform its mis-
sion while maintaining contact with one another. But fate stepped in, as it so
often does in war, causing the best-laid plans to go awry. It was a move that
failed, not because of an error in judgment or orders improperly carried out;
it was merely a matter of being in the wrong place at the wrong time. All cam-
paigns and wars bear witness to an event where fate steps in to alter the out-
come of a battle, or even a war. Stuart's raid was one of these unexpected
moments where nothing went according to plan, and fate took charge. While
it proved to be disastrous to the Confederate campaign, and was a prime rea-
son why the two armies met by chance on the fields of Gettysburg, it remains
a blameless act of fate, and not a willful error on the part of any officer
involved.

Regarding Lee's contention that the Army of Northern Virginia retained
sufficient mounted troops to adequately perform the duties of the cavalry, this
is a thinly veiled attempt to exhonorate his uncle and his immediate superior,
and to eliminate the situation with the cavalry from having any bearing what-
soever in the overall outcome of the campaign. While Lee argues that the Army
of Northern Virginia had sufficient numbers of mounted troops to sustain it,
and sets the number at over 6,000, he fails to mention the necessary detach-
ments made from this force during the march. The brigades of Generals Bev-
erly Robertson and William "Grumble" Jones had been assigned to guard
Snicker's and Ashby's Gaps and observe the movements of the enemy.[2] Each
forward step of Lee's army separated the main body from this cavalry force.
General John Imboden's brigade was assigned to cover Lee's left flank. In the
process of carrying out his mission, Imboden became entangled with the rem-
nants of General Milroy's command, fought a skirmish at Bloody Run, Penn-
sylvania, and did not return to the main body in time to participate in the
battle. It can be clearly seen that the subtraction of these three brigades would
have greatly reduced Lee's available cavalry from the 6,300 troopers Fitz Lee
assigns to the main army. What remained might have been sufficient for a cam-

paign like Chancellorsville or Fredericksburg, where the Confederates were operating on the defensive, within their own lines, on ground that was of their choosing and familiar to them, but it was hardly adequate for the campaign Lee was now conducting. An offensive drive, deep in enemy territory, required that cavalry screens be thrown out on all four sides of the advancing army. Lee lacked the numbers of horsemen to competently perform all of the duties required by the cavalry in such a massive undertaking. They were simply spread too thin to accomplish more than a minimum of the responsibilities normally entrusted to them. A case in point would be the chance encounter that touched off the great battle. Hill's corps, with Heth's division in the van, was marching blindly through open enemy country when Heth stumbled upon General John Buford's cavalry outside the town of Gettysburg. As Heth stated to Lee when asked why he had entered into a battle, despite orders against engaging the enemy until the main body was up, it had been felt that Gettysburg was defended merely by a small force of militia. Heth had no idea that a sizeable force from Meade's army was in his front when he allowed his men to charge the enemy blocking him from Gettysburg. The reason for this is that there was no body of cavalry in advance of Hill's corps providing the intelligence so crucial to command decisions. This was not an oversight. There simply was not enough cavalry to go around, as this glaring example illustrates.

Lee next examines the events of the evening of July 1 and the failure of General Ewell to secure the heights at Cemetery Ridge. His analysis is very detailed, and equally conflicting, citing the statements of several Union participants who were on the scene at the time. While he acknowledges that the ridge was held by no more than 1,200 organized troops, he goes on to speculate that any assault by the Confederates, at this time, might have been met by portions of the Second, Third, and Twelfth Corps, all of which had arrived in close proximity to the battlefield at that time. In doing so, he seems to be not only excusing Ewell's failure to act, but crediting him with making a good decision in withholding the charge. Robert E. Lee's orders to Ewell were to seize the heights "if practicable," and there was never a word recorded where Lee ordered Ewell to pursue the enemy once the heights were gained. Cemetery Ridge was the objective, not the Federal army, at this time. Lee wanted to hold this high ground and fortify it, seeing at once that it was the key position on the field. If this had been accomplished, Longstreet might well have gotten his wish to fight a defensive battle in the decisive contest of the campaign. The fact that portions of three Federal corps were several miles away should not have been a deterrent to seizing the heights, it should have been all the more reason for doing so. Ewell missed a golden opportunity to alter the course of history on the evening of July 1, and no amount of rationalizing on the part of Fitz Lee can account for that. One must remember the reason Lee was writing this narrative, however. He was responding to the paper written by Longstreet that had recently been published. His objective was to refute Longstreet's statements by defending the actions of his uncle and his direct superior. In defending his uncle, he was also defending his uncle's friends. Richard Ewell and Jubal Early had been staunch supporters of Robert E. Lee ever since the first dissension between Longstreet and the commander surfaced. Early, in particular, had been a crusader for the stainless reputation of Lee, and had been a tireless antagonist of Longstreet. Following Robert E. Lee's death, Early had taken up the gauntlet and become "Marse Robert's" champion, challenging any slights, real or imagined, to the memory of Lee. In defending his uncle, Fitz Lee could not single out two of his greatest supporters for criticism and censure. Indeed, he was a part of the group that sought to maintain his uncle's image by denouncing the charges and slanders being brought forth by Longstreet. To lay blame at the feet of Ewell or Early would be tantamount to agreeing with Longstreet and validating one of his claims, and that could never happen.

Lee then attacks the logic of Longstreets' statements concerning his meeting with Secretary Seddon and the supposed promise he had received from Lee that the campaign would be a defensive one in nature. He pays tribute to Longstreet's qualities as a soldier, and acknowledges his stalwart superiority as a defensive fighter, while pointing to his failures in exercising independent command. In other words, Lee is calling attention to his belief that Longstreet was quite capable when following the orders of a superior, but found desperately lacking when called upon to make the decisions of command himself. This foundation becomes the basis of the argument against Longstreet's claim that he had elicited the support of Robert E. Lee for conducting the defensively orchestrated plan of campaign he advised, and that the two were in perfect agreement with Longstreet's views at the inception of the movement of the army from Virginia. The reasons why this was unlikely to have been the case are clearly laid out by Fitz Lee, and he presents a credible argument that General Lee would never have constrained himself to such a limited scope of action, or subordinated himself to views of his subordinate, especially, as Fitz Lee carefully points out, since that subordinate did not possess the qualities necessary to exercise independent command decisions over such a large army.

Fitzhugh Lee now switches from the defensive and goes on the attack. He addresses the question of whether General Longstreet was dilatory in carrying out his orders for the attack on the Federal left on July 2. While most of his testimony concerning this topic cites General Lee's intention for an "early" attack, he does manage to slip in a reference to a "sunrise" attack. The issue of the "sunrise" attack has long been a point of contention between the supporters of Lee and Longstreet, and much has been written about it from either side. The historic record does not support the accusation that the attack was intended to be launched at sunrise, and the events that transpired on the battlefield seem to bear that out. Hill would have had to have his troops formed for battle in the early morning darkness in order to support such an attack, and Longstreet would have had to start his brigades moving even earlier. Activity on the Confederate side did not begin until the early morning hours of July 2, after daylight. As previously related, it seems certain that General Lee intended the attack to be made earlier, rather than later, and that a morning attack was what he was seeking, the idea of a sunrise attack is unsupported, and its circulation can only be the result of a desire to place Longstreet's actions in a light less favorable than they already were. Without going into a lengthy recap of the discussion already presented concerning the activities of July 2, it is safe to say that all indications point to the fact that General Longstreet was guilty of tardiness in launching the attack on the Union right. The testimony of Generals Ewell and Hill, the formation of battle lines at an early hour, the anxious anticipation so many reported seeing in General Lee's actions, all point to the conclusion that the blow was delivered considerabloy later than Lee had wanted and that Longstreet had been negligent in carrying out the wishes of his superior. Fitz Lee allows himself to enter into speculation about what the possible outcome of an earlier attack might have been, and he concludes that great victory might have been won if Lee's instructions had been carried out to the letter. It cannot be disputed that each passing minute decreased the possibility for success in the attack, and the Union army grew stronger and more organized with every hour that passed. Whether or not success would have been gaurenteed by an early morning assault is in the realm of speculation, however, and while it would have been more probable, it was not a certainty. The only thing that can be categorically stated is that by not attacking at an early hour another opportunity on the battlefield was surely missed.

General Longstreet's paper alleged that General Lee had shown remorse after the battle, and had told him that he regretted not adopting his plan of campaign. Longstreet says that Lee expressed to him that their efforts would have been crowned with success if he had only taken his subordinate's advice. Fitz Lee goes into a lengthy rebuttal of this claim, giving testimony from several individuals close to Lee in supporting his contention that Lee never uttered those words nor held those beliefs. In one of his few statements concerning the controversy, given before his death, General Lee flatly denies that he had ever agreed to Longstreet's advice about a defensive campaign, and states categorically that he would never have confined his actions by such narrow objectives. In fact, Lee disavowed any memory of the conversation at all, and could not recall it ever taking place.[3] *Why, therefore, would he tell General Longstreet that a plan he never remembered hearing about would have been successful if he had only adopted it? From Lee's own mouth came the most damning condemnation of Longstreet's assertions. The testimony provided by Fitz Lee serves merely as corroborative evidence. Longstreet was either remembering events as he wished to remember them, or was guilty of flat out fabrication in his allegation that Lee had given tardy approval to a plan he never remembered being discussed.*

Lee's letter to President Davis, offering his resignation for reasons of his failure to accomplish all that was desired, and Longstreet's letter to his uncle, following the battle of Gettysburg, are then presented in an effort to show that Longstreet felt himself superior to Lee and wished to free himself from subordination to his superior. Longstreet had tasted independent command at Suffolk. His next experience as a subordinate came in the Gettysburg Campaign, where his views and suggestions were constantly overruled by his commander. Before Gettysburg, Longstreet seemed content to be the commander of the First Corps, and Lee's trusted lieutenant. Following that campaign, he appeared restless with his assignment and openly sought transfer or promotion. General Joseph E. Johnston commiserated with Longstreet by writing "It is, indeed, a hard case for him, the Senior Lieut. Genl. & highest in reputation, to be kept in second place."[4] *Longstreet had even suggested to the Administration that he and Braxton Bragg change places. Longstreet would assume command of the Army of Tennessee, and Bragg would take over the First Corps. At any rate, Longstreet jumped at the opportunity to transfer, with his command, to the Western Theater, to aid in retaking Chattanooga from William S. Rosecrans and forcing the Federal army back from southwestern Tennessee. Longstreet's personal ambition, along with his critical comments concerning the Gettysburg Campaign, serves as the basis for Fitz Lee's allegation that Longstreet thought he was smarter than Lee and wanted to replace him. Fitz portrays Longstreet as thinking himself the "younger and abler man" Lee referred to in his letter of resignation to President Davis, and mockingly describes how he would have been received by the veterans of the Army of Northern Virginia. The fact is that Longstreet did desire promotion, and coveted his own command. It is the nature of a military man to seek such pro-*

motion, and Longstreet's achievments and service warranted an opportunity to show his abilities as an army commander. It must have galled him to see officers like Braxton Bragg, Kirby Smith, and John Bell Hood rise to the rank of full general while he remained the senior lieutenant general in the army. There is nothing underhanded nor unmanly in Longstreet's desire to attain the highest rank and responsibility his abilities could command. His natural desire for advancement only becomes an issue because of his criticisms of Lee's handling of the Gettysburg Campaign. When Longstreet rejoined the Army of Northern Virginia during the Wilderness Campaign, there is no evidence to support that he was anything but a dutiful subordinate. Sure, he frequently offered Lee his advice and views on tactical and strategic questions, but he had always done that, from his earliest association with Lee. His ambition is used to project an image of conspiracy in an effort to degrade his denigration of Lee's conduct at Gettysburg.

After Gettysburg, Fitzhugh Lee was promoted to the rank of major general. His cavalry division was instrumental in making it possible for the First Corps to secure the strategic crossroads at Spotsylvania Courthouse in advance of Grant's army. Toward the end of the war, with J.E.B. Stuart dead, and Wade Hampton transferred to North Carolina, Lee was placed in command of the cavalry of the Army of Northern Virginia. Following the war, he earned his living as a farmer in Stafford County, Virginia, until his election as governor of the state in 1885. In 1893, President Grover Cleveland appointed him counsel-general to Havana, Cuba. In 1898, when the Spanish-American War broke out, Lee was commissioned a major general of United States Volunteers. He served with distinction for three years, retiring in 1901 with the rank of brigadier general. Fitzhugh Lee died at Washington, D.C., on April 28, 1905. His remains were laid to rest in the Hollywood Cemetery, in Richmond, Virginia.[5]

Epilogue

The battle of Gettysburg was the greatest military struggle ever to take place on American soil, and a defining moment in the course of American history. Most historians credit it as being the crest of Southern fortunes in the war, and the beginning of the end for the South. Had Robert E. Lee's army been able to defeat Meade's Union forces there, it is entirely possible that the Confederacy could have prevailed in the war, and that America might have been permanently split into two nations. True, there were thousands upon thousands of Union troops in the field in other parts of the country, and the North would have had the capability to carry on the war, even if Meade's army had been defeated at Gettysburg, but the Federal government might possibly have concluded to give up its persecution of the war. The North was not fighting to defend its borders or to secure its status as an independent nation. The war aims of the Federal government were to conquer a portion of the country, then in rebellion, and to return it to the authority of the national government. If Lee's army had been able to brush Meade aside, and march on Washington or Baltimore, it would have shown the North, and the rest of the world, that Federal arms were incapable of acquiring the war goals it had established. How can you conquer an enemy when you cannot even protect your own capital and seat of government? While a Confederate victory at Gettysburg would not have assured that the South would have won the war, it certainly would have put them on a footing to do so.

The size, savagery, and cost of the battle, combined with its strategic and political implications, has always made Gettysburg the most important battle of the Civil War, and the most closely studied battle in American military history. The principle actors in the struggle immediately became famous, household names, with some rising to glory and honor that caused them to almost become legends. Every schoolboy knew the story of Pickett's Charge, which, in American history, became the rival of the famed charge of the British Light Brigade. The American people, both North and South, embraced the quiet fields of Gettysburg with reverent awe, a sacred spot where so many struggled, fought, and died for the cause they upheld, and a place where the finest qualities of American devotion, courage, and sacrifice were displayed, regardless of the flag the particular soldiers followed. From the time that the smoke first began to clear from the field, Americans clamored to get the details of the fight, to learn all they could about this great and tragic moment in history. Historians and writers obliged, as newspapers were filled with articles about the battle. Gettysburg has been recounted and debated in countless articles over the many decades that have passed since the armies marched away from its fields and hills. The various commanders on that field have been both praised and condemned for the parts they played in shaping the events that took place there. Gettysburg has become the most reported and written about event in American history, and the commanders who led the troops in that great struggle have become some of the most recognizable actors of the Civil War. It is for this reason that their personal recollections of the battle hold such great meaning for us, the students of the war, for they give insight to the actions of these men, both during and after the battle, that can be gained in no other manner.

The writing of this book serves to combine two important features for the reader. First, there is the aspect of history versus memory. Just because a person remembers an event in a particular way does not mean that it actually took place in that manner. Memory can sometimes play tricks, or can become confused and distorted. Second, there is the consideration that some officers may have had personal motives for "remembering" events in a particular way, either to enhance their own contributions, or decrease their own liability. Only by comparing their narratives with the historic record can we separate the fact from the fiction.

The controversy surrounding the battle of Gettysburg began before the smoke cleared from the field, and it will continue as long as the campaign is studied by historians and buffs. As human beings, we have an intrinsic need to be able to know the reason why things happen as they do. We also have a need to assess blame when things go wrong. As historians, we bring both of these human characteristics to our examination of the Gettysburg Campaign. Why did the battle turn out the way it did, and who was at fault? Since the South lost, we naturally concentrate more of our attention in trying to figure out what went wrong, or who was responsible for it going wrong. The errors committed by the victors may be casually examined, but the fact that they won usually prohibits any extended discussion of the failures.

The history of Gettysburg is filled with mistakes made and opportunities squandered, on both sides. The might-have-beens of this battle have become as important in the relating of the campaign as are the actual events that transpired. When history spawns debate it remains fresh and new and challenges the imagination, and this is the reason why Gettysburg will continue to occupy a revered place in the study of our nation's past.

Appendix: Organization, Strength and Losses of the Opposing Forces at Gettysburg

Army of the Potomac—Major General George G. Meade

I CORPS:
MAJOR GENERAL JOHN F. REYNOLDS

Headquarters: Killed 2, Wounded 3.

1st Division (Brigadier General J.S. Wadsworth): Killed 299, Wounded 1,229, Missing 627.

2nd Division (Brigadier General John C. Robinson): Killed 91, Wounded 616, Missing 983.

3rd Division (Brigadier General Thomas A. Rowley): Killed 265, Wounded 1,297, Missing 541.

Artillery: Killed 9, Wounded 86, Missing 11.

Out of a strength of 10,022, the I Corps suffered total casualties of 666 Killed, 3,231 Wounded, and 2,162 Missing = 6,059 or 60.45 percent.

II CORPS:
MAJOR GENERAL WINFIELD S. HANCOCK

Headquarters: Killed 1, Wounded 6.

1st Division (Brigadier General John C. Caldwell): Killed 187, Wounded 880, Missing 208.

2nd Division (Brigadier General John Gibbon): Killed 344, Wounded 1,202, Missing 101.

Artillery: Killed 27, Wounded 119, Missing 3.

Out of a strength of 12,996, the II Corps suffered total casualties of 797 Killed, 3,194 Wounded, and 378 Missing = 4,369 or 33.62 percent.

III CORPS:
MAJOR GENERAL DANIEL SICKLES

Headquarters: Wounded 2.

1st Division (Major General David Birney): Killed 271, Wounded 1,384, Missing 356.

2nd Division (Brigadier General Andrew A. Humphreys): Killed 314, Wounded 1,562. Missing 216.

Artillery: Killed 8. Wounded 81, Missing 17.

Out of a strength of 11,924, the III Corps suffered total casualties of 593 Killed, 3,029 Wounded, and 589 Missing = 4,211 or 35.32 percent.

V CORPS:
MAJOR GENERAL GEORGE SYKES

1st Division (Brigadier General James Barnes): Killed 167, Wounded 594, Missing 143.

2nd Division (Brigadier General Romeyn Ayers): Killed 164, Wounded 802, Missing 63.

3rd Division (Brigadier General Samuel Crawford): Killed 26, Wounded 181, Missing 3.

Artillery: Killed 8, Wounded 33. Missing 2.

Ambulance Corps: Wounded 1.

Out of a strength of 12,509, the V Corps suffered total casualties of 365 Killed, 1,611 Wounded, and 211 Missing = 2,187 or 17.48 percent.

VI CORPS:
MAJOR GENERAL JOHN SEDGWICK

1st Division (Brigadier General Horatio Wright): Killed 1, Wounded 17.

2nd Division (Brigadier General Albion Howe): Killed 2, Wounded 12, Missing 2.

3rd Division (Major General John Newton): Killed 20, Wounded 148, Missing 28.

Artillery: Killed 4, Wounded 8.

Out of a strength of 15,679, the VI Corps suffered total casualties of 27 Killed, 185 Wounded, and 30 Missing = 342 or 2.2 percent.

XI CORPS:
MAJOR GENERAL OLIVER O. HOWARD

Headquarters: Wounded 1, Missing 1.

1st Division (Brigadier General Francis Barlow): Killed 122, Wounded 677, Missing 507.

2nd Division (Brigadier General August von Steinwher): Killed 107, Wounded 507, Missing 332.

3rd Division (Major General Carl Shurz): Killed 133, Wounded 684, Missing 659.

Artillery: Killed 7, Wounded 53, Missing 9.

Out of a strength of 9,893, the XI Corps suffered total casualties of 369 Killed, 1,922 Wounded, and 1,510 Missing = 3,801 or 38.42 percent.

XII CORPS:
MAJOR GENERAL HENRY W. SLOCUM

1st Division (Brigadier General Alpheus Williams): Killed 96, Wounded 406, Missing 31.

2nd Division (Brigadier General John Geary): Killed 108, Wounded 397, Missing 35.

Artillery: Wounded 9.

Out of a strength of 8,589, the XII Corps suffered total casualties of 203 Killed, 812 Wounded, and 66 Missing = 1.082 or 12.6 percent.

CAVALRY CORPS:
MAJOR GENERAL ALFRED PLEASONTON

1st Division (Brigadier General John Buford): Killed 28, Wounded 116, Missing 274.

2nd Division (Brigadier General David McM Gregg): Killed 6, Wounded 38, Missing 12.

3rd Division (Brigadier General Judson Kilpatrick): Killed 53, Wounded 181, Missing 121.

Artillery: Killed 4, Wounded 19.

Out of a strength of 14, 973, the Cavalry Corps suffered total casualties of 91 Killed, 354 Wounded, and 407 Missing = 852 or 5.69 percent.

Army of Northern Virginia—General Robert E. Lee

I CORPS:
LIEUTENANT GENERAL JAMES P. LONGSTREET

1st Division (Major General Lafayette McLaws): Killed 313, Wounded 1,538, Missing 327.

2nd Division (Major General George E. Pickett): Killed 232, Wounded 1,157, Missing 1,499.

3rd Division (Major General John B. Hood): Killed 343, Wounded 1,504, Missing 442.

Artillery: Killed 22, Wounded 137, Missing 22.

Out of a strength of about 19,000, the I Corps suffered total casualties of 910 Killed, 4,389 Wounded, and 2,290 Missing = 7,539 or 39.68 percent.

II CORPS:
LIEUTENANT GENERAL RICHARD S. EWELL

Headquarters: Wounded 1.

1st Division (Major General Jubal Early): Killed 156, Wounded 806, Missing 226.

2nd Division (Major General Edward Johnson): Killed 229, Wounded 1,269, Missing 375.

3rd Division (Major General Robert Rodes): Killed 421, Wounded 1,728, Missing 704.

Artillery: Killed 3, Wounded 19.

Out of a strength of about 23,000, the II Corps suffered total casualties of 809 Killed, 3,823 Wounded, and 1,305 Missing = 5,937 or 25.81 percent.

III Corps:
Lieutenant General Ambrose P. Hill

1st Division (Major General Richard Anderson): Killed 147, Wounded 1,127. Missing 840.

2nd Division (Major General Henry Heth): Killed 411, Wounded 1,905, Missing 534.

3rd Division (Major General William Pender): Killed 262, Wounded 1,312, Missing 116.

Artillery: Killed 17, Wounded 62, Missing 1.

Out of a strength of about 23,000, the III Corps suffered total casualties of 837 Killed, 4,407 Wounded, and 1,491 Missing = 6,735 or 29.28 percent.

Confederate Cavalry:
Major General J.E.B. Stuart

Killed 36, Wounded 140, Missing 64.

Out of a strength of 12,500, the Cavalry Corps suffered total casualties of 240 or 1.92 percent.

Notes

(References are to works listed in the Bibliography, following)

General Oliver Howard

1. Warner, *Generals in Blue*, pp. 237–238.
2. Stackpole, *They Met*, p. 136.
3. *The War of the Rebellion*, Series I, Vol. 27, pt. 1, pp. 696–697, 700–702, 707.
4. Storrick, *The Battle*, p. 15.
5. *The War of the Rebellion*, pp., 696–697, 700–702, 707.
6. Warner, pp. 238–239.

General Henry W. Slocum

1. Warner, *Generals in Blue*, pp. 451–452.
2. *The War of the Rebellion*, pp. 758–763.
3. Clark, pp. 108–109.
4. *The War of the Rebellion*, pp. 758–763.
5. Warner, *Generals in Blue*, pp. 452–453.

General Abner Doubleday

1. Warner, *Generals in Blue*, pp. 129–130.
2. *The War of the Rebellion*, pp. 243–258, and *Battlefields*, p. 273.
3. *The War of the Rebellion*, pp. 243–258, and Johnson & Buell, p. 434.
4. Warner, *Generals in Blue*, pp. 129–130.
5. *New York Times*, April 1, 1883.

General Daniel Sickles

1. Warner, *Generals in Blue*, pp. 446–447.
2. Stackpole, *The Battle*, pp. 47–49.
3. Swanberg, pp. 173–174.
4. Stackpole, *They Met*, pp. 215–216.
5. Testimony of General Daniel Sickles before the Joint Committee on the Conduct of the War, February 26, 1864.
6. *New York Herald*, March 12, 1864.
7. Warner, *Generals in Blue*, p. 447.

General David Gregg

1. Warner, *Generals in Blue*, pp. 187–188.
2. Johnson and Buell, pp. 397–404.
3. *Ibid.*, p. 405.
4. Warner, *Generals in Blue*, p. 188.

General John Newton

1. Warner, *Generals in Blue*, pp. 344–345.
2. Stackpole and Nye, *The Battle*, p. 94.
3. *Ibid.*, p. 345.
4. *Ibid.*, p. 43.
5. Warner, *Generals in Blue*, p. 345.

General Daniel Butterfield

1. Warner, *Generals in Blue*, p. 62.
2. Johnson and Buell, vol. 3, pp. 411–412.
3. Warner, *Generals in Blue*, pp. 62–63.

Major General John Gibbon

1. Warner, *Generals in Blue*, p. 171.
2. Johnson and Buell, p. 387, and Wertz and Bearss, pp. 497–498.
3. Warner, *Generals in Blue*, p. 172.

Lieutenant General James Longstreet

1. Warner, *Generals in Gray*, p. 192.
2. Connelly, pp. 56–57.
3. Wert, pp. 244–245.
4. Johnson and Buell, vol. 3, p. 249.
5. *Ibid.*, p. 251.
6. Stackpole, *They Met*, p. 22.
7. Hollingshead and Whetstone, pp. 53, 58.
8. Dowdey, p. 373.
9. Johnson and Buell, vol. 3, p. 293.
10. *America's Civil War*, vol. 20, no. 3, July, 2007, p. 57.
11. *Ibid.*, pp. 58, 60.
12. Stackpole and Nye, *The Battle,* p. 96.
13. Smith, p. 67; Dowdey, p. 174; Lee, pp. 268–269; and Davis, p. 227.
14. Stackpole, *They Met,* p. 266.
15. Smith, p. 97.
16. Warner, *General in Gray*, pp. 192–193.

General Fitzhugh Lee

1. Warner, *Generals in Gray*, p. 178.
2. Longacre, *Lee's Cavalrymen*, p. 204.
3. Dowdey, p. 373.
4. Wert, p. 302.
5. Warner, *Generals in Gray*, p. 178.

Appendix

1. Stackpole and Nye, *The Battle*, pp. 94–96.

Bibliography

Books

Acken, J. Gregory. *Inside the Army of the Potomac: The Civil War Experience of Captain Francis Adams Donaldson.* Harrisburg, Pa.: Stackpole, 1998.

Battlefields of the Civil War. New York: Arno Press, 1979.

Clark, Champ. *Gettysburg: The Confederate High Tide.* Alexandria, Va.: Time-Life Books, 1985.

Coddington, Edwin B. *The Gettysburg Campaign: A Study in Command..* New York: Scribner's, 1968.

Connelly, Thomas L. *The Marble Man: Robert E. Lee and His Image in American Society.* Baton Rouge: Louisiana State University Press, 1977.

Davis, Burke. *Gray Fox: Robert E. Lee and the Civil War.* New York: Fairfax Press, 1966.

Doubleday, Abner. *Chancellorsville and Gettysburg.* New York: Blue & Grey Press.

Dowdey, Clifford. *Lee.* New York: Bonanza Books, 1965.

Downey, Fairfax. *The Guns at Gettysburg.* New York: Collier Books, 1962.

Groff, Tim. *Under Both Flags: Personal Stories of Sacrifice and Struggle During the Civil War.* Guilford, Conn.: Lyons Press, 2003.

Hollingshead, Steve, and Jeffrey Whetstone. *From Winchester to Bloody Run: Border Raids and Skirmishes in Western Pennsylvania During the Gettysburg Campaign.* Privately published, 2004.

Johnson, Robert Underwood, and Clarence Clough Buell. *Battles and Leaders of the Civil War,* vol. 3. New York: Castle Books, 1956.

Kantor MacKinlay. *Gettysburg.* New York: Random House, 1952.

Keneally, Thomas. *American Scoundrel: The Life of the Notorious Civil War General Dan Sickles.* New York: Nan A. Talese, 2002.

Lee, Fitzhugh. *General Lee.* Greenwich, Conn.: Fawcett, 1964.

Longacre, Edward. *General John Buford: A Military Biography.* Conshohocken, Pa.: Combined Books, 1995.

_____. *Lee's Cavalrymen: A History of the Mounted Forces of the Army of Northern Virginia.* Mechanicsburg, Pa.: Stackpole, 2002.

_____. *The Man Behind the Guns: A Military biography of General Henry J. Hunt, Chief of Artillery, Army of the Potomac.* New York: Da Capo Press, 2003.

Oates, Col. William C., and Lt. Frank A. Haskell. *Gettysburg.* New York: Bantam Books, 1992.

"Report of the Joint Committee on the Conduct of the War." Washington, D.C.: Government Printing Office, 1864.

Smith, Carl. *Gettysburg 1863.* Oxford, UK: Osprey, 1998.

Stackpole, Edward J. *They Met at Get-*

tysburg. Harrisburg, Pa.: Eagle Books, 1956.

Stackpole, General Edward J., and Colonel Wilbur S. Nye. *The Battle of Gettysburg: A Guided Tour*. Harrisburg, Pa.: Stackpole, 1960.

Storrick, W.C. *Gettysburg: The Place, the Battles, the Outcome*. Harrisburg, Pa.: J. Horace McFarland Co., 1932.

_____. *The Battle of Gettysburg: The Country, the Contestants, the Results*. Harrisburg, Pa.: J. Horace McFarland Co., 1956.

Swanberg, W.A. *Sickles the Incredible*. New York: Ace Books, 1956.

The War of the Rebellion: A Compilation of the Official Records of the Union and Confederate Armies. Series I–IV. Washington, D.C.: Government Printing Office, 1880–1901.

Warner, Ezra J. *Generals in Blue: Lives of the Union Commanders*. Baton Rouge: Louisiana State University Press, 1958.

_____. *Generals in Gray: Lives of the Confederate Commanders*. Louisiana State University Press, Baton Rouge, La., 1959.

Wert, Jeffrey D. *General James Longstreet: The Confederacy's Most Controversial Soldier*. New York: Touchstone, 1994.

Wertz, Jay, and Edwin C. Bearss. *Smithsonian's Great Battles and Battlefields of the Civil War: A Definitive Field Guide Based on the Award Winning Television Series by MasterVision*. New York: William Morrow, 1997.

Wheeler, Richard. *Witness to Gettysburg*. New York: Harper & Row, 1987.

Young, Col. Ford E, Jr. *The Third Day at Gettysburg*. Bethesda, Md.: Americana Stories, 1981.

Newspapers and Magazines

America's Civil War, July 2007, vol. 20, no. 3.

Civil War Times Illustrated, 1962, vol. 1, no. 7, and 1963, vol. 2, no. 4.

New York Herald, March 12, 1864.

New York Times, April 1, 1883

Index